Square Peg Square Hole

Keys to Find Your Niche in Life

Helen M Hamilton

Balboa Press books may be ordered through booksellers or by contacting:

Balboa Press
A Division of Hay House
1663 Liberty Drive
Bloomington, IN 47403
www.balboapress.com
1-(877) 407-4847

ISBN: 978-1-4525-3494-7 (e)
ISBN: 978-1-4525-3493-0 (sc)
ISBN: 978-1-4525-3495-4 (hc)

Library of Congress Control Number: 2011907613

Printed in the United States of America

Balboa Press rev. date: 6/27/2011

Dedication

With many blessings to younger generations, this book is dedicated to reopening awareness to your own magnificence and the all embracing love that has and always will be your constant companion within.

Helen

TABLE OF CONTENTS

Introduction

About Helen
My Experience in the Schoolroom of Life
About My Peg

"Life in the world should consist of only two things, that which helps us grow and that which helps others grow."

Lester Levenson

The inspiration for this book comes from my heartfelt desire to assist others who like myself travel the road of life seeking to recover their self-worth and to find and awaken to their true selves. It is also for those seeking to find right employment for their unique and special talents.

ABOUT HELEN

I had been happy as a young child. However, as a young teenager, I thought I should have been a boy. I outgrew my friends by five inches. I tended to be strong and heavyset. When I would pat my friend on the back, she would almost keel over. I didn't recognize my own strength. Indeed, I would even play with my younger sister as if I were a boy. I yearned to be a boy because I thought I was a wrong person.

When my girlfriends began dating, no boyfriend ever came calling to take me out. I was taller than the boys were until my last year in high school. Plus my strong demeanor overpowered them. Even later in life with a husband and children, I didn't know who I was or how I fit in.

After I had been married for nine years, the joy I used to experience left my life. My early childhood happiness was long gone. I allowed myself to slip until I totally lacked self-worth. I constantly compared myself to others around me and felt I didn't measure up. I thought I wasn't good enough or perfect enough.

Then I began to slowly put the pieces together. It took fifteen years to pull myself out of the lack-of-esteem hole I created. With the help of key psychological tools described in the following text, I stopped trying to be something I wasn't. At last I came to a growing level of self-acceptance of who I am. Realization then dawned about what I can contribute to benefit others and the whole. I now accept myself. It is okay to be me just as I am.

"If you make friends with yourself you will never be alone.'

Maxwell Maltz

My Experience in the Schoolroom of Life

"The difference between school and life? In school, you're taught a lesson and then given a test. In life you're given a test that teaches you a lesson."
Tom Bodett

The descriptions and personal stories that follow illustrate several of the tools—the major keys—that helped me find and accept myself. I rediscovered my natural inherited qualities, my abilities, and how I could contribute in the world. I call the tools I used keys because they unlocked doors within me when I permitted myself to change my unsupportive behaviors, opening me to deeper wisdom and a deeper acceptance of myself. Many of these doors could only be passed through when I gave up an outmoded way of being or an ineffective way of thinking.

The keys took me out of unsuccessful employment. They placed me in the correct working environment for my natural motivational tendencies. They provided me with an understanding of my body's needs. They shone a light on my relationships with others and led me deep into understanding myself as a spiritual being.

When I review my life, especially when looking back over the last forty years, I can see the process of change I traversed, not only clearing unwanted energy blockages caused by negative patterns but increasing my vibratory frequency through the years. I am able to assimilate now in a way I could not even approach or understand earlier when I was mired in my pessimistic personality. The somewhat convoluted pathway I followed through my explorations eventually readied me for deeper spiritual understandings, an open heart, and awakening of my abilities.

I began my journey as a critical, loud, harsh, unkind, and negative self, who was selfish and entirely self-critical, always comparing myself to others and finding myself wanting. My journey to change my self-worth has cleared away most of my negativity and has released many energy-blocking patterns of behavior. Now I can say I am tolerant, much kinder, thoughtful of others, even compassionate, more positive in my outlook, and no longer judgmental. A serene peace and stillness often fills my being. Through self–acceptance, I have stopped judging and criticizing myself, accepting myself as I am—as I truly am. In all of its imperfection, my life is perfect.

Major shifts in my perspective of who and what I am often came to me from books and workshops. I am still discovering even deeper levels of self than I ever could have imagined. My experience is yours to embrace. I offer it as a mirror to help you to know yourself, to enjoy yourself, to enjoy how you fit in with others, to enjoy your work, and enjoy your life.

This is a story of key discoveries in my long life as I approach my seventy-fourth birthday. I delve into the many ways in which I began to understand and accept my uniqueness as a human. Learning about how my ancestors influenced my present life and how I am a continuum of an energy field was important in my life. I describe how to master mind techniques to remove emotional blocks and obtain goals. Perhaps you will improve your communication skills in relationships through my stories, preventing in your life what cost me so dearly in mine. My experiences in learning to understand my body's needs and all the lessons I have learned about losing weight and regaining health are also mentioned. I present my memoirs as an aid in the sincere hope you, dear reader, will find beneficial assistance for your own journey to wholeness as well.

About My Peg

Do you remember the child's toy called a bingo bed? The little bench with different-shaped holes cut through it and the brightly colored pegs to be hammered into the right-shaped hole? Some were round, some were square, some were triangular, and some were even shaped like stars. For much of my life, I was a square peg trying to fit into a wrong-shaped hole.

It has taken me many years to master becoming a square peg in a square hole. I misspent much time as a square peg trying to fit into a round hole in life, and I continue to progress in self-acceptance and deep spiritual awakening. While recovering my self-esteem took me many years, I desire that your journey may be shortened through tips you find in my stories of the major and minor tools that assisted me in my growth.

It took me too long to recognize my experiences are self-created and serve as learning moments. My most devastating moments were not problems but opportunities for growth. Along the way, I received valuable assistance from teachers, books, and workshops allowing many positive changes to restructure myself. Everything facilitated my journey, whether it taught me a better way to do something or a new way to think about myself.

I genuinely hope you receive the blessing of learning from my life experiences, which are incorporated within these pages.
"Life can only be understood backwards, but must be lived forwards."

Soren Kierkegard

Keys to Life Enjoyment

Purpose of Life
Importance of Self-understanding
Happy Self-fulfillment Is Possible
What Do You Really Want?

Purpose Of Life

The purpose of life is to experience the experiencing of experience.
The Evergreens (channeled by Michael Blake Read)

I had worked myself up to such a tizzy over nothing! I left home for the airport at 5 a.m. on my way to a seminar in Las Vegas. I budgeted plenty of time, leaving over an hour and a half before my flight to move through customs and security—at least, I thought I budgeted plenty of time! Long lines of people looped around the airport as several flights were all processed at once. At the counter, the clerk shocked me by saying I would have to pay $28 to check my only bag! I thought, There's no way I am going to pay extra! Instead of checking it, I would carry it on board along with my shoulder bag.

I sailed through customs, but then I arrived at excruciatingly long lines for the security checks. The security personnel processed two lines at once. I watched the time tick away until it was my turn at last. I took off my shoes, lifted my bags onto the conveyer belt, placed my two plastic regulation bags of liquid items in the bin for the scanner, and walked through the arch. Oh goodness! Did I leave my manicure scissors and metal nail file in my suitcase? I suddenly wondered. Yes, the scanner picked them up and I had to allow the female security officer to open all my bags.

After removing the items, she presented me with two options: She could confiscate my scissors and nail file, or she could place them in an envelope at the cost of one dollar per day until I returned to retrieve them. I chose the retrieval option since replacing them would've cost more than the fee for five days in storage. I was escorted to a desk placed beside the serpent-like line of people waiting to go through security. I filled out my envelope and then had to return to the long line.

I glanced anxiously at my watch and thought, My flight will be boarding so soon. Oh please, hurry! I eventually endured the same procedure in the second security line. This time a taciturn security officer greeted me. He objected to my several items in the regulation clear-plastic bags for liquids. He suggested I step out of the line to prepare another retrieval envelope or relinquish some items. He insisted the one bag I could take with all the remaining items must be tightly closed.

Stressed and a bit flustered, I opted to throw away my little sunscreen container and managed to stuff everything into one closed bag. This time my luggage went through the scanner and the security officer discovered another object, my cruet bottle with a metal spout on it used for a nighttime sipper bottle. I suppose it looked like the beginnings of a Molotov cocktail to him. Over my agitated protests that my luggage had just been searched minutes ago by the other security line, he insisted I once again open my bags. Growing increasingly upset, I knew I had very little time to find my departure gate.

But at last, I was free of security. I raced down the corridors. By the time, I arrived at my gate, breathless and afraid I had missed my flight, the plane announced its final boarding call.

I made it, but emotionally I was a mess. However, as I progress in my spiritual development now, I know if I had accepted what was actually occurring in each moment, I would have been left in a state of calm peacefulness—instead of emotional turmoil.

Remember the movies Forrest Gump and Napoleon Dynamite? Both Forrest and Napoleon had many things happen to them, but they always remained unruffled by their experiences. They just accepted what occurred. They realized what is happening today was already created some time ago in the etheric realms. Stop resisting. Just accept what is occurring peacefully and life will move smoothly and easily.

The true function of life is not letting the challenges we face or our perceived shortcomings snag our process or catch us on their jagged edges. Life is just simply about living every moment in acceptance of what is present, from a depth of peace and stillness, responding and not reacting to whatever is occurring now. Life is about returning to self-love and enjoyment. Life is about caring and loving and giving. Life is about returning to oneness with true understanding.

Life is based on our choices. Realize as I did, I can choose to live focused on my failings and disappointments or I can choose to concentrate on my daily successes however little they may be. You can approach life from the negative view of the glass being disappointingly half-empty or the positive view of the glass being only half-full with room for lots more to be added.

"Though a man go to battle a thousand times against a thousand men, if he conquers himself he is the greater conqueror."

The Dhammapada

Importance of Self-Understanding

Unless I can operate freely guided by the flow of knowledge within my heart, my life can seem fraught with problems and resulting unhappiness. I sometimes forget I have been given the power to change myself. But I know I am a truly creative being with God-given abilities. Until I regained self-understanding, I didn't recognize who I was. I didn't know where I fit or belonged. My focus was on my lack of self-worth, causing me bouts of depression and periods of discontentment. Learning about myself, embracing my uniqueness, and accepting how I fit into the whole was extremely important. Self-understanding is key to enabling me to function as I am meant to in life. The tools to enable you to also fit your square peg into the right square hole are available all around you.

Happy Self-Fulfillment Is Possible

"Self esteem is the experience of being competent to cope with the basic challenges of life and of being worthy of happiness."

Nathaniel Branden PhD.

Until I discovered who I was and found my place within the properly shaped hole, a major part of living on this planet involved feeling unworthy and unhappy.

Who are you? Do you know where you fit in life? Can you be happy if your square peg isn't sliding into the right square hole, which matches your natural talents and abilities? Each of us is incredibly unique. The world needs every person to participate in life with our God-given abilities. We often lose sight of the fact we are part of a greater whole. But each of us has a role to play as part of that whole.

No wonder I was so filled with negativity, criticism, and lackluster achievements. It took many years of unfulfilling employment until the simple tool I describe later put me on the right track. Can you be happy at work in a round-hole job if that role doesn't fit your square peg?

Can you find the right life partner if you haven't found yourself? Entering relationship without being a whole person eventually contributed to my marriage failure.

Can you be happy without discovering your best fit in life—your niche in life? I know I wasn't. We are all parts of a beautifully choreographed humanity. I didn't realize my unhappiness was adding to the general misery of all of us.

Yes, you can find yourself and your best fit in life. But you don't need to follow my path of failed efforts and non-fulfillment. I invite you to take a shortcut and learn from my experience. Discover how you fit in. These tools can help make your self-discovery easy.

You really are a beautiful person. Your gifts are unique, and they are needed in this world. You can find your okayness and freedom to be just as you are. Surprising peace and happiness will arise in you as you find your niche in life—as you at last fit your square self into your own square hole. You always belonged there but did not recognize or believe it was possible for you. You deserve to feel at home here in this incredible world. We need you. We want everyone to find his or her rightful place.

What Do You Really Want?

"Low self-esteem is like driving through life with your hand brake on"

Maxwell Maltz

Are you unhappy enough, unfulfilled enough, or depressed enough yet to be ready to change? What do you really want from life? Ask yourself and allow an honest answer to arise from your heart.

If you think the answer is a bigger house, a new baby, or more money, you are badly mistaken. You will discover the answer is finding yourself. Make peace with who you really are, who you already are. Uncover your own unique way to contribute to the whole. What I have discovered may provide the help you need to see yourself anew. I present a variety of avenues for you to explore, each of which helped me to find myself. I sincerely hope they help you too. Life is far too short to spend so much of it putting yourself down, criticizing your actions, or finding yourself wanting.

You too can find enjoyment, inner peace, and happiness when your square peg fits easily in the square hole of life.

Chapter 1

ANCESTRAL KEYS

Finding Out I Am a Square Peg

Energy Vibration
My Peg's Genetic Inheritance
Amazing What the Eye Reveals
Iris Structures
Other Iris Indications
Denny's Workshop
Discovering Relationship
My Peg's Family-Tree Connection
Healing From Inherited Distortion
Solving My Parents' Marriage
Rayid for Your Peg
Transfer from My Peg's Ancestors to Successors
Ancestral Lesson Keys

WHO AM I? WHAT CAN I LEARN FROM MY ANCESTORS?

"Personality is generally genetically determined."
Denny Ray Johnson

Along my journey to find myself, an important healing discovery stands out; I learned my peg was born with a built-in personality determined by my ancestors before I was born. I found it very freeing to learn about my peg's natural talents and abilities, which had been programmed into my DNA. This knowledge transformed my perspective so much I would like to share it with you. Let's look at the basics of Rayid™, a system for understanding the genetics of personality developed by Denny Johnson, and how this relates to you, dear reader.

Energy Vibration

"Beyond the personalities they contain, each grandparent contributes a different and specific energetic vibration to the development of the grandchildren. The number of possible combinations creates the infinite uniqueness in all of us."
Denny Ray Johnson

Importantly, I realized I actually reside as a strand of continuing energy. Ancestors in my family tree pass the energy of life down to me along this strand. Like a continuous strand, my energy field transfers information from one generation to the next. It animates my body and shines out of my eyes for others to see. Connected by a spider-web type of filament, I am part of a continuous stream of energy running within my family members. Amazingly, because we are all connected, when I change myself, not only does my energy field change but those of both past and future generations do as well.

My Peg's Genetic Inheritance

"The iris of the eye is like a fingerprint. It is a long-term genetic pattern, a kind of blueprint of inheritance."
Denny Ray Johnson

Until I learned of Denny Johnson's work with the iris, I hadn't thought much about the personality traits I inherited from my ancestors. I recognized my fair skin, dark blonde hair, and blue eyes had been passed down from my Scots and English parents and grandparents. Those inheritances were obvious and understandable. Further, I realized tendencies to act in certain ways also ran in my family. While I recognized these influences, I didn't realize a map existed to assist me in understanding and balancing these inherited patterns. In fact, my irises display that map!

Amazing What the Eye Reveals

Perhaps my fascination with eyes originated as a result of being partially blind. But the information I gained through Denny Johnson's book, *What the Eye Reveals*, and through attending his workshops certainly enhanced my self-understanding. I began to understand the dark spots, the petal-like openings, and straight, thickened strands in my iris were clues on a map, telling me of the genetic personality I inherited.

Surprisingly, my eye structure communicated a wealth of information on a sub-conscious level to others.. For example, my iris reveals certain tendencies to act and react. The fibers, colors, and spots in my iris actually predict my inherited behavior tendencies. Further, the markings types and locations disclose different, important facets of my personality and emotional legacy. Patterns and ways of relating to others had been incorporated into my being from thirty-two of my ancestors going back over four generations. They passed down to me whatever emotional energy blockages they did not resolve in their lives. However, my blind eye remains a veiled mystery since it is covered by cataracts.

The iris map can be compared to an inherited computer hardware directing the software of my personality. The basic iris structure does not change throughout life. Color spots called jewels may be formed in early childhood. Certain color shifts within the iris record changes in the brain's hemispheric dominance, reflecting introversion or extroversion. These modifications occur as I learn to balance my personality.

You and I are meant to be free-flowing energy beings, able to respond without restriction to the occurrences of our lives. Every time you suppress a response to an event, however, you create blockages in your energy flow. These stoppages trigger emotional responses. When these emotions repeat often enough, they soon turn them into habitual ways of responding. Soon a blockage in energy flow is created. In time, this habit goes underground below your awareness, continuing to occur unconsciously—just like driving a car became second nature after you had driven for a while.

Further, if I die without freeing the flow in these habitually energy clogged areas, the following generation inherits the emotional blockages displayed by a corresponding feature in their iris maps. My children's irises will show indications of these accumulated and still remaining blockages. It is then up to my children to try to solve the unbalanced energy patterns they inherit. My family unit provides opportunities to release patterns to achieve balance.

Iris Structures

In his study and development of Rayid™ (a system for understanding the genetics of personality through the study of eyes), Denny Johnson asked a friend to photograph people's eyes. Denny then posted the enlarged pictures around his apartment. Through a series of deep meditations on specific markings in the irises, he created eye maps. He compiled the maps to form an interpretive mapping system. Through the mapping system, Denny Johnson was able to recognize attitude and behavior traits (similar to the iris maps used in iridology). While iridology maps the physical traits, the Rayid™ system maps the emotional traits that form our personalities.

> "The human iris is a pattern revealing how we think, act and choose relationships" (*What the Eye Reveals*).

As Denny focused on a specific spot or an opening in a particular location in an eye, he would receive a vision indicating the type of inherited emotional experience that had created it. He states, "By understanding the structure of the iris, we can determine how a person learns and changes; how that person expresses himself through gestures and words, and how social and intimate relationships are formed" (*What The Eye Reveals*). Denny categorized several different features, which I'll mention here.

- **Stream**-type irises have many close filaments radiating from the iris center and indicate sensory, kinesthetic, and verbal elements. The energy output connected to this category is constrictive.

- **Flower** structures are openings in the irises like flower petals and relate to feeling, emotional, and social aspects. The energy output associated with this category is expansive.

- **Jewels** are color spots in the irises and indicate thinking, analytical, and verbal features. The energy output for this type is constrictive.

- **Shakers** combine all three previous types and are split, alternating between them, and extremists. Their energy output is expansive.

- **Combination** types will exhibit tendencies of several fiber types with corresponding balance challenges.

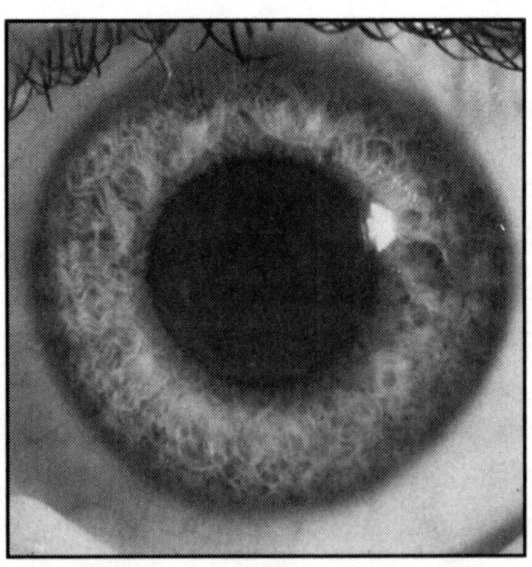

Openings like flower petals indicate a Flower iris structure.

Flowers learn best through hearing. They are visual and expressive with their hands. Flowers are feeling, emotional, spontaneous, and social. They often use expressions like "I feel" or "I see." They are drawn to Jewels for romantic relationships. (Dark band around periphery is a Ring of purpose. Further description follows.)

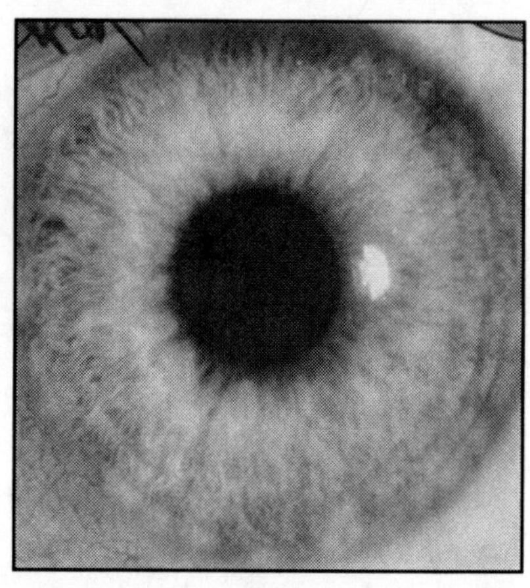

Long, tight, straight fibers indicate a mostly Stream iris structure.

Streams are intuitive and learn best through experiencing their lessons. They are physical, mental, intuitive, and sensitive. Receptive to everything, Streams are sensory, kinesthetic, verbal, sensitive, and mediators, although they are often in motion and seldom at rest. Stillness brings out their greatest potential. They often say, "That touches me" or "I can't stand that." They are attracted to jewel-flower combination types for relationship. (Evidence of concentric ridges called the Ring of Freedom, as well as a Ring of Expression indicating an extrovert has become introvert are shown as thickened fibers around the pupil, described later.

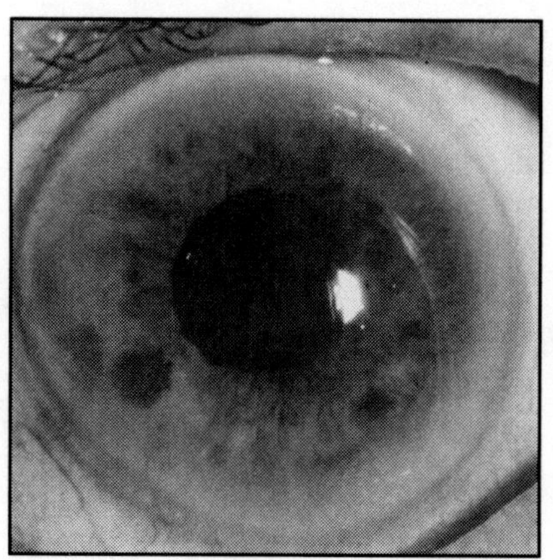

Color spots indicate a Jewel iris structure.

Jewels learn best through seeing. They are thinking, analytical, verbal, and independent. They often find self-acceptance and change difficult. They are frequently philosophers, critics, and planners.

Jewels say, "I think" or "I hear." They are attracted to the visual expressions of a Flower for romantic relationships. (White Ring of Determination described below).

Shaker iris structure combines flowers, jewels, and streams.

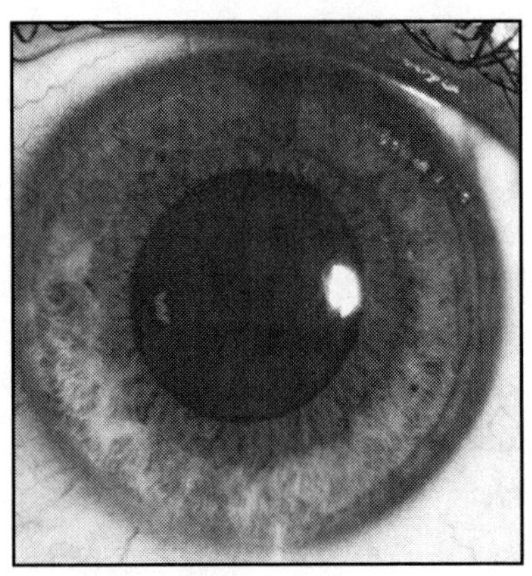

Shakers learn best while in motion or being touched. They have a full range of feeling and half the range of hearing and seeing. By nature, they are extremists. They are split between the attributes of the Jewel and the Flower, and they alternate between extremes of being. They are zealots of new ideas. Devoted and loyal, they tend to be pioneer types, inventors, explorers, or motivators. They can reach great heights of originality and accomplishment or be in the depths of self-abuse and destruction. They are attracted to Streams for romantic relationships. Nature enhances their intuitive intake. (Some evidence of Ring of Freedom.)

Other Iris Indications

- **Left- or right-brain dominance** is shown by stronger color and more jewels or fiber differences and in physical characteristics as well. Color changes at the top of the iris can show if a person has switched dominance (for example, from left to right brain).

- **Ring of Expression** is indicated by thickened fibers noticeable in a circle away from the center of the iris with less fiber showing within the ring closest to the pupil. When a density of fiber fills in again around the pupil, it indicates a switch back to introversion. These are the inward or outward movements of emotional and physical vitality called introversion or extroversion.

- **Ring of Determination** is the white band around the iris perimeter. It shows hardening of arteries and hardening of attitude as well as a determined or decisive nature. It mostly occurs in people over forty. The traits exhibited within the complete structure will determine whether the person is in or out of balance.

- **Ring of Purpose** is a continuous dark band around the iris periphery caused by a lack of fiber. People with this ring constantly seek their special purpose in life. Their great strength will be poise and calmness. When unbalanced, they will exhibit certain tendencies based on their complete eye structure.

- **Ring of Harmony** is a series of white or yellow dots or clusters around the iris toward the outer edge that can indicate high ideals and expectations of others. It may also well indicate certain health tendencies that can lead to exhaustion.

- **Ring of Freedom** is a series of concentric ridges that circle around the iris suggesting an accomplishment oriented nature. The expression they designate can be in or out of balance.

- **Hemispheric Dominance** is indicated in pupil size of one eye compared to the other plus color above the iris. The right eye denotes left-brain dominance and the father. The left eye indicates right brain dominance and the mother.

Denny's Workshop

"By understanding the structure of the iris, we can determine how a person learns and changes; how that person expresses himself through gestures and words, and how social and intimate relationships are formed."

Denny Ray Johnson

After I began to invest time in Denny's theory, I was presented with the opportunity to attend one of his workshops. Denny's assistant photographed all of the attendees' eyes. Denny then projected everyone's pictures in turn onto an overhead screen as he explained what he saw and identified our types of structures. He classified us into shaker, stream, flower, or jewel structured, right- or left-brain dominant, and introverted or extroverted. Denny also told us whether we learned best through seeing, hearing, feeling, or a combination of skills and described some of our strengths and weaknesses. A person trained in Rayid iris interpretation can easily perceive the inherited patterns.

As my eyes were projected, Denny referred to me as an extremist-type shaker, which explained so much about my natural abilities and tendencies. I sat in his workshop astounded by the information and its accuracy. I recognized I am naturally a zealot for new concepts and ideas. While I am devoted and loyal, I either achieve great success or great failures. Indeed later in a private session, Denny told me I could be a teacher, healer, or witch! any one or all three.

Discovering Relationship

"The human iris is a pattern revealing how we think, act and choose relationships."
Denny Ray Johnson

As Denny commented and showed set after set of pictures on the screen, he walked up the stairs of the theatre touched a man and then walked over a row to tap a woman on the shoulder. He said, "You two are a relationship. Your structures complement each other. You are a flower extrovert structure, and you are a jewel introvert structure with related attraction repulsion patterns in each of your irises."

The two, who did not know each other, were surprised and peered more closely at each other. Their opposite iris patterns were two sides of a pattern of attraction. If they joined together as a couple, they would share the learning experience needed to balance the pattern.

At the workshop's conclusion, I purchased Denny's book and two magnifying mirrors to look at my own and other's eyes. One was a concave mirror magnifier that could be held up to the cheek to view your own eyes. The other was a battery operated lighted magnifying lens to look through at another's eyes. To confirm the truth of what I had heard, I determined to research and confirm Rayid by looking into my friends and family members' eyes.

I arranged for family eye photographs. It became apparent my mother had a large number of jewel spots in her eyes. Since a jewel's preferred mode of receiving information is visual, I understood why my mother did not seem to take in auditory information very well. She had to see a new concept to fully digest it. She was a voracious reader.

Taking the mirrors to my office, I checked the eyes of my staff and partners. Harold and I had just added a new partner, Shirley, to our management business. Soon after, Harold ambled into my office saying, "I can't stand how Shirley is always waving her arms about. It is so irritating. She is so emotional."

After Harold left, Shirley slid softly in and said, "I don't think Harold likes me."

However, after I examined their irises and they, taking the magnifiers, looked at their own and each other's eyes in turn, suddenly I exclaimed, "You are a relationship. Shirley is a flower, and Harold is a jewel!"

The two of them stared closely at each other. Within two weeks, they sheepishly admitted they were now seeing each other and soon after moved in together. As a couple, their qualities complemented each other, and they were both very happy together through their remaining lives. Further benefitting their relationship, Harold was a Nine personality on the Enneagram, and Shirley was a Seven. Her outgoing qualities complemented Harold's peaceful nature and helped to draw him out. He in turn provided a calming influence for her. (We'll focus more on the qualities of the Enneagram in the following chapters.)

My Peg's Family Tree Connection

Denny discovered "there is a living connection between all members of the family tree … The tree is a living symbol of our inheritance and of the continuous flow of love and light from our ancestors, nourishing and guiding us from generation to generation" (www.rayid.com).

My birth order in the family is also significant. I demonstrate distinct physical and personality qualities of a second child girl behind a male firstborn. Birth order shows how I will act within the family.

Eye structure differences between family members can also shape their interrelationships. For example, a mother and daughter with the same eye structure will have a difficult relationship. Denny details the varieties of relationships in his books. One feature, for instance, was about the tendency for abuse in a relationship, which shows up as strong features in the lower lateral segment of the iris.

Healing From Inheriterd Distortion

The iris structures hint at aspects of our lives where we need to find corrective balance. If these imbalances remain unresolved for a few generations, the next generation of children may even be born with related physical or emotional disabilities. This can occur if certain problems of imbalance pass down from up to four sets of parents and grandparents. Parents by not resolving their own inherited behavior patterns unwittingly cause these issues. In acting out their blocked inheritance, they even continue to add to these patterns. Increasingly unresolved patterns intensify the distortions within each succeeding generation.

Once he gained this understanding, Denny was able to initiate healing of children born with severe developmental problems by nurturing the children with corrective energy practices. Through the appropriate application of male or female energy, the children's severe developmental imbalances were largely corrected. Denny, with the parents' and volunteer's efforts, was able to restore the children's energy field balance, which greatly reduced their impairments over time.

Denny displayed several amazing pictures of children he had diagnosed and treated in Norway. In one case, nine-month-old twins were blind, deaf, and curled forward with their heads on their stomachs, a sad situation caused by inheriting too much powerful feminine energy from their ancestors. Generations of strongly dominant women had married very submissive men. This had resulted in an imbalance in energy flowing through the governing and central meridians such that the meridians running up the back of the girl's bodies were far stronger than the front meridians, thus causing the forward curl of the baby's bodies. The parents, desperate for a solution, sought Denny Johnson's help after doctors had told them nothing could be done for their girls and to just let them die. However, the second set of pictures of the twins (at age two and a half) showed they had recovered a normal upright structure and were now able to walk normally. Denny told us the twins had recovered their hearing but still had sight impairment after several years. The healing was performed by having men hold the girls twenty-four hours a day; the men also talked to the girls while they were in the alpha or sleeping state. Contact with female energy was denied until the imbalance had righted itself sufficiently to largely reverse the disability. This was effective because the girls' impaired development resulted from the too strong feminine presence in their mother.

In another photograph, a sixteen-month-old boy was arched backwards with his eyes rolled into his head because he had received too much male energy. However, Denny correctly diagnosed and treated him with amazing results. The photos displayed vast improvements in the children's disabilities after being treated with the right kind of continuous nurturing. After being shown those photographs, I realized the importance of correcting inherited imbalances.

Solving My Parents' Marriage

"Your behaviour with the world will be the same as it is with your parents."

Lester Levenson

Using the knowledge I gained from Rayid™, I understood why I had been attracted to my husband. Patterns in my genetics sought the balance of an opposite pattern in order to heal. Each successive generation tries to enter a relationship with a partner that will help them solve their parents' marriage difficulties. Often the offspring do not realize they are doing this. They have, however, been attracted to their spouse because each partner shares one side of an inherited problem; this common problem draws them together. After examining the relationships in my family through the generations, I could clearly see this pattern in operation.

My genetic inheritance (acting as a continuous energy conduit) drew me to others in an attempt to solve inherited emotional problems. For example, I was unconsciously attracted to my husband because he was very much like my father in temperament. In order to correct the imbalances in my parents' relationship, I found a partner who mirrored my father. Through my marriage, I attempted on an unconscious level to make corrections in our relationship to benefit my inherited energy stream. My children also found marriage partners seeming to mimic my qualities or the qualities of my husband. Our children also unconsciously attempted to improve the imbalances they inherited from us. Their children are doing the same—unknowingly trying to solve their parents' marriage weaknesses.

As an example, my parents originated from different social backgrounds (my father from a farm background and my mother from city society). They divorced after seventeen years when my father, who had physically abused my mother, was unfaithful and left to marry his secretary. Consequently, I as a member of the professional class married my husband who was from the working class. While my husband and I instinctively resolved to not continue the physical abuse present in my parents' relationship, mental abuse still occurred in our relationship. My husband was also unfaithful like my father, but we stayed together for twenty-nine years before separating and divorcing. Continuing the cycle, my city-raised daughter married a man from a rural Japanese background. Happily, they continued to resolve the energy balance; they celebrated their twenty-fifth anniversary with a reconfirmation ceremony and are still together.

In another example, my mother did not communicate much with me. She seemed to live in her own isolated world. As she was very critical and argued with her own mother every few days, I did not want to emulate those traits. I rejected her tendencies towards social climbing and arguing and disagreeing with her mother. However, I also choose to live in an isolated way. Regrettably, I also did not communicate well with my daughter. But my daughter also rejected my way of relating and communicates almost daily with her daughter, thereby correcting my imbalance. Through the generations of each family, the subsequent members try to harmonize the energy stream running through them all from their ancestors to the current generation and even to the yet unborn generations.

Rayid™ For Your Peg

Denny's remarkable work expanded into understandings of humanity's interrelated family tree and birth order relationships. In addition to iris interpretation, these enable an even greater understanding of who you are.

You may be thinking this sounds interesting and be wondering, How can I find out what my eyes reveal? What strengths and weaknesses have I inherited that I need to understand and resolve? With the help of a Rayid™ practitioner, a map of your irises can provide you with the information to help you understand, rebalance, and heal your inherited patterns. Denny's work continues through Rayid™ International and the Unitree Foundation. Details of how to reach them appear in the bibliography at the end of this book.

Transfer From My Peg's Ancestors To Successors

Until I examined my past, I didn't understand there is a transfer of energy to a successor in the family when a family member dies. The unresolved patterns within the deceased family member's energy field pass on to another in the family whose energy most resonates with that of the deceased. When my father died in 1989,

I inherited his energy stream of pessimism and negativity. While I had been happy and joyful, I found myself mired in negativity and pessimism once again. It took me many years and periods of depression to work through this added inherited energy and again reach a more positive frame of mind.

When my mother died in 1999, I inherited her energy of loving to read the newspaper each day. I am seemingly addicted to reading the paper even though I have no wish to fill my mind with such constant negativity. I also inherited her fear energy of not having enough money and becoming a bag lady living in poverty. Once again, I added another energy challenge to master.

Ancestral Lesson Keys

1. You are born with an inherited personality.
2. Each of us is a strand of energy linked to our ancestors.
3. When you change your behavior patterns, you affect both your ancestors and your progeny.
4. The Rayid™ (meaning Ray of the Soul) iris maps developed by Denny Johnson provide maps of inherited personality behavior qualities.
5. You are meant to be free flowing, responding without restrictions to occurrences.
6. When you suppress a response, you stop the flow.
7. An habitual repression of energy flow becomes a blockage in your energy field and a routine way of responding to similar situations.
8. If you do not correct these energy-flow blockages, your children will likely inherit them.

9. Iris structures show many inherited qualities, including the way you think, process information, learn, and express yourself.
10. You are drawn to relationships with partners to balance out your inherited behavior tendencies.
11. The birth order in a family also provides clues to your behavior.
12. The right nurturing applied to babies can heal development impairment.
13. You likely will choose a marriage partner to solve your parents' marriage problems.
14. When your family members die, they pass on their energy stream to the remaining family members.

Chapter 2

PERSONALITY KEYS

Healing My Square Peg Begins

The Effect of My Peg's Personality
Core Values
Personality Development
Self-acceptance
Self-worth
Daily Prayer of Acceptance
Serendipity and the Enneagram
The Enneagram Symbol
Formation of Nine Basic Personality Types
Finding My Peg Is a Three
My Healing Begins
Reacting and Responding
More Gifts
Your Peg's Turn to Find Itself
Find Yourself through Avoidance
More Clues on the Triangle
A Peg's Relationship to Time Provides Clues
Moving Against the Arrows
Personality Lesson Keys

HOW HAVE I BECOME WHO I AM? SELF-DISCOVERY

The Effect of My Peg's Personality

My personality—how was it formed and what really is it? The Evergreens, a channeled voice that spoke through the sleeping body of Michael Blake Read, beautifully provides an analogy that describes the effect of personality. The channeled voice points out that my personality drives the direction in my life, likening my personality to that of a man riding a bicycle. The cyclist, my personality, rides over the flat surface of the deck of a huge aircraft carrier ocean liner with the ocean liner illustrating my life. As the man on the bicycle cycles rapidly around the deck, he gives instructions to the ship. The cyclist moves quickly over the ship's deck, turning first one way and then another as he points and says to the ship "Go this way" or "Go that way," and the huge ship responds. It slowly takes him in the direction of his accumulated instructions. My personality created through my daily choices thus directs my life.

Core Values

I inherited and adopted certain core values. Some were good and useful, but many were not. I accepted the core values of being a good person, truthful and open, but at the same time, I believed and formed the value I was not good enough, I was unworthy. I accepted a core belief I had to achieve to be OK. I accepted that failure was bad; I believed if I failed, I was unworthy. Very self-critical, I measured myself against other people or some impossible and unattainable standard. Through constant comparison, I eventually created my lack of self-value through non-acceptance of myself.

I live by my core values, as do we all. Our actions are colored by these very deeply held self-beliefs. Because these values form and shape us, they become deeply embedded in our sub-consciousness. Our actions flow from them most often unconsciously.

Personality Development

Each decision I made in life added to my core foundational patterns. Gradually I built up habitual ways to respond to input based on my experiences. I sought to avoid pain and to enhance pleasure. Over time, these perceived needs and beliefs grew into trees with many connecting branches of experiences. Eventually the roots of these trees were no longer kept in my consciousness but became buried deep in my mind. Whether I am aware of my now unconscious beliefs or not, they still influence my decisions and choices each moment.

I also began to develop a picture of what and who I was. I began to perceive myself in certain ways based on the personality I had developed.

Self-Acceptance

"There is no weapon more powerful in achieving the truth than acceptance of oneself."

Swami Prajnanpad

While I suffered from low self-esteem, I didn't realize self-acceptance was even possible. I always wanted something, and I constantly criticized myself. I lacked self-acceptance. With my many healing changes, I'm now able to achieve a large degree of self-acceptance.

I realized self-acceptance means accepting without reservation everything about myself, without the need to change or regret my strengths or weaknesses. I must accept my perceived shortcomings, all the mistakes, without any reservation or conditions. Acceptance includes self-forgiveness for my perceived failings, accepting both fear and love, accepting my life is a blessing and a gift, and I can learn, change, and grow.

Profound acceptance entails an open heart ready to receive whatever the day may bring with complete loving recognition of what actually occurs in the moment. Self-acceptance doesn't mean I have to be perfect—just that I accept what and where I presently am.

Self-Worth

"Self esteem is the reputation we acquire with ourselves."
Nathaniel Branden, PhD

As a small child, I unconsciously added to my inherited personality. Because I was also self-critical, I saw myself as unworthy. My natural self-esteem gradually disappeared until I lost my sense of self-value. I covered up my natural state of loving acceptance with inherited and environmentally induced patterns. I no longer felt consciously aware of the patterns my responses were ruled by.

What is self-worth? It's a proper view of yourself, knowing you have value as a being, as a person in the world and you're contributing to the whole in some way. I began to restore my sense of self-worth when I accepted myself in a new way, discovering my old, unhealthy pattern of relating to myself had been untrue and based on a false belief. With this new understanding, I also understood others around me better.

Spirit woman Lise Storgaard, who sadly died in a vehicle accident last year, wrote a very effective daily prayer of acceptance, which I have used often to open to complete acceptance:

DAILY PRAYER OF ACCEPTANCE

I accept myself completely.
I accept my strengths and my weaknesses, my gifts and my shortcomings.
I accept myself completely as a human being.
I accept that I am here to learn and grow, and
I accept that I am learning and growing.
I accept the personality I've developed, and
I accept my power to heal and change.

I accept myself without condition or reservation.
I accept that the core of my being is goodness and that my essence is love, and
I accept that I sometimes forget that.

I accept myself completely, and in this acceptance I find an ever-deepening inner strength.
From this place of strength, I accept my life fully and
I am open to the lessons it offers me each day.

I accept that within my mind are both fear and love, and
I accept my power to choose which I will experience as real.
I recognize that I experience only the results of my own choices.
I accept the times that I choose fear as part of my learning and healing process, and
I accept that I have the potential and power in any moment to choose love instead.

I accept mistakes as a part of growth.
I am willing to forgive myself and give myself another chance.
I accept that my life is the expression of my thought, and
I commit myself to aligning my thoughts more and more each day with the thought of Love.
I accept that I am an expression of this Love.
I am Love's hands, voice, and heart on Earth.

I accept my own life as a blessing and a gift.
My heart is open to receive, and I am deeply grateful.
May I always share the gifts that I receive fully, freely, and joyfully.
I accept all that I was, all that I am, and all that I choose to become.

Serendipity and the Enneagram

"Finding one's Enneagram type is meant to be a self-enlightenment which leads to authentic personal freedom on a level never before experienced."

Maria Beesing, Robert Nogosek, Patrick O'Leary

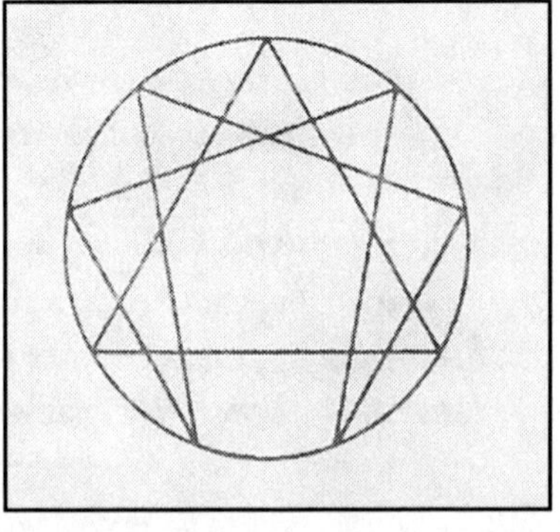

On a quiet weekday afternoon, I snuggled into my chair to do some leisurely reading. Completely unaware of what was about to happen, I made one of my first life-changing experiences reading an exceptional book. I accepted the book's message about personality development and discovered I was perfect just as I am. Although the writers use the word God to describe the Divine, Truth, or Higher Self, you can use whatever term you are comfortable with.

The day I purchased the book seemed uneventful enough. Entering a New Age bookstore, I sought out the spiritual section.

The clerk who greeted me asked, "What kind of book are you looking for?"

"I want to find something about the Sufis," I replied.

"If you are interested in the Sufis, you'll be interested in another book," she said as she went to fetch a book from the Psychology section. She placed the book, *The Enneagram, a Journey of Self Discovery*, into my hands telling me, "This information has come from the oral tradition of the Sufis."

As I took the book from her, it opened to a section called Number Three. Immediately I recognized I was reading a description of myself. Intrigued I bought the book along with a book of Sufi stories, beginning another life-altering experience caused seemingly by chance, a serendipitous happening. One of life's great "ah hahs."

Back at home, sitting in my favorite recliner, I opened *The Enneagram* once again to the section about Threes, finding a statement that the compulsion of Threes is to avoid failure. Ooh! That's dead on, I thought. I took a short test of twenty questions; most of them seemed to fit me. Fascinated, I flipped through the book reading every section about Threes.

The Enneagram Symbol

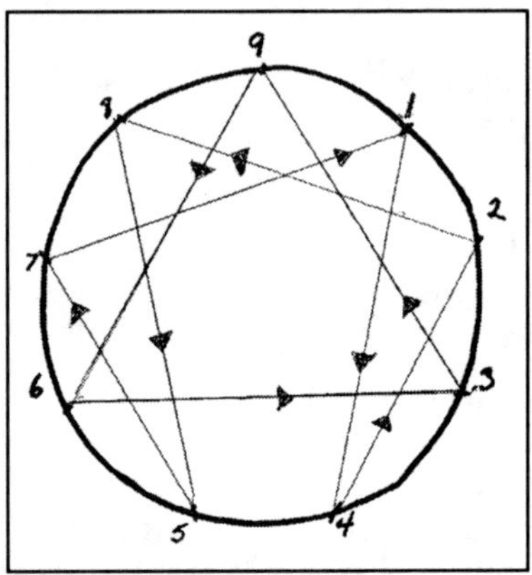

The Enneagram is a very unique symbol delineating the flow of energy within a completing cycle of change. Each person can find their description in the qualities ascribed to the Enneagram. When the categories do not seem to fit well, it is likely other aspects, perhaps inherited aspects, are also present.

A process or cycle begins at number nine and traverses the circle from number one back to nine in a clockwise direction. A completing process must move first in an outgoing movement, reach a change of direction, and then return to its starting point having gained the experience of the process. Then the process begins again but on a higher octave. As the energy moves outward, new energy comes in at several points to maintain the circular flow of the process. Without these points, the energy would not remain within the movement forward of the cycle process.

A triangle is set within the circle. At the three points of the triangle intersecting with the circle, energies from outside enter the process, which is necessary to continue the flow of the process in a direction toward its completion. At the three point, something is added. At the six point, something is removed The nine point represents a place of balance between the two. Nine, being both the alpha and omega point, is the start of a new cycle of progress as well as the point of completion of another. The lines within the circle represent internal flows within the process moving in the direction of the arrows.

For a more complete description of the Enneagram symbol and the laws describing its formation, please go to Chapter 11 Spiritual Keys: The Future of Mankind.

Formation of Nine Basic Personality Types

At some point in the past, the Sufis superimposed the acquired personality tendencies of all persons onto the Enneagram symbol. The nine basic types of personality represented all of humanity. In *The Enneagram*, I read about how the nine different personality types described in the book are formed at a very early age. Each person makes decisions based on their limited experience of life, selecting from three distinct self-concepts (or ways of looking at the self) and three distinct preferred modes of behavior (or ways of relating to the world). These decisions become a strategy to defend and protect the self. The three concepts of self are:

1. "I am bigger than the world."
2. "I must adjust to the world."
3. "I am smaller than the world."

The three behavior modes are:

1. "to act against the world (aggressive behavior),"
2. "to act towards the world (dependent behavior),"
3. "to act away from the world (withdrawing behavior)."

I conjectured that these behavioral choices could perhaps occur in young children based on their experiences.

- For example, a child's concept of being bigger than the world might form when all of the child's needs were immediately met as a young baby. For example, when the baby was wet, it was changed; when it was hungry, it was fed, and it was loved. That child would think it must be bigger than the world because whatever the child wanted was provided.
- Likewise, another baby might develop the concept of adjusting to the world based on a different experience. Sometimes someone would come to feed and change it, but sometimes no one would come when it cried to be changed or fed or held. That baby might decide it must adjust to the world.
- The baby left without its needs met when it was hungry or wet might conceive the idea it must be smaller than the world.

Having developed a concept of itself relative to its surrounding world, the baby would then make a choice to act outwardly against the world, to act towards the world, or to act by withdrawing from the world.

Finding My Peg Is A Three

"The Enneagram is intended to help persons see themselves in the mirror of their minds, especially to see the images of personality distorted by basic attitudes about self."

Maria Beesing, Robert J. Nogosek & Patrick H. O'Leary
(The Enneagram)

Threes make decisions to adjust to the world and to act aggressively.

For most of the early years of my life, I wanted to be a man; I thought I was the wrong person, that I was really more a man than a woman. I was tall, large, loud, powerful, and aggressive in my actions. But girls, I thought, were supposed to be small, dainty, feminine, simpering, yielding, and quiet. Until I was forty years old, I thought I didn't fit in properly because I didn't possess any of the gentler qualities of womanhood.

What a revelation and healing this book was for me! I am okay! It is okay to be me—just as I am! These concepts literally changed my life. The restoration of my self-esteem took a big leap forward.

My Healing Begins

Reading further, I found diagrams, which showed "traps," that can be healed by "holy ideas" for each type of personality number. The trap for Threes is efficiency. Threes are obsessed with efficiency. I had to agree. To counter this, they need to abandon themselves to God's will, offering their lives in service in happy submission to God's plans for their lives.

The next diagram showing "passions" can be healed by "virtues" startled me once again. The book said the passion of Threes is deceit. I was shocked! Me deceitful? Surely not! I pondered the idea for a moment and shamefacedly had to acknowledge I really was deceitful. I put on a false front, a mask, submerging and hiding my real feelings while I tried to become what the people around me wanted me to be. Not only that, I took photocopies from the office copier and did not pay for them. I also didn't declare everything in my suitcase to customs officials when crossing the border.

Having completely recognized myself in the descriptions, I immediately made a decision to embrace the healing virtue of Threes—truthfulness. Henceforth, I would be totally honest and truthful—well, at least in all of my dealings. I recognize the times when I submerge my true feelings behind a mask of persona, which still causes me concern. Fresh tears come as I write this. I am still not as in touch with my feelings as I need or want to be; however, I continue to grow and learn.

The Enneagram describes how Threes use their feelings for everything, including thinking. As a result, they often are not in touch with their feelings since they find it hard to differentiate between their emotions and their thoughts. I now spend time examining what it is I truly am feeling when I notice my mood.

Sometimes tears come as I focus on what I am really feeling. Other times I recognize I am depressed. Rather than reacting to sadness by masking emotions with another activity such as eating, as has been my pattern, I stop to acknowledge and feel the emotion. Often that acceptance changes my mood for the better.

Reacting and Responding

"Anything that bothers you is not outside you: the bother is within you."

Lester Levenson

The Enneagram also describes spontaneous movements of "consolation" and "desolation" affecting each personality type. Consolation comes from responding to balance your personality type.

Desolation comes from reacting, in a manner that further unbalances your personality. We all must recognize the difference between reacting or responding to other persons and situations. Reacting is an expression of defense of my personality. Reacting is rejecting what is occurring, wanting a different outcome.

Responding is acting in service to God and in harmony with the experience of what is actually occurring at a particular moment. With the ability to respond comes an awakening of the fruits of the spirit: love, joy, peace, patience, kindness, goodness, trustfulness, gentleness, and self-control.

More Gifts

The Enneagram contained wonderful therapeutic powers for me. It enabled me to understand and love myself as I truly am and provided great healing of my self-esteem. I was also able to see what number types my family members were. I now honor their differences accepting them as they are. As I interact with them, I understand better why each person acts the way they do.

After absorbing the concepts, greater tolerance was just one more gift I received along with the most wonderful gift—a massive increase in self-esteem. My serendipitous experience with *The Enneagram* changed me permanently. I went on to read a number of books detailing personality and the Enneagram but none were so clear and direct. May God bountifully bless the writers for the healings they have brought me and others.

Your Peg's Turn to Find Itself

You, too, can find your basic personality structure, embrace the change, increase your self-worth, and then honor it. Honor who you have created yourself to be. Learn to be comfortable in that role as your part of our wonderful greater whole.

Find Yourself through Avoidance

One of the easiest ways to start is to find yourself through what you avoid in life and locate the defensive strategy you've developed to secure security and meaning in life. While you may not yet perceive it, it is an underlying problem in your life. The problem must be faced head on if you are to grow and change.

For example, my biggest avoidance was failure. I was afraid to fail, so sometimes I wouldn't even try. I thought, I can never be good enough so why should I even start? My compulsion greatly influenced how I considered myself in relation to others. Because I was not aware of the subtle hidden impact it exerted on me, I made decisions based on fear of failure. I held myself back for far too many years.

What is your avoidance? What is your Achilles heel? You need to discover it and accept or exorcise it through self-reflection and change. The avoidances of each personality type are listed below:

1. Ones avoid anger.
2. Twos avoid need.
3. Threes avoid failure.
4. Fours avoid ordinariness.
5. Fives avoid emptiness.
6. Sixes avoid deviance.
7. Sevens avoid pain.

8. Eights avoid weakness.
9. Nines avoid conflict.

My mother was a ***One***. She avoided expressing anger because she was a perfectionist, but her annoyance came out as carping and criticism. As a One, she did not feel comfortable unless everything she perceived in her outer world was perfect. As the brunt of her criticism was directed at me, I found her hard to live with until *The Enneagram* helped me to understand why she acted the way she did.

One of my sons is a ***Two***. He does not feel comfortable unless he is helping others. He needs to be needed by others. He feels he only has value when he is relating to others. As a result, he does not honor or acknowledge his own needs. Because he is a truly caring person, people take advantage of his willingness to help.

As a ***Three***, I grew up thinking I only had value if I succeeded. I placed my identity in the role I had. Because I also sought approval from others, I assumed a persona, a mask covering my insecurity. Living inside this persona, I did not realize I was not totally honest in the way I presented myself to others.

A friend who is a ***Four*** avoided being ordinary because she felt she was different from others. Her life as a child had been tragic. It made her feel special to be unique. She would wear unusual clothing and try out atypical hair colors in order to stand out and be seen as different. She often succumbed to melancholy.

A very bright young man I knew was a ***Five***. He avoided emptiness through storing knowledge. He desired to fill his inner emptiness because of a lonely upbringing as an only child. He withdrew from others in order to think, observe, and gather knowledge. He didn't enter fully into life but watched from the sidelines. He spoke so quietly I had to strain to hear him. He feared sharing what he knew, worrying it would leave him empty. A miser, he kept his wisdom to himself and his money as well.

An older lady in our group was a ***Six***. Concerned the rules be completely obeyed, she allowed herself no deviance. Obeying the law was very important to her. She was anxious, fearful, and insecure. She worried about making a wrong decision. She was dependent on others. Being part of a group and loyal to her group was important to her. Needing to be secure motivated her life.

Another close friend was a ***Seven***. She avoided pain whether it was mental or physical. She was optimistic and fun loving. She would distract herself from anything perceived to be painful with pleasurable activities. She was a great marketer and networker. She did not always complete her tasks if they involved difficulty and pain of any kind. She seemed oblivious to others who were in distress.

A man in one of the buildings I managed was an ***Eight***. He abhorred weakness and would bully other residents. He was a strong man and the other residents in his building feared him. He perceived the other residents as weak, which triggered his own fear of weakness. When I stood up to him, speaking to him forcefully, he would accept it because he respected my strength. He would then meekly back down from his threatening stance.

One of my close friends was a ***Nine***. He could not stand conflict or violence of any kind. He experienced life with an even energy level. Tension took too much out of him. He was a peacemaker who tended to be lazy but was extremely lovable. Likely because he had grown up in an orphanage, he could not believe others loved to be with him. He felt lacking in value. His energy was very balancing.

What number are you? Simple quizzes in *The Enneagram* book will help you see yourself in a true light. Honestly exploring within yourself may bring up pain as you begin to see what you are. Sincerely looking at yourself will lead you to discover how you have chosen to be in the world. Honesty will enable you to begin to see the personality you have structured. *The Enneagram* guides you to see truthfully and then to embrace the appropriate healing changes in your life. It can be hard to accept the truth about yourself. But it is oh so worth it in the end. *The Enneagram* can be a major turning point in your life as it was in mine.

More Clues on The Triangle

In progressive cycles of development and growth, we move around the outer circumference of the Enneagram circle. Moving around the Enneagram from a new beginning to completion, the energy lines within the design connect us to certain viewpoints of the cycle process. At each point of development, sighting along the connecting lines enables us to view future possibilities or look at our experiences.

The personality types finding themselves on the triangle points—the Three, Six, and Nine—will also express a recognizable energy. These points are places where energy enters the cycle to help maintain its direction. This incoming energy redirects the movement of processes of change in a person's life. Without redirection, the process may not reorient itself into a completing pattern.

- As a Three, I am at one of the points of incoming energy to maintain the direction of the process. I love to gather and provide helpful information to others for their gain.

- My friend who's a Six was at the opposite incoming energy point. She would provide cutting comments to tear me down to let go of something that wasn't serving me.

- Another friend who is a Nine (the point of incoming energy) provided an example of balancing both energies in a harmonious positive way. Conflict upset him. He always sought peaceful solutions.

Do you recognize any of these qualities in yourself? Are you a Three, Six, or Nine (one of the triangle points)?

You also have ways of relating to the energies of thinking, feeling, and responding from your instinctive gut reaction. If you are located on the triangle points, you will find your response to energy input is distorted. The point positions represent the strongest use of one or another response system.

- For example, as a Three, in the heart of the feeling center, I did not recognize I use feeling for thinking and gut responses. Feeling is so strong and a natural part of my personality that I have confused it. I misused it by turning for guidance to my feelings in place of thinking or instinctive gut recognition.

- A Six is at the heart of the thinking center and will use thinking for feeling and instinctive gut responses.

- A Nine is at the heart of the instinctive gut center and will use instinctive gut responses in places where thinking or feeling would best be turned to for guidance.

A Peg's Relationship to Time Provides Clues

When we are being compulsive, we each will relate differently to time.

1. Ones feel dominated by time. They feel there isn't enough time to accomplish things properly. They feel chained to time.

2. Twos experience time depending on whether there are interpersonal encounters. Without it, time has no meaning.

3. Threes experience time as a means to get somewhere. Because they are achievement oriented, they seek efficient use of time. They tend to take on too much and try to do too much for the time available to them. (This describes me perfectly.)

4. Fours measure time by how much emotional intensity it provides. Time will either fly or drag on according to the intensity of their experience. They tend to be late unless they anticipate the appointment will be an experience of deep involvement.

5. Fives watch time go by. They want to examine every aspect of an activity to understand it and are miserly with their time, believing there are many things to comprehend and observe and not enough time to do it.

6. Sixes relate to time as an authority, a boss. Completing things on time is very important to them. They try to keep their deadlines. They typically arrive or leave on time.

7. Sevens find time to do more fun things. Time is expandable if they are having a good time. They often have trouble being on time. Future planning is important but getting down to achieving their goals is not, so they become procrastinators.

8. Eights don't let time control them; they control time. They will go at their own pace, but often arrive ahead of time. If they are involved in something significant, time is not an issue. They keep moving with a quiet impatience.

9. Nines find being on time is not important so long as they stay on schedule. Each moment of time has the same length. They need to follow schedules and try to keep emotional content low. They find changes in schedule upsetting.

Moving Against the Arrows

The interplay of energy flow within a process is indicated by the directional arrows in the Enneagram symbol. My growth can be enhanced by resisting moving in the direction of the easy flow. By moving against the arrows, I strengthen myself in beneficial ways.

The Enneagram gives excellent details about the ways to heal your personality disorders by moving against the arrows. You can heal your unbalanced self by moving against your compulsions, passions, traps, and denials to accept and embrace your virtues, pride, redemption, and holy ideas. Used copies of *The Enneagram, a Journey of Self-Discovery* are available at Amazon.com (See the Bibliography for other information).

Personality Lesson Keys

1. You direct your life through daily moment-by-moment choices.
2. Your deeply held beliefs become your core values. If these are negative and not serving your greater self, they need to be changed.
3. Unconscious beliefs influence your moment-by-moment decisions.
4. Your self-perception is based on your core beliefs.
5. Total acceptance can restore self-worth when you recognize your true inner nature is Love.
6. You are perfect just as you are, and it is okay to be just you.
7. The Enneagram is a Sufi symbol used to describe the formation of distinct personality types and how they function.
8. The Enneagram is also a unique symbol delineating the flow of energy within a completing cyclical process of growth and change.
9. The Enneagram personality descriptions can allow you to accept your idiosyncrasies as an individual.
10. The Enneagram personality types can facilitate you (like me) in your understanding of your family members and acquaintances, enabling you to be more tolerant of their differences.
11. What you avoid experiencing can help you to identify your Enneagram personality type.
12. Your self-concepts develop at an early age from your perception of your relationship to the world and how to act within it.
13. You can heal your dysfunctions by moving against your compulsions and passions, denials and traps, toward embracing and accepting your virtues, pride, redemption, and holy ideas.

14. You can heal your perceived dysfunctions by embracing an opposite quality—a virtue to heal a passion.
15. Reacting is a defense of personality to what is occurring.
16. Responding is acting in harmony with what is occurring.

Chapter 3

MORE PERSONALITY KEYS

Expanding My Square Peg Self-Knowledge

Cycles of Existence
Mid-Life Crisis
Channeled Guidance
Cycles of Astrology, Numerology, and Tarot
Fitting My Peg into Astrology Cycles
Uranus' Generational Cycle
Numerology Lays out My Peg's Future
Kabbalah & Tarot Awaken My Peg to Spirit
Higher Arcana Keys
Palmistry, Re-Birthing, Hypnotic Regression, & Shamanic Practices
Seeing My Peg's Creations
I See My Peg as I Am, the Result of Me
People Love to Help Pegs Get Sorted Out
Personality Lesson Keys

OTHER SELF-DISCOVERY METHODS

I view my incarnation as a human as a great gift, although it took many years before I could understand and appreciate it. Through my studies I came to realize I am actually spirit that chose to be embodied (incarnated) in form as a human to gain experience. To experience the experiencing of experience. I believe the purpose of becoming human involves gaining love and wisdom, and rediscovering our true selves within. We each enhance our being with our many experiences and differences. First I explored many fields, learning more about myself and how I fit into the wholeness. Then later when I had restored my self-esteem sufficiently, I eventually realized all that is necessary is to live from my innermost being. In my search for meaning, my questing mind voraciously explored many esoteric systems of wisdom. I describe a few of them below.

Cycles of Existence

"The pulse of life is one of cycles and rhythms. There is a rhythm to the seasons and to the ocean tides, there are cycles in the growth of plants and in the course of night and day. Whether we speak of the life of a star, a planet, a tree, or a human being, there are observable cycles of birth, youth, maturity, old age, and death."

Dr. Donald M. Epstein

Through many different sources, I came to understand how cycles of rhythmic waves affect and govern all aspects of my life. Sometimes reading about a type of cycle would lead to a deep knowing inside; allowing myself to be in harmony with the greater and lesser cycles brings more inner peace. Another value in learning to understand various personal and universal cycle systems entailed the development of my feeling of belonging to a greater universal reality.

Of course, we are all familiar with the cycles of waking and sleeping, the seasons of the year, or the phases of the moon. Birth began my life cycle, and passing through death will take me into a new cycle in another dimension. However, innumerable cycles exist, many moving within each other. Cycles are rhythmic rays of energy that fluctuate in distinct frequencies and waves or pulsations. Cycles within cycles affect every aspect of our bodies and lives. Moving within greater cycles are lesser cycles within these major flows.

The ancients related the energy experienced within a particular part of a cycle to the effects caused by the rotation of the seven known planetary influences. Not only did they recognize the planets influenced the days of the week but also shorter periods within a day. In attempting to harmonize with their surroundings, the ancients aligned their daily activities to the functions and qualities of these cycles.

Consequently, the days of the week were deemed to follow the order of the planets. Sunday was the day of the Sun, Monday the day of the Moon, Tuesday the day of Mars, Wednesday the day of Mercury, Thursday the day of Jupiter, Friday the day of Venus, and Saturday the day of Saturn. Then the cycle repeated. Each planet represented a prototype of certain energies. Sunday was the start of the cycle and had the quality of creativity, promotion, advancement, and individuality. Monday was the day of the Moon with the characteristics of co-operation, power to influence others, domestic affairs, and changing moods. A day of action would be best on a

Tuesday for Mars was seen as the influence of aggression, energy, quarrels, war, and physical exertion. Mercury's day, Wednesday, was for communication, intellect, mobility, science, and education. Jupiter's day, Thursday, was a day of optimism, luck, abundance, and higher thought. The day of Venus on Friday would be for rest and leisure and was seen as best for beauty, affection, happiness, and arts and crafts. Saturn's Saturday was for growth, planning, concentration, and real estate. Saturday being the last day in the cycle also became a holy day, the Sabbath. In modern times, we shifted the start of the cycle of days to Monday from Sunday and unbalanced the whole ancient rhythm of natural living.

In addition to systems of astrology, numerology and more popularly known cycles of existence are the daily energy cycles known as biorhythms, which chart emotional, mental, and physical highs and lows on a daily and weekly basis. Daily cycles can be plotted to form biorhythm charts indicating the highs and lows of different energy cycles impacting your body each day.

Additionally, we experience cycles of human development as we grow from babyhood to old age. Knowing about the cycles of existence enabled me to see and accept where I was in life's progression. Understanding the cyclical nature of living provided a type of framework for my life.

Each embodiment incorporates experiential stages of learning to be human, which must be mastered in a given lifetime. The stages follow a predictable, cyclical growth pattern related to seven planetary influences. Further, each individual life is divided into periods of seven years. From birth to age seven, under the influence of the sun's creativity, a child is involved in rapid physical development and mastery of form. From age seven to fourteen, a child experiences emotional development through often painful trial and error as he learns cooperation in the family. The Mercury years from fourteen to twenty-one are spent in action and rebellion against the status quo, preparing for a separate life away from the family. From twenty-one to twenty-eight, Mercury's influence teaches thinking and reason. By age twenty-eight to thirty-five, a person experiences expansion and creates goals to move toward. By age thirty-five to forty-two, a more relaxed awareness develops. The final cycle from age forty-two to forty-nine heralded the end of life in ancient times. In that cycle, we experience discipline and practicality.

Following the last cycle, the cycles begin to repeat themselves, adding greater depths to each stage of mastery. From age fifty to fifty-seven as the new cycle begins, one explores new creativity and spiritual life influences. From fifty-eight to sixty-four, one relaxes into cooperation and family concerns as grandparents and guides of the new generation. From sixty-five to seventy-two, in action and rebellion against our aging forms, world travel frequently occurs. Ages seventy-three to eighty focus on our diminishing capabilities of memory and the development of wisdom and reason. Now with greater life spans and the addition of two new planetary influences (Uranus and Neptune), we expect to live longer.

Mid-Life Crisis

"The cycle you are working on is the cycle called 'yourself.'"
Robert M. Persig

At midlife, having reached the apex of the inward flow of the life-force cycle, the energy begins to reverse. While most are not consciously aware of how these cycles affect them, they still experience them. At the start of the energy-flow reversal around age forty-eight to fifty-four, many people may feel they have somehow missed out on something. The incoming life-force energy cycle begins its reversal, returning to the source and to death. Most people do not realize what they experience at this mid-point is due to the change in direction of the energy flow. The midlife crisis occurring in some people at that age is caused because they intuitively sense or feel the change in energy. Men, especially those who have strived to build something in their lives, often experience a midlife crisis. In order to recapture some of their earlier more vibrant energy, men seek out younger women to help revive their energy for life.

Women also go through midlife entering menopause and cessation of their production of ovum. I began my inward return gradually, experiencing physical decline, then the balancing and smoothing out of emotional highs and lows. Now in my seventies, I note my wrinkles and memory weaknesses as part of a general decline leading toward eventual withdrawal of my life force and spiritual preparation for death.

Everything is also in a constant state of change and growth, continually evolving into more. Levels of development occur within the same cyclical space and time, evolving from the tiniest particle into energy then matter and to ever greater expansions of growth, complexity, and change. From a particle to an electron, to an atom, into a molecule, into a cell, and on to become the community of an organ—a variety of ever-larger processes of growth affects humanity as a whole.

I learned about another interesting lesser cycle from Annie Besant; this cycle appears to influence whole groups or nations of people who incarnate together to learn the same lessons. People incarnate in areas suitable for the stage of development they are to experience. Annie suggests mastering the physical world through survival is an early human incarnation event. Many people struggling to survive in Africa presently share this experience. In subsequent incarnations, emotional qualities are developed, such as caring for one's self and learning to care for and get along with others. This stage progresses into learning to accept responsibility, to be dependable and accountable, perhaps through being a servant. The next progression leads to caring enough for the good of another, or the whole, to lay one's life down for others as soldiers do. With the development of mental abilities, the stages lead to mastering the gaining of material possessions and perhaps wealth. Then the next stage of progression may see the loss of those possessions with the realization they did not bring the happiness they seemed to promise. With the release of the attachment to possessions and by embracing other altruistic qualities, the final stage of the progression involves gaining spiritual perspective.

One of the wealthiest nations, the United States, now experiences the loss of material possessions. Perhaps through the suffering, more and more people will open to the awareness there is something more than just physical existence. They begin to become spiritual seekers. At the spiritual stage, a person becomes conscious of his/her innermost being and the dimensions beyond the physical levels. To fully awaken to the pull of their innermost being, the control of one's existence must ultimately be given to the real self within.

"It has now been demonstrated that mankind is subjected to vast, perhaps cosmic, forces that determine his actions. These forces determine booms and recessions, prosperity and depressions... They control or at least influence man's susceptibility to various sorts of disease. They change man's mood from liberal to conservative and back to liberal again."

E.R. Dewey

Cycles not only impact my daily life, but they affect humanity as a whole. When I read J. G. Bennett (author of *The Enneagram* and a disciple of the great spiritual teacher G. I. Gurdjieff), I discovered the cyclical nature of many different aspects of life. Bennett plots a number of progressions in the symbol of the Enneagram, in particular, describing the progressive cycles of the earth (which he names the biosphere).

Mr. Bennett describes how humankind as a whole continually moves toward a greater embodiment of the many levels of development and a deeper understanding of itself over an immense span of many eons on earth. Using a circular diagram divided into four quadrants, he illustrates the cycles and stages of development. Each quadrant of man's development takes eons of time. Through these major cycles, humankind moves from its beginning as animal man at the apex of the current cycle through the quadrants.

Imagine progressing clockwise around the perimeter of a circle divided into four sections: physical development, emotional development, mental development, and spiritual development. Each quadrant section of ninety degrees of the circle represents a specific type of quality for humanity to master. Beginning at the top of the circle and moving clockwise through the quadrants, humankind has progressed downward through physical development and emotional development. Humankind as a whole has mastered physical and emotional qualities and abilities and is now on the upward arc passing through the quadrant of mental development. The final spiritual quadrant will eventually be traversed to return this great cycle to its end and the beginning of the next cycle. Ultimately, humanity becomes a new, highly evolved, spiritual creation ready to begin another cycle of existence as the cycle returns to its beginning but on a higher level. At several points of the cycle, outside energies help maintain the circular progression toward its conclusion.

Accepting Mr. Bennett's information and looking at what he charted of our past, humankind is likely on a threshold about to transition into new levels of awareness. His description enables me to accept the major changes happening on earth as this new era is ushered in. I sense the higher frequency of energy that humankind now moves into as this change occurs. These higher frequencies disturb people who have not yet begun to harmonize with their present energy frequency, especially if they cling to dark or evil ways.

Additionally, a member of the Theosophical Society, in a compilation called *The Solar System* by A.E. Powell, describes how the earth may move within its cycle of existence over millions of years from its birth in creation to its final demise (as do other parts of our solar system).

Channeled Guidance

One must be careful to properly discern the legitimacy of channeled guidance (information received while an individual seeks guidance from ethereal spirits); however, channeled information can be a source of great guidance. Accordingly, I benefited from video sessions of Ramtha, who was channeled by Jayzie Knight and another channel, Lazarus. As mentioned previously, I also attended a number of sessions of The Evergreens, channeled by Michael Blake Read.

Further, Dr. Jerry Jampolsky introduced me to *The Course of Miracles* in 1980 when he came to lecture at the Palliser Hotel in Calgary. *The Course of Miracles*, a channeled work, along with the teachings of Dr. Jampolsky enabled me to make many beneficial changes.

Many channels claim to be Mother Mary, Jesus, or various angels. However, through my later spiritual teachers, I learned a truly high-frequency spiritual being would never impose his or her energy directly into a person. Their frequency of energy is so high and of such great intensity the shock to the body receiving their energy could be very damaging.

Cycles of Astrology, Numerology, and Tarot

"My experience with the Tarot and Astrology is that both are outer expressions of veiled 'magical' truths."

Max Freedom Long

Additional self-healing came about through my explorations of the ancient arts of astrology, numerology, and the Kabballah. While not as momentous as learning of the Enneagram, seeing my personality relative to cycles of existence was illuminating. I began to see that cycles of influence governed my life and where my square peg fit into a greater scheme of things.

The ancient metaphysical systems of astrology, numerology, and tarot all provided ways to explore the cycles of my life experience, enabling me to understand who I am and providing glimpses of my future. As part of one universal being, I am affected by the vibrations governing our whole universe. I feel better and more alive when I am in harmony with these energy cycles. Gaining cycle knowledge helped bring me to a place of peace and acceptance. My correspondence to the whole as measured through these systems can tell me how my personality will be impacted as I move through the cycles of my existence.

Fitting My Peg into Astrology Cycles

"Astrology is the study of the correlations that can be established between the positions of celestial bodies around the Earth and physical events or psychological and social changes of consciousness in man."

Dane Rudyar

While astrology is an art and not a science, it describes cyclical movements and changes occurring not only in the heavens but in individuals. While we observe the cycles of heavenly movements, they also have corresponding effects on earth. Thus my experiences relate to the cycles of the whole earthly and universal being.

The information provided by Charles F. Haanel in "*You*" overviewed how the vibrations of the planets and the ether we reside within affect our lives. He described how we are influenced from birth by frequencies and vibrations from planetary, solar, mental, electrical, celestial, cosmic, light, sound, color, and heat sources. A particular movement causes each vibration in accordance with cosmic laws.

The moment of birth (or actually conception) placed me into an energy field of form at a particular place and time. The position of the planets at the time of my birth exerted an influence on the ether and thus on me, which began to shape my life since all life resides within one field of ether. Movement shapes the ether and becomes energy in a variety of vibrations and forms. Through long astronomical study, the ancients recorded the effects of each planetary influence on life in their communities. These qualities formed a basis for understanding the world. From their studies of a particular planet or placement within the cycle of the heavens, they prepared charts of the heavenly influences to predict the future.

Astrology states the placement of the planets at the time of my birth impacted my life. I learned about myself through my astrological sign qualities and the positions of planets within an energy cycle pattern named Taurus. As a Taurean, I display many of the basic qualities ascribed to the sign of Taurus. Because birth time and location determine the energy field qualities and effect the planetary positions will exert through life, all Taurean's lives while experiencing certain basic influences will differ.

My birth horoscope chart shows the planetary positions; however, the planets representing life forces continually change their locations in the heavens. Thus as shown in progressed charts, I am continuously affected by the changing, planetary interplay. They either harmoniously enhance my activities or I conflict with them as they touch my inborn energy patterns. For instance, Uranus indicates types of disruptive transforming and renewal experiences within one's deepest being as it breaks down old established patterns. In my birth chart, Uranus is conjunct my sun in the seventh house of my zodiac cycle, not only giving my personality (the Sun) sudden insights but drawing me into unusual relationship experiences for my growth. Now Uranus, whose cycle is 84 years, has moved to Pisces in my fifth house of, creativity, children, love affairs, speculation and personal risks. During its transit in Pisces I have speculated and lost financially, have seen old patterns excised, but have also seen my creativity sparked.

Uranus' Generational Cycle

The cycle of Uranus also impacts humanity as a whole. Plotting a complete 84 year cycle around a zodiac circle divided into quadrants, the effect on humanity as a whole of a cycle of Uranus can be traced. Starting at Aries the first quadrant including Taurus and Gemini can be likened to spring, a child and physical development. From Cancer through Leo and Virgo to Libra the second quadrant can be likened to youth, emotional development and summer. At Libra the midpoint, energy changes from incoming to returning. Following around the circle from Libra through Scorpio and Sagittarius to Capricorn we have maturity, mental development and autumn. The last quadrant from Capricorn through Aquarius and Pisces once again to Aries takes us through old age, spiritual development and winter. In 1928 Uranus was in Aries at the beginning of its cycle. In 2010 Uranus completes its cycle and returns to Aries to begin again. When Uranus reached Libra in 1969 humanity was at a mid-point crisis of change, the cold war.

Now we have been traversing through the disruption and death of systems that must change readying ourselves for the birth of new ways of being with each other and our innermost reality as we enter Aries.

Also affecting humanity, along with Uranus in Pisces are Neptune in Aquarius and Pluto in Capricorn. Neptune is higher sensitivity, higher psychism and a wish for ideal states. Pluto is rebirth, regeneration and produces natural disasters while it releases new values.

Capricorn represents perfected mastery, matter, height of worldly ambition, and crystallization. Aquarius represents social consciousness, blends reason and intuition, is altruistic, reforming and visionary. Pisces is sensitivity, changeable, surrender, break down of structures for evolvement.

Humanity as a whole is going through great upheaval and change. If successful in allowing the breakdown of our crystallized ways (Pluto in Capricorn), our re-forming and spiritualizing of society (Neptune in Aquarius), and willingly going through the transforming death of our old ways (Uranus in Pisces), humanity will ready itself for rebirth of a new way of more harmonious life as we begin a new cycle.

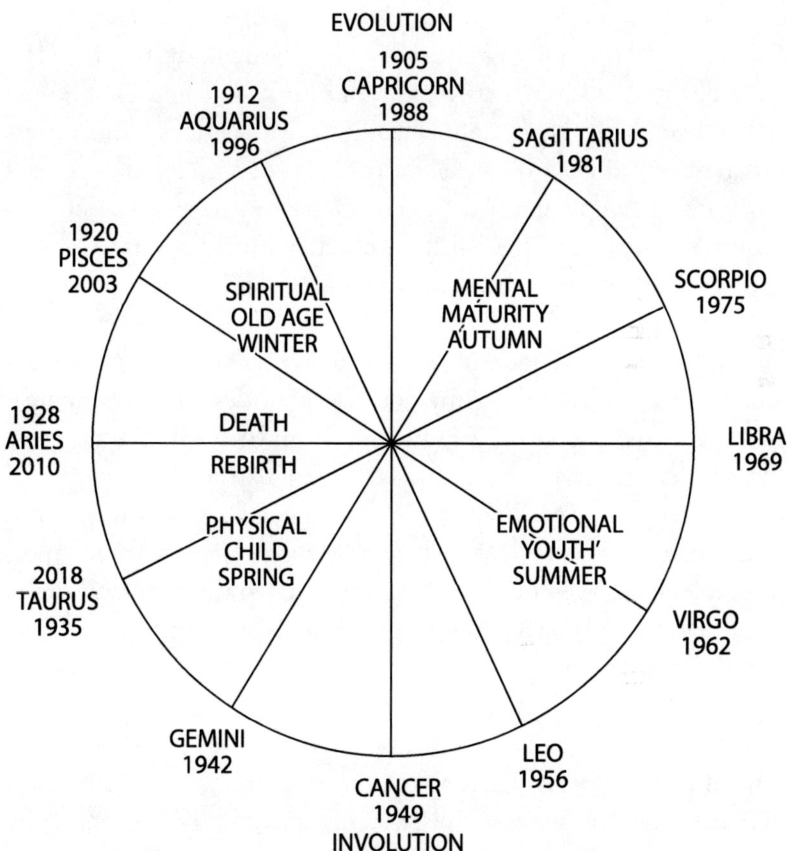

URANUS CYCLE=84 YEARS=MAN'S GENERATIONAL CYCLE

Chinese astrology also describes my experiences in life. I am a fire ox. True to Chinese astrology projections, this past year has been a difficult one for oxen. Many of my financial and other projects went awry.

I reviewed a number of books and over several years had personal readings performed by several astrologers. However, I found the descriptions given by Dane Rudyar in *The Astrological Houses, The Spectrum of Individual Experience* to be particularly helpful. The book describes each planet's position in the zodiac houses and how they relate to the expression of certain qualities. I used the charts generated by an astrological computer program to identify the positions of the planets. Then I put Dane's descriptions of planet-position qualities together with the chart. My interest was so piqued I then did the same for each of my children and grandchildren.

Similarly, *An Astrological Mandala: The Cycle of Transformations and Its 360 Symbolic Phases* by Dane Rudyar describes astrological symbols based partly on a reinterpretation of the Sabian system. It presents archetypical meanings related to the 360 degrees of human development. It gives the meanings of symbols in relation to a structured process of growth in consciousness. Archetypical principles operate in our lives connecting us to the historical cycles of humanity's existence. You may wish to explore this deeper level of self-development.

Other energy influences are also at work in my life so I cannot solely rely on an astrological chart to tell me what to expect. However, it does shed light on some of my basic qualities and the choreography of my life by a divine source. On a greater scale, our planet cycles through the twelve signs of the zodiac every 26,000 years. We are leaving the age of Pisces and entering the age of Aquarius. We can expect greater awareness of our humanity as a whole and the knowledge that we are all interconnected within one universal being.

Numerology Lays Out My Peg's Future

Omnia in numeris sita sunt. (Everything is veiled in numbers)
Faith Javane and Dusty Bunker

Delving into the Kabbalarian system of numerology, I received a private reading from a Rosicrucian, which provided more awareness of self. It detailed what I may experience in my life cycles. At the age of seventy-four, I can see many personality experiences referenced in numerology have been completely accurate.

Numerology (an ancient system of vibration used to determine your path within the cycles influencing your life) is also derived from cycle information. Through many years of refinement, ancient spiritual seers transcribed the meanings of vibration into alphabets. Ancient languages such as Hebrew and Greek have not only alphabetical letters, but each letter also corresponds to a number vibration. Even English letters have numerical correspondences, but they are not widely known. Numerology uses these numerical values derived from the vibrations embedded within the letters of our names and birthdates. The meanings of number vibrations and their values were compiled into lists applying to each number.

- Number 1 represents a new beginning, restlessness, urge to action, a start in a new direction.
- Number 2 represents secret workings, compromise, and peace.
- Number 3 represents the union of 1 and 2, creativity, expansion, and growth.
- Number 4 represents the form built as a result of the merger of 1 and 2 and the expansion of number 3.
- Number 5 represents the experience needed to function in the

new form in the world.

- Number 6 represents love, balance, and harmony through finding the right relationship to function in number 5.
- Number 7 represents physical completion, mastery, and turning within to rest and listen.
- Number 8 represents the results of past efforts, responsibility, and karma.
- Number 9 represents final ending, completion, reward, and transition into the next cycle.

All letters in ancient alphabets correspond with number vibration values. Their values are shown in the following table reduced to a single number.

A	1	N	14 =5
B	2	O	15 =6
C	3	P	16 =7
D	4	Q	17 =8
E	5	R	18 =9
F	6	S	19 =1
G	7	T	20 = 2
H	8	U	21 =3
I	9	V	22 =4
J	10 =1	W	23 =5
K	11 =2	X	24 =6
L	12 =3	Y	25 =7
M	13 =4	Z	26 = 8

The totaling of numerical values of each letter in a birth name and each number in a birth date provides a specific number connecting to personality qualities. The total of my birth date equals the life-lesson number 5 correspondingly described as being here to learn and experience the value of freedom.

My life-lesson number is derived through the addition of my birth-date values. It represents what I must learn in this life and indicates what career path to choose. The number 5 indicates I am here to learn and I value freedom. I will have a quest for knowledge, be an avid reader, fluent talker, and versatile doer. My talents prepare me for dealing with the public and having a literary career. I find it fascinating to see my condominium management career was very much involved with people and now I have rediscovered my love of writing.

My soul number is derived by adding only the vowels of my birth name, which totals 11. The numerological description is one of being an old soul and having learned much about the mysteries of life and death.

My outer personality number vibration of 5 is derived from totaling only the consonant values in my name. Among other qualities it describes how others see me as having natural curiosity and likely to take chances. It points out my desires can lead to excesses in eating, drinking, drugs, and sex. Looking back, I certainly did overindulge in both sex and eating and have been a high-risk investor.

My path of destiny number is derived by adding the total of all the vowels in my birth name, then the total of all the consonants in my name, leaving them in unreduced form. Then by adding the two totals together, I obtain my path of destiny number, which is a 7. The text describes my destiny is to develop my mind to be a teacher of ethics, a philosopher, or mystic who can reveal some of the mysteries of life to the world. I am entering a new cycle, a new beginning. If I had kept my square peg more attuned to the information, I may have foregone some of the life tests I experienced. Numerology pointed out I would face a test in number 14. Sure enough, I have struggled with my version of a life test through being overweight most of my life.

The most excellent numerology books I discovered are *Numerology and the Divine Triangle* by Faith Javane and Dusty Bunker and *Numerology and Your Future* by Dusty Bunker. The second book shows how to work out your ongoing cycles of days and years. Your life progresses in a series of nine-year cycles. Each year will include particular qualities related to its numerical value. You can determine what will happen to you on any given day, week, month, or year.

Kaballah and Tarot Awaken My Peg to Spirit

"The Tarot need not imply that our fate is bound to overtake us, but rather it indicates how we may best go forth to meet our destiny—that we have a choice."

Susanne Judith

My greater understanding of placement in life came from the symbol known as the Tree of Life in the ancient Hebrew system of Kaballah. The Tree of Life is a map of the journey of the individual soul down from the source and the return to the source once again. More about this journey is written in the Spiritual Keys chapter.

The archetypes displayed pictorially on Higher Arcana Tarot keys are linked to both the zodiac and planets of astrology as well as to numbers.

Higher Arcana Tarot Keys

The Higher Arcana Tarot keys shown are based on Hebrew letters. The Tarot keys pictorially represent archetypal life patterns that speak to our subconscious minds. They provide another way of exploring our cycles of existence. They contain numerical, zodiacal, and planetary correspondences along with many others such as musical, psychological, and so on. The seventy-eight keys of Tarot are divided into two groups: (1) the Higher Arcana corresponding to numbers zero to twenty-two and (2) the Lower Arcana in four suits numbered from twenty-three to seventy-eight (often pictured as four suits of playing cards).

Most people are familiar with Higher Arcana Tarot keys used as picture cards for divination by psychics. They, however, actually show the spiritual cycle of progression of humans to become awakened beings. More information about the Tree of Life and the Higher Arcana keys follows in the Spiritual Keys chapter. Additionally, an excellent description of the meaning of the Tarot keys can be found in *Numerology and the Divine Triangle* by Faith Javane and Dusty Bunker.

Imre Vallyon, The Foundation for Higher Learning

Imre Vallyon, The Foundation for Higher Learning

Palmistry, Re-Birthing, Hypnotic Regression, and Shamanic Practices

While I also explored palmistry, graphology, re-birthing, hypnotic regression, and shamanic practices, they did not provide major assistance in my search for self-discovery and how I fit into the world. Although palmistry was an interesting study, it did not lead to major self-understanding. Intriguingly, I watched how various lines on my palms changed over the years. For instance, my lifeline forked and shortened, perhaps foretelling a shortened length of life. My eldest son's lifeline was short, and indeed he died in an accident at age thirty-six.

In my foray into re-birthing, I once entered a state of breathlessness and peace while performing continuous breathing and lying motionless but conscious of the facilitators discussing and marveling at my state.

Additionally, mental pictures from my experience of hypnotic regression are still with me. During the regression, as I went deeper, I came to an experience at age eight. The relived experience was one of extreme joy at having received a boxed set of Eagle Prismacolor pencil crayons. I had not experienced joy like that for many years.

Then the facilitator took me before my birth in this reality to several prior experiences. In one, I particularly noted the color and sense of the sky (which had a haunting northern quality) while I was on a Viking-type sailboat. I saw myself as a woman bound to a mast and being beaten. I can still picture the tan garment she wore made of a coarse hemp material.

In another regression, I was surprised to look at my feet and see I wore curled-toe dancing slippers. When I went to my home, I lived in a tan stucco building on a street where sewage ran in shallow trough-like channels down the sides of the roads. The connection to dancing seemed to be born out in my present life since I love creative dance.

In yet another experience, I saw myself as a balding man of about fifty wearing a type of toga. I stood in a marble-columned building. I could look out of the columns and see the ocean. Then I walked down some steps to meet others. When I went home, it was very Spartan with a heavy table. I experienced his loneliness. In my current existence, I have chosen to be somewhat of a loner. My living room furniture seems also to be related. The coffee and end tables are heavy, square, oak pieces with simple uncluttered lines.

A similar experience of regression through Core Belief Engineering took me back through my birth to a place before I was born where I resided in the universe in some way. I enjoyed such a feeling of bliss. It stayed for a while but gradually dissipated during the day. This beautiful sensation may have been one reason I began to search for spiritual meaning in my life.

Seeing My Peg's Creations

Seeing takes on profound meaning as I begin to look at just what I have created of my life. I now recognize I have fashioned all of my experiences. I have chosen my responses, my sadness, my happiness, my depressive states, my lack of outer harmony, and my sometimes-unhappy personality. I see I have chosen how I will act.

I see how I let negative thoughts bring negative pessimistic events into my life.

Seeing the truth about myself was not easy. It came with tears and painful anguish welling up from my heart. I had to allow it, to sit in it. In allowing it to be expressed, the blocked energy stored within me began to lessen and be released. My resistance to my good has brought me pain and suffering. My outward search for what I felt was missing in my life has been a tragic mistake. My focus on myself, my needs, and my wants has been a misdirection of my life—all those wasted misspent years. I now see how I never needed to suffer if I had followed the divine plan laid out for me from within.

I See My Peg As I Am: The Result Of Me

"If you want reality to be different than it is, you might as well try to teach a cat to bark. You can try and try, and in the end the cat will look up at you and say, 'Meow.' Wanting reality to be different than it is, is hopeless."

Byron Katie

When I gain understanding and recognition of my unique talents and abilities, I am better prepared to allow myself to flow with life as God or my Higher Power intended. I can stop resisting my good. I didn't realize I opposed my good by clinging to what I wanted to have happen in my life. I insisted on my wants, my needs, and my desires for things to differ from reality. My studies began to show me my present experiences resulted from my past thoughts and actions. What held me back in life was my lack of acceptance of what is, of what I had already created. Now seeing the truth of what I have done, I am making corrections.

I had known for many years I lived life from an incorrect perspective. I saw I focused on the world, ignoring my inner self. Living with an outward focus only on the material world while ignoring my inner world was a misdirection. Outer life is meant to be an expression flowing from within the Self, a harmonious flow directed without self-interest

I only focused on myself and what I wanted or needed. Had I paid attention to what was within, I would have enjoyed living in the world. I would have been more concerned for others than for myself. The more I had given to benefit others, the more I would have received. A rewarding life is not about what I can get for myself but about what I may give to others.

I had to look at the truth within me. It was so easy to be hard on myself for all my failures. "Don't be so hard on yourself," I continuously reminded myself.

You must realize like I did you cannot beat yourself up for past actions. The past is already gone. You created today yesterday. There is nothing you can do today to change yesterday. You must forgive the past and move into the new direction of self-acceptance and self-love.

People Love to Help Pegs Get Sorted Out

Advice from friends and family was sometimes enough to help me find my way again when I was disturbed. But there were several times when my problems seemed overwhelming. I lost sight of my self-worth and direction. I was disturbed, not knowing which way to turn to solve my dilemmas. At several points in my life, I sought professional help through marriage and personal counseling about how to resolve my situations. Being mired in my subjective difficulties my view was too narrow, while the professional's objective view opened me to see a wider range of solutions. I wondered, Why did I suffer so long before reaching out for needed assistance? Seeing a psychologist was of great help in addition to accepting direction from a personal coach and mentor. These trained people provided me with support to set me in a new direction, leading me to create better habits and recover my sense of value. A personal or life coach can also direct you to an appropriate solution. They can provide the support needed to change your life. Their simple suggestions can set you in a new direction as they did for me. Joining networks or Master Mind groups can also provide a support group for specific business or other areas.

Personality Lesson Keys

1. The purpose of existence is to gain love and wisdom and rediscover our true selves within.
2. You are influenced by vibration.
3. Cycles of many kinds of rhythmic energy waves affect and govern all aspects of your life.
4. Through embracing cycle knowledge, you can recognize your unity within a greater universal reality.
5. We all experience seven growth and development cycles.
6. Daily biorhythms chart changes in energy levels in physical, emotional, and mental areas.

7. You can experience a midlife crisis when the incoming life-impulse energy reverses to outgoing.
8. You are more, never less.
9. Humanity evolves as a whole as it goes through major cycles over hundreds and thousands of years, changing from animal man to a yet-to-be-realized spiritual being.
10. In the great cycle, humankind is on the threshold of mental development.
11. People incarnate to learn social lessons of survival, responsibility, service, sacrifice for another, material gain, material detachment, and realization as spirit.
12. The earth itself may be following its path of return to the source.
13. Channeled information is not all from exalted higher-level beings.
14. Studying cycles, astrology, numerology, and tarot can provide new insights into who and what you really are as a tiny part of a universal being.
15. The map of the Tree of Life can illustrate your inner journey beyond mere physical existence.
16. Your life has been choreographed by a greater divine being within.
17. Regression, rebirthing, and breathing practices can open your awareness to spiritual experiences.
18. Recognize you create yourself and your experiences.
19. Seeing truthfully with acceptance enables the release of unbeneficial patterns. Recognize the need to focus and live your life from within instead of focusing and living your life from without.
20. A rewarding life comes through service to others.
21. Explore getting help from mentors or Master Mind groups.

Chapter 4

EMOTIONAL KEYS

Removing the Burs and Splinters in My Peg

WHAT PART DO EMOTIONS PLAY IN WHO I AM?

My experiences and insights may help you to see more clearly the emotions you also have created that no longer serve you.

EMOTIONAL KEYS

"There is a gulf between the self we show to the world and the self that we keep hidden within. The result of this split is an inner parade of doubt, fear, and anxiety every time those hidden feelings are threatened with exposure."

Harold H. Bloomfield, M.D. & Robert B. Kory

Emotions are stored feeling experiences. Because I allowed them to burrow into my sub-consciousness, clearing the feelings blocking my energy was key to my recovery. Releasing blocks to my energy flow freed me to experience life more openly and fully.

Once I have created and repeated a way of responding to feelings, I have simultaneously fashioned an emotional pattern. This pattern will occur every time I experience a similar situation. I may have formed emotional responses to situations no longer serving my needs; yet they still appear when situations trigger them—especially my patterned responses to feelings of not being good enough or not being lovable. These may have been created at a very early age in response to particular situations. Unfortunately, I still allow these patterns to replay repeatedly, strengthening them over time until I actually believe them to be true. These patterns become blocked expressions or energy-flow blockages. Any experience triggering this emotion is now perceived as painful so I do things to avoid the feelings. I block the feelings. It seems easier to accept the original idea behind the emotion than to face it squarely and ask if it is still true.

"Blocks are exactly what the name implies, the lingering residue from some unreleased emotion which continues to obstruct a genuine expression of feelings."

Slow Motion Miracles, Geraldine Smith Stringer by Sherry Sleightholm

If I allow myself to see truly, the very act of seeing brings about a release of stored energy. Seeing truly begins the healing process of releasing energy stored as the patterned response. When I clearly view what I have created, the seeing is often accompanied by tears of release coming up from my inner being and then subsiding, leaving me beneficially changed. Later I notice the emotional pattern has been reduced so the experience has subtly freed me.

My Peg Is Devastated

In my era, a woman was still considered the chattel of a man. With successive generations, much has changed. Thankfully, this situation is no longer true for my grandchildren with each person coming to marriage as equals. But in my time, society expected many girls to marry and be looked after by their husbands like any other type of property. When my parents divorced, it was almost unheard of at that time. I recall the special visit the next-door neighbors made to our house, the only time I think I ever saw them in our house. Sitting tensely in the living room, the neighbors said they would still speak to my mother. In contrast, many others in her circle of engineers' wives ostracized her.

I still recall the severe emotional pain of abandonment I felt when sitting for lunch at the old enamel-topped kitchen table when my mother told me and my two siblings that my father and she were divorcing and he was moving away permanently. I jumped up in pain, my heart rent from my body. I loved my father dearly even though he could sometimes be too harsh. At twelve years old, I doted on my father. How could I accept he would not be home with us anymore?

In reflection from the perspective of many years later, I recognized that to cushion myself from the pain, I developed a protective emotional block. Somehow, I took on the belief I had been abandoned because I wasn't good enough. Unconsciously through my teen years, I began to assuage my stifled feelings with candy and food. However, as every problem is an opportunity, I now know I needed to experience what I did for some reason.

"The good thing about the past is it's over."
Richard Bandler

My Pregnant Peg Gets Married

I was in love with my boyfriend and a bit starry eyed. I used to spend long hours lying on the couch in our living room listening to the dreamy music of James Last while I created loving fantasies of being held in my boyfriend's arms. Although we came from different backgrounds, we often shared long conversations until the wee hours of the morning while we sat in the car. We enjoyed our times together. Because of my strong sex drive and poor understanding of how easily one can get pregnant, backseat-of-the-car-fumbling sex led to my pregnancy at age eighteen. When I told my boyfriend

I was pregnant, he accepted the responsibility, and we discussed getting married. My mother was upset when I told her. She and my father felt their dear daughter had ruined her life.

My divorced parents, living in different cities, arranged a meeting in a downtown hotel room with my boyfriend and me. My father offered to schedule an abortion for me, but I could not kill the unborn life growing within me. So with my parents' sad agreement, my boyfriend and I planned to be married. Very happy and in love, the thought of marriage was a special dream I carried within me. I was working at a summer job downtown at the Calgary Tourist Information Bureau at the time. Situated nearby were pawnshops with inexpensive rings displayed in their windows. I longingly gazed at the rings as I walked by, hoping we could afford a ring. I fantasized of our beautiful life together.

My mother gave us the opportunity to receive the grand sum (in those days) of $250 for our new life if we chose not to have a fancy wedding ceremony and reception. We accepted and arranged for a simple wedding. Mom helped me find a simple white suit for my wedding apparel.

We were married August 10, 1955 at the Rundle Memorial Church on Banff Avenue with two close friends as our witnesses. No photographer would come out on short notice so only a couple of Brownie camera photos commemorated the occasion. The four of us enjoyed an elegant meal at the Banff Springs Hotel where we received several congratulatory telegrams from my uncles and my aunt. After an evening spent with our friends having drinks at a picnic shelter, we spent our wedding night in a bed and breakfast in Banff.

On our return to the city, my grandmother hosted a small reception for us in her home. We located a small basement suite to rent where I became a housekeeper in between bouts of morning sickness. I was glad to get away from my mother's constant criticism and enjoyed setting up house. While at home, my mother had still carped at me not to forget the salt, pepper, cream, and sugar when I set the table. I had been setting the table since I was three for heaven's sake! In charge of my own home, I lived in a false euphoria between the times I had to wash dishes in the only sink (which was in the bathroom) and when I was throwing up from morning sickness.

One night in our early days while my husband and I were disagreeing, he raised his hand to hit me. I sidestepped him and parroted a phrase I had heard from my mother, "A man never strikes a woman." My husband dropped his hand and honored the statement. He never hit or abused me physically. However, I was so forthright, outspoken, and loud voiced my husband began to criticize me with verbal brow beating. I embarrassed him in social situations, so he tried to tone me down. He also attempted to maintain the dominant position in our relationship. Over the years and through continual criticism (first from my mother and then from my husband), I lost my sense of having any value.

Bermuda Becomes Home

My husband had arranged to become an articled Chartered Accountant student in Bermuda for the grand wage of $75.00 a month so off we went in early October six weeks after marrying. With my mother's guidance about the formality of English life in Bermuda, I packed the silver tea service I had received as a wedding gift along with rayon tablecloths in a wooden crate to be shipped to Bermuda. On the flight, I wore my sheared fur jacket for the last time. It was far too warm to ever need it in Bermuda. After boarding at a lovely home in Warwick, my husband and I found a suite in an old home close to Hamilton where I set out to become a good wife. I learned to cook a few meals my husband enjoyed, and each week I dutifully polished that silver tea service that was never used.

One early morning a few months later, I rode to the hospital in Hamilton, Bermuda, on the back of my husband's motorcycle with my labor pains growing more and more intense. Once in a hospital bed with the contractions coming every few minutes, I watched the sun come up, go down, and then come up again. After forty hours of strong labor, I tearfully despaired my baby would never arrive. Finally after being put on Demerol to relax my taut stomach muscles, my son was born the following morning on March 29, 1956.

Back in Calgary, my mother fashioned a false report of my son's 8 lb 6 oz. birth weight saying he had been born prematurely at 5 lbs. and 6 oz. It would've been so detrimental to her social upbringing and situation to let anyone know I had been pregnant when I married. I went along with it for her, falsifying my son's weight on my birth announcement cards.

In those days, women were kept in hospital for eight days after the birth of a child while we learned to nurse and wash our babies. Once home in our apartment again, I didn't know what to do. I had to call the doctor. I didn't know whether to oil my son's bottom or use baby powder. I was so uninformed and ill equipped to be a mother. Finally, I purchased a baby book printed in the 1920s.

Following its dictates, I began to give my son sunbaths out on the porch for a minute at a time front and then back. How he survived my fumbling attempts at motherhood I don't know, especially the times I let him cry in his crib because I could find nothing wrong with him.

I recall his scream and my horror at accidently pricking his skin with the diaper pin when he was five months old. Cloth diapers were vogue in those days. I washed them in the bathtub each day using an old metal scrub board. My knuckles were often raw and bleeding. The landlady didn't like the baby's poop being washed down her drains so we had to find a new place to live.

We found a furnished lower suite in a house back in Warwick. Our bedstead had been painted so many times it was scaly and rough to the touch. Our mattresses were cotton tick covers filled with straw. On occasion, spiders as large as my hand would crawl on the wall over the head of the bed. By now I had become accustomed to the little gecko lizards running about on the ceilings catching insects. But I never grew used to the huge, omnipresent cockroaches that even flew at mating season each August. When a cockroach would wave its antenna at me, I would cringe in fear. Nor did I enjoy the black lines of ants trailing along the electrical lines and entering the house making a beeline for my sugar canister. Amazingly, they could squeeze under the tightly closed lid.

When the sweet bananas would ripen in bunches on the tree at the back of the house, I would make everything I could think off with bananas, trying to use them all up before they rotted—banana bread, banana donuts, banana pie, banana pudding, etc. Each week I dutifully polished the still-unused, silver tea service displayed on the top of its wooden packing case. Our friends were fellows from my husband's office. They were into football, not the niceties of tea service.

I was so naive and immature when I married. I had led such a sheltered life. I knew nothing about the seamier side of life about abuse, prostitution, and other crimes like rape. I also knew nothing about caring for a baby. But by age twenty-one, I learned much about life I hadn't known even existed. I had really been too young and inexperienced to marry.

We moved again to a nicer, furnished, second-floor suite in Mount Vernon. Here I became lonely and depressed as I had to give up my cashier's job at a furniture store when my son became ill. I couldn't bring myself to wash the dishes for days at a time. They would be stacked up all week until I had no more to use and would be forced to wash them. Out of loneliness, I invited myself for coffee at another young woman's apartment in the building, until she tired of me constantly being at her place. I was too isolated with only my young son for company.

In the semi-tropical climate, pests were a problem. Sometimes at mealtime, my husband and I would hear a noise from the stove. Looking over, we would spy a mouse perched on the edge of the dinner pot watching to see whether we had heard him. We then discovered a nest of mice lived in the insulation between the oven and warming oven. We had a wire mesh, freestanding cupboard called a food safe that had a sort of extended ring around each leg like a dish. Some people kept these dishes filled with ant poison. One day I went to get out my tablecloth only to discover termites had riddled it with holes along with the wooden bottom of the buffet drawer.

I became pregnant again in August, and one night in the early days of my pregnancy, I reached to put on my pajamas. As I slid my leg into the pajama leg, out ran a cockroach. Terrified, I screamed. Over the next three hours, my husband caught a number of cockroaches while I cowered in fright at the onslaught.

After close to two years in Bermuda, we returned to Calgary. I was six months pregnant with my second child, a girl. Over the next several years, I had two more boys and lost another in a miscarriage. I busied myself being a happy homemaker in my mother's rented home, since she now lived in Spain.

Several years later, Mother lent us a down payment, and we bought our first bungalow in Lakeview, a new district in Calgary. I enjoyed creating a gravel patio area surrounded by trees and bushes where I would sit for hours looking into the flames of a wood fire in my stone fire pit.

Unborn Pegs Feel Our Fear

Many years later, my then sixteen-year-old daughter attended the University of Alberta for Pre-med. In a science class, she went to a jar of live cockroaches to pick out a specimen to dissect. As she approached the jar, she fainted in panic and fright. Yet at no time in her life had she ever seen a cockroach since she had been born in Calgary. I realized her experience of fear was tied to my fear of cockroaches while she was still in the womb. It became clear to me we transfer our feelings to the unborn child in the womb even while it is just a tiny embryo.

LIFE-CHANGING DEVASTATION

I was the innocent happy homemaker busily looking after my four children and doing some volunteer work. I lived in a state of joy. I trusted my husband when he told me the reason he had been away until the early morning hours was because of a work situation. I naively accepted what I was told on the occasions when my husband didn't come home at a decent hour or was away for the night.

One evening as I happily watched the flames of a fire in the seclusion of my patio and fire pit, my husband (thinking I may have enjoyed myself too much at a Jaycette convention I had gone to in Edmonton) told me he had been unfaithful with his secretary. I was shocked and devastated. I ran into the house to our bathroom, beside myself with grief. My husband followed, trying to explain, but I was dreadfully hurt. At age twenty-seven, my rose-colored world crashed around me. My belief in my husband looking after me died. All the joy drained away from my life and was never recaptured. My trust shattered, my love for my husband shrank. This was the most devastating blow I had ever experienced in my life.

As the days passed, we stayed together, but I began to see things differently. I could no longer believe a man would look after me. I had to take responsibility for myself and for what I wanted out of life. I began the journey to recover my self-worth and to become fully self-responsible.

I sought the kind of work I could do from home with a young family. Over time, I sold Tupperware, Avon cosmetics, and Sarah Coventry jewelry and worked as a telephone solicitor for a milk product. I would go to sales parties in the evenings when my husband could be home with the children. When my youngest son was in the second grade, I began to work as a cashier at an airport gift shop. I realized if I wanted to do things I enjoyed like attending live plays or symphony concerts, instead of just sitting with my husband and his cronies in the beer parlor night after night, I would have to begin to create opportunities for myself. By the time my children were young teenagers, I took up hot air ballooning and bought a small sailboat after taking some lessons.

It took over fifteen years to restore my sense of self-value. As I recovered my naturally dominant self, it also changed our marriage relationship balance. Now being the more naturally dominant partner in the relationship, I unfortunately belittled my husband when I was provoked. The trust in my husband was never recaptured. We had an unconscious pact to stay together until the last child left home. My youngest son stayed until we pushed him out to live on his own at age twenty-two. As I began to grow in a more spiritual way, the gap between my husband and I deepened, and after twenty-nine years of marriage, I chose to leave. We went our separate ways and divorced a few years later.

Looking back through the years, my experience with his infidelity shocked me into a necessary stage of growth. Without it, I would never have begun taking responsibility for my life. I can imagine I must have chosen to experience this lesson for the growth it enabled. I also may have remained stuck in low self-esteem had I not gone through what I did.

Willingness To Pull Out My Splinters

My unhappiness brought me to a state where I could change. The pain of suffering my husband's infidelity and my perceived low self-worth eventually led me to embrace change. I became willing to examine my beliefs and to make changes. Nothing can improve without the willingness to go through the pain of change. Only when I was unhappy enough was I willing to face what I needed to in order to change. Change can only be embraced when one is willing to step into newness, new ways of responding and being.

Accepting Change

"The first step toward change is awareness. The second step is acceptance."

Nathaniel Branden, PhD

Various methods helped me to see what I needed to alter and then gave me the tools to implement change. It was not an overnight process, but a cumulative one that took place over a number of years. Perhaps if I had had the guidance of a mentor or nurturing parents, the period it took to change may have been shortened.

Letting My Peg Experience Its Feelings

"All negative emotions block the life force. All positive emotions increase it."

Imre Vallyon

Feelings are experienced as a flow of energy moving through the body. It is so important to experience feelings in each moment whether happiness, anger, or grief. All too often, I had stifled my feelings. This pent-up energy created strong emotions and energy blockages in my body. These trapped feelings constricted my energy flows sometimes leading to states of dis-ease in my body. Now I've learned expressing my feelings as they occur can prevent the storage of damaging emotions.

"I was angry with my friend
I told my wrath, my wrath did end.
I was angry with my foe:
I told it not, my wrath did grow."
William Blake

RELEASING LONG-HELD GRIEF

For many years since the loss of sight in my left eye in an accident, I experienced a deep toothache type of dull pain inside my head, which ran behind my left eye down to the area behind my upper jaw. Like many things that are daily occurrences, I learned to live with the constant discomfort. Then one day I was liberated from the grief and longtime nagging ache through holding a dialogue with my left eye with the help of a Core Belief Engineering facilitator. Core Belief Engineering is an effective therapy that has a base in neuro-linguistic programming. Aided by the facilitator, I conversed with my subconscious self. The facilitator suggested some questions to be repeated to my subconscious mind, eliciting replies in a self-dialogue in order to bring repressed thoughts and feelings to the forefront. In doing so, these stored emotions were then transmuted and changed through use of touch anchors and other simple techniques.

As the facilitator led me through the questions for my blind eye, it became apparent I had not expressed the anger and grief surrounding the loss of my sight, and I began to cry very deeply for several minutes. As a twelve year old at the time of the accident, I had immediately gone into the mode of "what's done is done, let's move on." I had not expressed my anger or really grieved the loss of my sight. Now at last, deep anguished tears came and washed away the toothache of pain. Emotions suppressed for over thirty-three years were at last expressed, bringing healing. The discomfort immediately disappeared and has never returned. New beliefs of love and clear seeing were then installed. No matter how many years the grief and anger has been held, I've found relief with this simple technique. You can reach a Core Belief Engineering practitioner through their webpage at www.corebelief.ca.

Healing the Last of Grief

While attending a workshop, we discussed the subject of death. I expressed how painful my experience had been on the first day of grief over my son's death in an automobile accident. The knowing facilitator realized the very fact that I had brought up the topic indicated there were still feelings to be dealt with.

She coaxed me to summon the feelings surrounding my memory of that day and to see them as a cloud placed in front of me. When I had done so, she told me to reach out and pull the cloud of emotion into my being, into my heart, and to just be present with it, allowing myself to feel it fully. I recreated the memory, reached out, and gathered the cloud of feeling into myself, and for about ten minutes, I was almost overcome as I felt the feelings and the pain in and around my heart. At last these remaining feelings, having finally found expression, were released and disappeared. Now my mourning period truly concluded. I could easily talk about my son or think of him without any remaining anguish.

Removing Burs by Healing My Attitudes

"They are just little things that happened in the course of the day , and you brushed it under the rug and you moved on. However, it's still within you emotionally. If you don't deal with it, it builds up. Then something else happens, then something else happens, and pretty soon you've magnified three or four little things into an attitude. That attitude then becomes a perception, and that perception then becomes an experience of how you see the person or how you see life. On a regular basis, you just visualize and see those things, and you consciously release them."

Rev. Michael Beckwith

One of my biggest roadblocks (and one I observed with many of my friends) was being too self-critical. I was so hard on myself for my perceived mistakes. With the help of Jerry Jampolsky's attitudinal healing, I changed my attitudes and allowed self-forgiveness; consequently, my healing catapulted forward.

As an impatient driver, no one would let me into his or her driving lane nor would I let other drivers into mine. I was often angry and annoyed with others on the road. All the slowpokes always seemed to be in front of me too. My energy field communicated my anger to other drivers and triggered similar responses in them. Then a gem of a book inspired me to change my attitude and improve my life. Many years ago, good fortune led me to discover Gerald Jampolsky's *Love is Letting Go of Fear*. Jerry's simple phrases (quoted below) suggested a change of my mind was in order:

Do I choose to experience peace of mind or do I choose to experience conflict?

Do I choose to experience love or fear?

Do I choose to be a love finder or a fault finder?

What we experience is our state of mind projected outward.

We cannot change the external world nor can we change other people.

We can change how we perceive the world, how we perceive others, and how we perceive ourselves.

I am determined to see things differently.

These phrases truly touched me. I had inherited and added to a critical faultfinding streak in myself. The awareness it made others and me unhappy finally dawned on me. I began to practice changing my attitude while I drove, shifting from an attitude of impatience and anger to one of loving, peaceful acceptance. What an amazing difference it made! Almost immediately, people would easily let me into their lanes. Pokey drivers would even move over to let me pass by. How is this possible? I wondered. Are they reading my mind? At that time, I did not yet understand we are really all connected. We are in touch with each other and communicate on subtle levels.

After my surprising success in driving, I began attitudinal changes in other areas of my life. Once again, Jerry Jampolsky's healing words and guidance provided a profound lesson in forgiveness:

Inner peace can be reached only when we practice forgiveness.

Forgiveness means correcting our misperception that the other person has harmed us.

When we see our only function as forgiveness, and are willing to practice it consistently by directing our minds to be forgiving, we will find ourselves released and set free.

One evening my husband tearfully announced his business was in financial trouble. He informed me we must sell our beautiful, just-completed penthouse within a week. I was shocked and began to cry. That we were not doing well financially was a total surprise. I had put my heart and soul into creating my "okay" space around me. I had lovingly designed and looked after all the construction details, expecting to live there the rest of my life. Recalling Jerry Jampolsky's guidance, although I was heartbroken, I was able after a few moments of tears to let my dreams go. Shaken and saddened, I forgave my husband completely (or so I thought). I put our penthouse up for sale the next day. Because of our exceptional improvements, we sold it to a cash buyer within a week.

We rented a pleasant spacious townhouse. Still saddened at our loss, I could not even put up pictures or paintings. I left all the walls bare for eight months. Then my husband planned to hold an office Christmas party in our home. He began to put up the pictures aided by our youngest son. I burst into deep sobs. I had invested myself completely in the design and construction of the lost penthouse, and I now realized I hadn't been able to bring myself to devote my energy in a property again by decorating it. While I believed I had completely forgiven my husband, I had actually only forgiven him about ninety percent. My forgiveness fell short. With this recognition and its accompanying tears, the last bit of forgiveness was released.

Our thoughts, feelings, and bodies communicate with us in subtle ways. Listen to what your feelings and behaviours say. Simple awareness can lead to positive change. Even inherited attitude tendencies can be released once you see them.

As I write this, I realize I regress in driving courtesy when I feel I am taken advantage of, for example, where I have been waiting in a long line to merge due to a driving lane being closed for construction. Other drivers drive down the closed lane then expect to push in ahead of me. They have waited perhaps a minute to my ten or more. It annoys me. Oh! Oh! Time to practice letting go again!

Allowing Myself to Forgive Myself

"If you talked to your friends the way you talk to yourself, you probably wouldn't have any friends. We are harder on ourselves—and meaner—than we are to anyone else."

Sean Stephenson

Forgiving myself has not been as easy as I would like. I often fell back into my "I'm not good enough" patterns and rejection patterns too easily. I was very self-analytical. Measuring myself against what I perceived to be the perfection of others was a major mistake. It did nothing but enhance my low self-worth. I'm never pretty enough, thin enough, good looking enough, or bright enough, I thought. Since thought is a creative force, my constant analysis only emphasized and strengthened my shortcomings. Until I accepted myself warts and all, so to speak, every putdown created a less-than-perfect existence. How could I admit I had created my own painful experiences and then forgive myself for having done so?

The last time I was nearly thin I allowed myself to be drawn into too many one-night stands with unsuitable partners; I had sex because I was so desperate to be loved. Seeing what I had been doing with men I would not consider life partners, I suppressed my sexual desire. My shutdown was so effective that where before my vibes were attractive to men, now they were not. But that shutdown handicapped me. I had blocked myself from love even of myself.

It took me years of gaining understanding and releasing patterns that did not serve me to come to a place where I could at last forgive myself for all the negativity I created. It also took deeper spiritual understandings about my underlying identity as a being of Truth. Inner self had always loved and cared for me so tenderly and steadfastly. Nothing in my life needed to be changed to receive my inner being's love. It had always completely accepted and loved me without any reservation. Until I cleared my patterns enough to realize a bit of my inner nature, I was blind to my inner lover, who was always there, just waiting for me to recognize it. Self-forgiveness was part of freeing myself to see truly.

Taking On Other Peg's Vibrations

We may unknowingly take on other's vibrations, believing them to be our own. As a result we may create unbeneficial patterns of behavior. I recently realized as a young pre-school child I had taken into myself the vibration of my parent's abuse of each other. I recalled having snuck out of bed, going down to sit trembling on the stairway landing between the main and upper floors of our house while my parents had a nasty fight below me. While it was out of my eyesight, it wasn't out of earshot or out of my imagination. Sitting there I was trembling with fear and terror. Wrenching tears came up as I relived the memory of those frightening feelings. Now, looking back, I recognized this may have been the start of my fear of men that had lasted well into my twenties. To begin to release from my body the vibrations I had taken on I did prayers for forgiveness and releasing outside influences while touching grace points on my hand. Taught to me by Ellena Lieberman, the technique helps to clear the vibrations taken on from others that were not mine. (Contact information is in the bibliography).

Awakening to Enjoyment And Passion

"Ah, today is a wonderful day. It's a great day to be alive…to learn, to give, to grow, and to achieve your dreams."

Mike Brescia

I received some pointers from the channeled voice named the Evergreens during a 1985 winter gathering in Devon. I learned I did not need to suffer. Suffering is self-created. I could live life in enjoyment. It was as if a switch had been turned on inside me. Then as I ate supper and conversed with several others at the sessions, I ventured out of my shell and realized I had developed enough knowledge and self-esteem to share information to help other people.

Later in the evening, all the participants gathered for a group session with the Evergreens. As the "voice" contacted each person, it would ask, "What do you want?" And the person receiving advice would reply.

When my turn came, the Evergreens asked me, "What are you doing, Helen?"

Startled, I replied, "I am gathering information to begin to impart it to others."

They said, “Does a reservoir have to be full before serving water to the city?”

I smiled and replied, “No.”

They said, “How full is full?”

I replied, “I am full enough already.”

“Yes. You know what we mean. Now go and do.”

I replied “All right.” Turning to the organizer, I told him that I would be available to talk at the next workshop. He suggested I fill the slot at the next Evergreen gathering. In preparation for my presentation, once more I was inspired by a book—*Move Ahead with Possibility Thinking* by Robert H Schuller. It so excited me I even had business cards made called The Art of Winningness along with badges and hand mirrors with the slogan “Love and EnJoy” surrounded by symbols for success, love, money, and happiness: a heart, a happy face, a star, and a dollar sign. I even had several T-shirts painted with the symbol as well. A dear friend helped me type my constant revisions, and in May, I presented to about thirty-six attendees.

I taught on the topic of how to find the joy in life through enjoyment. During the presentation, I had each participant look into large hand mirrors I had supplied and say they loved themselves. Some found it hard to do. I also passed around a very large soft teddy bear nicknamed Dr. Many Hugs. Some of the participants felt so nourished while hugging the bear they did not want to let the bear go. At the end of the workshop occurring over parts of two days, I had participants choose gifts from many of the self-help books I had benefited from (like Leo F. Buscaglia's *Living, Loving and Learning*, Jerry Jampolsky's *Love is Letting go of Fear*, and several of Robert Schuller's titles). I only asked they pass them on to others after they had read them.

The Evergreens encouraged me to acknowledge and to begin to share what I had learned. The Evergreens also directed me to look into the Tarot, so I took a course and learned how to tune in to and do Tarot divinations. While on a train ride to attend a family reunion, I sat in the bar car doing free readings for others on the train. Fascinatingly, I could do a spread of higher arcana cards for a person totally unknown to me and have them respond and gain benefit from the reading. Now, of course, I know we are all connected through our shared common mind. Through recovering my self-esteem, I realized I wanted to reach a deeper level of fulfillment through exploring spirituality.

Negative to Positive

"A bad habit can be quickly changed. A habit is the result of concentration of the mind. You have been thinking in a certain way. To form a new and good habit, just concentrate in the opposite direction."

Paramahansa Yogananda

Moving from a negative point of view to a positive one has been a long journey. In addition to inherited tendencies, I had patterned myself after my father's example of pessimism. It became part of my submerged subconscious way of being. I saw the glass of life as always half-empty and not good enough. Yet in a life of duality, the opposite way of viewing life was also always present, seeing the glass as only half-full with lots of room for more to be added. Both aspects were present, but one operated in the foreground, and the other was submerged. I began to see how I responded with negativity and pessimism. I would not be happy unless I changed. I made a conscious effort to go to the opposite positive view of a negative sensation or experience. I began to realize the opportunity in a problem. I employed many helpful tools to change my perspective.

Lessening Depression

"Every smile makes you a day younger; every sigh makes you a day older."

Chinese Proverb

Because of my negative outlook, I often experienced depression. If I did not measure up to my unrealistic standards, of course I did not feel good about myself. Over time, these accumulated feelings became a type of depression always overshadowing my existence. Changing my attitudes about myself reconciled many of the overshadowing experiences of depression. Sharing my problems with another and approaching things from another perspective sometimes was all I needed to brighten my life. Several times, I successfully sought out psychologists for help.

As I made beneficial modifications in my attitude, my inner demeanor changed. My depression lessened. Of course, not all depression is caused by emotional patterns. Depression may be caused by the body's response to chemical imbalances or not getting sufficient sleep.

Powerful Pull of Sex

While my early experiences were more minor, many girls have had difficult unwarranted sexual experiences in their early childhood. Experiences of fondling or abuse at a young age can interfere with a girl's normal sexual development. This is especially true if she has no support to assist her with the feelings generated. Several encounters—one of fondling in a crowded elevator and another of being trapped by young boys exploring sexuality when I was a preschooler—affected my own emotional development.

The subject of sex had been taboo in my dear mother's home. She had been shocked and unable to consummate her marriage for several weeks when she entered marriage without any knowledge of intercourse. She wanted to make certain I at least knew about sex, since anything to do with sex was a hush, hush subject in her day. I was fourteen when I remember Mother coming into the bedroom, shutting the door and sitting me down on the edge of my bed while she explained "the birds and the bees" to me. She told me the basics about sex but not about its powerful urge to seek completion once awakened nor did she mention ways to prevent enticing a sexual encounter.

One of our strongest sensations when aroused is that of sex. As a teenager, I discovered, once aroused, sexual urges can be almost overpowering. The first time a boy touched my breasts over my sweater, I cried as unusual powerful feelings were aroused. On our next date, I sought out the feeling, strongly desiring to be touched again because the feelings had been so pleasurable. Nature's powers to reproduce are very strong. It is wise not to disregard that power. Had I been forewarned and known how to prepare by not letting myself be drawn in by a touch or a kiss, I would have been better equipped to handle the powerful and consuming urge to union. I could perhaps have prevented being lured into intimate situations before I was equipped to handle the quick arousal of feelings. Ultimately, my poor preparedness led to my marrying at eighteen because I was pregnant.

Continuously Accepting Change

"What you resist persists. What you oppose, you become. What you fear remains. And anything you cling to turns to dust."
Imre Vallyon

Life is change. When I was young, I did not want anything to change. But regardless of my wishes, things always change, an obvious universal law. By resisting change, I blocked portions of the energy flow from moving through my being. My practice was to avoid the feelings of failure, rejection, or self-belittlement.

With every small choice to act or to reject a feeling in response to what was happening in my environment, I created a huge tree of emotional blockages. Each small action or inaction was added to the branch containing a prior situation and response. Eventually, I grew many branches in a giant response-patterned tree. In time, each branch went underground into my subconscious automatic memory where it became a patterned way of responding to specific input. I formed a paradigm putting roadblocks between me and my efforts to change. Healing my impossible multi-branched tree began with seeing I needed to change, that I wanted to feel better about myself and to fit in better with others.

I now allow myself to continuously accept change as I see opportunities presented for self-improvement. When I am ready to review a particular blockage in my personality, it will pop into my awareness. Allowing myself to see clearly where I have taken missteps often leads to painful remembrances. In the past, I would shut down at this point. I sit completely within the feeling generated while letting the emotional pain be felt and allowing my deep wrenching tears to flow. Understanding comes as the energy is released. It enables me to see what I had done years before to create the blockage as well as what can be done differently.

A similar new situation no longer bothers me as deeply since some of the blocked-energy twigs have been pruned away. Looking back, I can see these small steps of release have led to major changes in self-acceptance. I could not see the deeper levels of blockage until I released lesser levels, the twigs on the tree of emotional branches.

Helpful Healing Methods for Pegs

Over the years, I explored many healing modalities. Several of the most effective I experienced are Neuro Linguistic Programming, Core Belief Engineering, the Emotional Freedom Technique, and the Sedona Method. The Work developed by Byron Kadie is also very helpful to release unproductive patterns of belief. (Contact information is included in the bibliography.)

NLP (Neuro Linguistic Programming) taught ways to understand how my mind affects my body. NLP is based on the connections between my neurological processes, my language, and my behaviors. When I first tried an NLP technique of talking with my body, I experienced surprising constrictions in my stomach muscles as my body responded to the questioning techniques outlined in the book *Frogs into Princes*. I attempted to put in place a new pattern regarding my food addictions. The change lasted a few days until I rewired my pattern so I could continue to receive the negative benefits the eating pattern gave me.

"I tell you plainly about your defects. If you do not heal the sore places in your mind, you will wince every time that others rub them."
Paramahansa Yogananda

Core Belief Engineering enabled me to dialogue with my subconscious mind to follow the branches of a tree of belief down to its root core. Finding the origin of a pattern can help the pattern be released using specific anchoring and techniques. NLP forms the foundation for Core Belief Engineering. I had the good fortune to be trained as a Core Belief practitioner by the founder, Elly Roselle. Many practices over several days helped me to become more open. I found core belief work especially beneficial in releasing myself from pain and restoring my self-worth. The knowledge gave me an understanding of how our minds create patterns and beliefs.

In another practitioner training session, the students were asked to get in touch with our male and female selves. I began my questioning, asking to speak to my female self. I responded in shock and surprise to the picture and voice that appeared to me. In my mind, I saw a voluptuous naked woman clutching a velvet maroon curtain about herself as she peered from behind it. The tassels led me to believe it was a bordello curtain she hid her body with. In a strong sexy, somewhat derisive voice I heard her say, "Yes, dearie." In our following conversation, I realized my feminine side was the strong side of my personality. When I asked to communicate with my male side, an older grey–haired, wise man appeared. He was quiet and peaceful. Once again, I was surprised because I had always thought I was too masculine, that my assertive strong demeanor was a masculine quality. However, I discovered it was actually the other way around. When each part had been spoken with, we were instructed to bring them together. My male and female halves kissed and united. I realized at the time something in me had healed.

Following my practitioner training, I used the techniques to help others. Sometimes my results as a facilitator surprised me since the technique is very simple. One lady I assisted healed herself from severe migraine headaches. Another man let go of his fear of being in business and started a painting business the following week. I helped one lady see she programmed her excessive smoking habit by constantly telling herself she "was fuming." Her body was only trying to comply with her instructions.

EFT (Emotional Freedom Technique), developed by Gary Crain, provided a simple process of releasing my emotional blocks through repetition of phrases while successively touching points on my body's meridian system. Using simple tapping techniques, I (along with many people) experienced permanent results covering a wide range of personality pattern problems and a variety of fears.

The Sedona Method, developed by Lawrence Levinson and now continued by Hale Dwoskin, has also been very effective. In the Sedona Method, I explored individual emotions with several simple sentences to release blocks to total openness of being. The key is acceptance of what is and/or allowing it to be changed. I found the simple questioning technique to also be very effective in my self-healing.

The Work by Byron Kadie is another method of questioning your perceptions to get at the truth underneath. This method of self-inquiry is very beneficial for releasing false perceptions especially in relationships with others. In the process, a person reviews their perceptions to find out whether they are really accurate.

Seeing Growth Through My Peg's Diary

Keeping a diary or journal of my peg's activities and periodically reviewing it has enabled me to see I am changing in positive ways. I record noteworthy incidents as well as my significant dreams and the incidents of deepening understanding of my true spiritual nature. As I step forward in life, it unfolds behind me.

Emotional Lesson Keys

1. Repetitions of an emotion create patterns, which block energy flow in a part of the body.
2. Feelings are meant to flow through you without restrictions.
3. Clearing blocked emotions that no longer serve you is the key to recovery.
4. Resisting change blocks energy flow.
5. Stored emotions can cause physical symptoms of illness like aches and headaches or worse.
6. Healing begins with seeing the need to change.
7. Seeing why feelings were not freely expressed brings about the release of the stored energy pattern.
8. Stay with the painful feeling, and the energy holding the blockage gently begins to release.
9. When you try to protect yourself from pain by tightening and holding back your feelings, you create blockages in your energy.

10. When a painful emotion is not given expression, you may begin to find a substitute way to placate your feelings with food or candy.
11. Unexpressed emotions gradually become hidden from view in your subconscious mind. Yet they still control your behaviour.
12. Another's energy may have been taken on and thought to be your own. Clear it using prayer and forgiveness techniques.
13. Constant comparison to others is harmful to your self-worth.
14. Mental abuse can be as destructive to your self-worth as physical abuse.
15. Depression can be caused by loneliness and isolation as well as accumulated feelings of low self-worth.
16. Recognize a problem is also an opportunity when seen from its opposite pole in duality.
17. Fear and other experiences can transfer to your unborn baby in the womb.
18. Once lost, your trust in another may not easily be regained.
19. Willingness is a key to allowing change.
20. Entrusting your life to another to look after you is a failure of self-responsibility.
21. Learning to take full responsibility for your own life is a major key.
22. Only you can achieve what you wish in life.
23. Your experience is a projection from your mind.
24. Forgiveness is a major key; self-forgiveness heals.
25. Thoughts, feelings, and your body all communicate with you.
26. Your suppressed feelings can block you from love, even of self.
27. Suffering is self-created.
28. Hugs are healing even from a soft teddy bear.
29. You see yourself in the mirror of others, but you project and create the mirrors.

30. We are all connected through our shared mind.
31. Sharing a viewpoint can aid clarity and true seeing.
32. Many helpful inspirational books and tools like EFT, Sedona Method, Core Belief Engineering, the Work, etc. are available to assist in restoring self-esteem.
33. You see your improvement only as you look behind at where you have been.
34. Be prepared; once aroused, sex is a powerful force seeking its release in union.

Chapter 5

BODY & HEALTH KEYS

Studying My Pegboard Home

BODY & HEALTH LESSON KEYS

Self-Discovery Through My Body Temple

"The main and final objective of health is continuous and unconditional happiness."

G. Vithoulkas

As a youngster, I did not really reside in my body. I totally ignored what it needed. Because I was so focused on other things, I forced my body to accept my poor treatment. I never befriended it. Even now, I still occasionally overrule my body's desire to go to bed early if I am doing something I enjoy. However, I have learned a great many things about the functioning of my body, especially concerning eating, health, and weight loss. I also began to take responsibility for any medical problems I encountered, no longer just blindly trusting a doctor to know what is best for my body.

Physical Keys

Health Is My Peg's Choice

The secret of health for both mind and body is not to mourn for the past, nor to worry about the future, but to live the present moment wisely and earnestly."

Buddha

I reside in a physical form that communicates with me. Have you ever thought about how your body communicates with you? Our bodies talk to us in physical ways such as feeling happy or thirsty, by being rested and alert or tired and sleepy, by having aches and pains, and by creating health or dis-ease states. Exercise or lack of exercise, food and drink choices, social life, thoughts, and emotions all affect our health. By trusting your own judgment and listening to your body, you can take better care of your health. By doing my own research, I have placed the care of my body into my own hands, and you can too.

Initially, I needed to understand how my peg functions. Then I needed to respect and honor my body and provide it with what it needs. My extremist nature would keep me up long after my yawning body told me it was time to sleep. I disliked exercise, regarding it as a punishment, a waste of time, and boring. I disliked it so much I seldom gave my body any. I ate foods that disturbed my body and became addicted to carbohydrates. I found it annoying that eating wheat products would make me congested because I was addicted to bread products and ate them often. I had a sweet tooth. I wouldn't stop at one cookie; I would eat the whole package trying to fill a craving that had nothing to do with my body's needs.

Any time I suffered from dis-ease, it acted as a clue for a better understanding of my body's functioning. Gradually, I began honoring my body and respecting its needs, forming major realizations and improving my health tremendously.

All healing is the result of a decision to get well. No one can heal for you.

Healing My Peg Body

"Illness is a message from your body telling you that you need to change something in your life."

Dr. Mike Samuels

For too many years, I overlooked the importance of the right food and adequate rest to heal my body. My body often responded with sickness to an imbalance, trying to achieve balance by causing a rash or other noticeable change. However, I began to recognize these clues. For instance, if I eat too much chocolate, my face may break out with acne. If I allow my body to become too acidic with an overconsumption of carbohydrates or acidic foods, I will invariably catch a cold or flu or other illness.

Blocked Feeling Causes Dis-Ease

Other dis-ease states have occurred, which depend upon the part of the body affected and intensity of my withheld feeling. My replayed memories or repressed self-recrimination, further decrease my energy flow and add to my blockages. In time, my belief system became unknown to my conscious mind even though it could still manifest as a physical ailment. My beliefs developed their own identity and struggled to defend themselves by becoming unconscious.

Body-Type Key

"The human body is a divine idea in the mind of God. He made us from rays of immortal light and encased us in a bulb of flesh. We have placed our attention on the frailties of the perishable bulb rather than on the eternal life energy within it."

Paramahansa Yogananda

Part of my program of self-discovery involved gaining awareness of the unique body that houses me. I tended to think humans all have the same needs. But I discovered people are simply not the same. The health needs of one person can be the total opposite of the needs for another. The food one person thrives on may cause illness in another. One person's meat may be another person's poison. The exercises building a strong body for one person may be too strenuous for another. Some of my friends succumb to different illnesses than I do. Yes, we are different. I have learned to honor and respect my body type. I can feed and exercise my dear body according to its needs, enabling me to be healthier and happier.

Dr Abravanel's books on *Body Type Diet* and *Body Type Program for Health, Fitness and Nutrition* helped me to recognize my body structure, showing how body structures can be classified into several types. Each body type is ruled by a gland, giving each type unique recognizable structures. To be maintained at its best, each body type has different food and exercise requirements. Each body type develops and is ruled by the hormones of the strongest gland in the body.

Dr. Abravanel classifies three types of structures for men:

1. Adrenal type
2. Thyroid type
3. Pituitary type

Dr. Abravanel also classifies four types of structures for women:

1. Adrenal type
2. Thyroid type
3. Pituitary type
4. Gonadal type

He developed a list of questions about food preferences, activities, and energy levels to help you to determine your type, including external physical appearance. A look in the mirror at the shape of my face and body confirmed my body type.

- A pituitary type has a childlike, round quality to their features. They seem to have a childlike outline with baby fat all over. (That was not me.)

- The adrenal type has a stocky body with a strong thick trunk and legs. (No, again.)

- The gonadal type has a problem with keeping weight off. They have a small waist and protruding rear-end. (My rear-end is nearly flat.)

- The thyroid type has an almost flat rear-end and a curvy body fuller in the middle. The head tends to be long and the face slender. (Bingo!)

Similarly, the science of Metabolic Profiling has further refined Dr. Abravanel's work to help direct people to the best techniques for their individual body health. Each body type requires different foods to maintain its energy levels due to its different hormone and chemical makeup. I used the information and questionnaire to determine my glandular type. Trial and error helped me find what my body needs. These clues soon led me to an understanding of the best food choices for my specific thyroid body style. Following Dr. Abravanel's suggestions, I was able to lose some weight and no longer felt tired in the afternoon.

My Peg Is Fiery

I also explored Ayurveda as I attempted to understand my body's function and needs. Ayurveda is an ancient comprehensive system of health originally transmitted by the seers of India. It has been in use for over 5,000 years. The science takes into account the whole person and one's relationship to the five elements found in nature: ether, air, fire, water, and earth. The system seeks to harmonize a person and the natural world, including the effect of the seasons of the year. The science of Ayurveda works to balance the inner physical being with the outer natural world.

The combination of elements forming the basic constitution of an individual is determined at conception and remains constant throughout one's life. A person's ancestors have genetically predetermined this makeup. But throughout a person's life, the body will respond to environmental changes. Certain foods will nourish the energy of the body while others will be detrimental to achieving harmony and a sense of balance in life.

I determined my constitution was primarily a Pitta-Kapha dosha (or type)—pitta being fire and water and kapha being earth and water. Vata, which is actually the principal of movement in the body, is represented as ether (or space) and air. All constitutions contain all three doshas—Pitta, Kapha, and Vata—but one or more will dominate. When the doshas are out of balance, disease originates. The following list is taken from *The Ayurvedic Cookbook* by Amadea Morningstar with Urmila Desal.

"To balance my Pitta I need:

- To keep cool,
- Avoid excess heat, steam, and humidity.
- Avoid excess oils, fried foods, caffeine, salt, alcohol, red meat, and hot spices.

- Emphasize fresh fruits and vegetables.
- Enjoy ample amounts of milk, cottage cheese, and whole grains.
- Emphasize sweet, bitter and astringent tastes in my food choices.
- Get plenty of fresh air.
- Trust my feelings and express them in ways supporting me and those around me."

To balance my Kapha I need:

- "To get plenty of physical activity every day.
- Keep my consumption of fat to a minimum, including fried foods.
- Avoid iced foods and drinks, sweets, and excessive amounts of bread.
- Choose food which are warm, light and dry.
- Drink no more than four cups of fluid each day.
- Emphasize pungent, bitter, and astringent tastes in my food and herb choices.
- Luxuriate in fresh vegetables, herbs and spices.
- Get enough complex carbohydrates to sustain me and maintain an adequate energy intake.
- Allow excitement, challenge and change into my life as much as possible."

Those Vata types (ether and air types) need to:

- "Keep warm.
- Choose warming foods and spices.
- Avoid extreme cold, and cold or frozen foods and drinks.

Minimize your intake of raw foods, especially raw apples and members of the cabbage family.

- Take it easy on most beans, with a few key exceptions
- Make sure your food is warm, moist and well lubricated. Soup, hot drinks, and rice with a little oil or butter in it are some examples.
- Emphasize sweet, sour and salty taste in your food choices.
- Keep to a regular routine.
- Create as safe, calm and secure environment as you can."

I could identify with much of the material. A Vata friend used to walk around with a hot-water bottle just to keep himself warm enough during his stay in Canada one summer. As a Pitta type, I cannot bear saunas or steam rooms, which overheat me.

Ayurveda explained my acidic digestive system (fire) and why I do not enjoy hot weather. Since my system is already hot, it needs to be balanced by coolness. Through the science of Ayurveda, I also learned about the crevice in the center of my tongue. It indicated problems with my lower back I had suffered with most of my adult life. The vertical ridges on my fingernails indicated a malabsorption problem. I learned about the six tastes (sweet, sour, salty, bitter, pungent, and astringent) and how they affect digestion and health. I made a Pitta cooling spice to put on my foods to aid my digestion, but I didn't make sufficient changes to release my excess weight.

My Peg Is An 'O' Blood Type

"It makes sense to believe that you are what you eat. Many people with poor diets suffer from weak immune systems. A balanced diet strengthens the immune system and acts as a defensive nutrition insurance policy to protect you from disease."

The Formula, a Personalized 40-30-30- Weight Loss Program by Gene and Joyce Daoust

When I began to read *Eat Right 4 Your Blood Type* by Dr. Peter J. D'Adamo and Catherine Whitney, I discovered another aspect of my body's relationship to food. Dr. D'Adamo found different blood types benefit from different foods, thereby flourishing on different diets. He describes how their blood types affect their immune systems, leading some people to resist certain disease states more easily than others do.

The original and oldest blood type he identified is O (for old), which is followed many thousands of years later by the adaptive type A (for Agrarian). Centuries later, Type B (for Balanced) was named and followed only about a thousand years ago by type AB (for modern). Following his description of the history of humanity's development into different blood types, he describes the changes that occurred in their food sources. Type Os began as hunter-gatherers thriving on meat. When good hunting became scarce, these people migrated to seek better food sources. To supplement their diets, a branch of humanity settled into communities and grew grain crops. These dietary and lifestyle changes affected their digestive and immune systems altering their blood type to A. These agrarian blood types gradually became light-skinned Caucasians and developed an ability to digest grains.

Following the migration into the Himalayan areas, Type B was formed through dietary changes adding milk and the products of domesticated animals along with grains and meat. The last modern blood (Type AB) is rare. It is an intermingling of Type A (a Caucasian group) with Type B (a Himalayan group) inheriting the food tolerances and immune system changes of both groups.

Dr. D'Adamo points out the blood types developed differing immune systems, so certain illnesses occurred in certain blood types, such as peptic ulcers being more common in Type Os who have high stomach acid. Type As tend to develop stomach cancer due to low stomach acid and lack of Vitamin B-12. The risk factors for Type As indicate they "are biologically predisposed to heart disease, cancer, and diabetes … Type Bs are usually able to resist many of the more severe diseases common to modern life, such as heart disease and cancer" and if contracted "are more likely to survive." Their systems do, however, "seem to be more prone to exotic immune-system disorders, such as multiple sclerosis, lupus, and chronic fatigue syndrome."

Using Dr. D'Adamo's descriptions and knowing I had Type O blood, I realized why I absorbed some foods better than others. While people with Type O blood did well on high protein diets, people with Type A could not. Dr. D'Adamo identified the strengths of each physical type. For instance, my O Type "carries a genetic memory of strength, endurance, self-reliance, daring, intuition, and an innate optimism" They also have inherited "focus, drive and a strong sense of self preservation." Fueled by a high-protein diet, my type requires heavy physical exercise. Otherwise, we "become depressed, despondent and overweight."

The book also describes the best diets for each body type. Some of the headings and descriptions from the book are listed in the following:

"Type O: The Hunter

- Meat eater
- Hardy digestive tract
- Overactive immune system
- Intolerant to dietary and environmental adaptations
- Responds best to stress with intense physical activity
- Requires an efficient metabolism to stay lean and energetic"

Type Os "thrive on intense physical exercise and animal protein." To lose weight, they must "restrict consumption of grains, breads, legumes and beans … Gluten in wheat and wheat germ acts on Type Os metabolism inhibiting insulin metabolism, and interfering with the efficient use of calories of energy." It "clogs the works." Type Os "have a tendency to have low levels of thyroid hormone because of a tendency to not produce enough iodine … Certain beans and legumes, especially lentils and kidney beans, contain lectins" whose effect on Type Os is to make their muscles "less 'charged' for physical activity" thus contributing to weight gain. "Type Os burn meat as fuel."

For Type Os, foods encouraging weight gain are wheat gluten, corn, kidney beans, navy beans, lentils, cabbage, Brussels sprouts, cauliflower, and mustard greens. Foods encouraging weight loss are kelp, seafood, iodized salt, liver, red meat, kale, spinach, and broccoli.

This Type O information is very true for me. I had always wondered why I would lose extra weight the day after a meal of shrimp and also found the same thing is true of strawberries. Only recently have I accepted and acknowledged I need to be gluten free in order to feel my best. While I have disliked exercise because I perspire so profusely, I always feel better afterwards. In fact, I recognize sitting at a computer for long hours is hard for my body which needs to be physically active.

"Type A: The Cultivator

- The first vegetarian
- Reaps what he sows
- Sensitive digestive tract
- Tolerant immune system
- Adapts well to settled dietary and environmental conditions
- Responds best to stress with calming action
- Requires agrarian diet to stay lean and productive"

Type As do best on "soy proteins, grains, and vegetables." It is particularly important for sensitive Type As "to get their foods in as natural a state as possible: fresh, pure, and organic … Type As ultimately store meat as fat … Dairy foods are also poorly digested by Type A and they provoke insulin reactions."

For type As, foods encouraging weight gain are meat, dairy products, kidney beans, lima beans, and wheat (in overabundance). Foods encouraging weight loss in Type As are vegetable oils, soy foods, vegetables, and pineapple.

"Type B: The Nomad

- Balanced
- Strong immune system

- Tolerant digestive system
- Most flexible dietary choices
- Dairy eater
- Responds best to stress with creativity
- Requires a balance between physical and mental activity to stay lean and sharp"

For Type Bs, foods encouraging weight gain are corn, lentils, peanuts, sesame seeds, buckwheat, and wheat. All of them also affect the efficiency of type Bs metabolic process, resulting in fatigue, fluid retention, and hypoglycemia. Foods encouraging weight loss are green vegetables, meat, eggs/low-fat dairy products, liver, and licorice tea.

"Type AB: The Enigma

- Modern merging of A and B
- Chameleon's response to changing environmental and dietary conditions
- Sensitive digestive tract
- Overly tolerant immune system
- Responds best to stress spiritually, with physical verve and creative energy
- An evolutionary mystery"

For Type ABs, foods encouraging weight gain are red meat, kidney beans, lima beans, seeds, corn, buckwheat, and wheat. Foods encouraging weight loss are tofu, seafood, dairy, green vegetables, kelp, and pineapple.

PEG MERIDIANS & VIBRATION

"The doctor of the future will give no medicine but will interest his patients in the care of the human frame, in proper diet, and in the cause and prevention of disease."

Thomas A. Edison

Science has recognized our bodies with all of their cells, electrons, and spaces contain a massive field of vibrational energy. Our bodies are actually electric. The vibrational movement of the body's particles oscillates faster than we can perceive, so we may erroneously believe our bodies are made of solid matter. However, our bodies are in a constant state of change as new cells are formed and old ones die, but these changes are not noticeable to us on a moment-to-moment basis. I'd accepted a belief system that said my body is a solid form. But since my body is electric, it can be influenced in subtle ways by healing sciences working at the electrical level.

Within my body are pathways of energy currents. These channels called meridians conduct energy through my various organs in distinct pathways. Chinese medicine mapped these pathways and represented them with the elements of earth, fire, water, metal, and wood a second fire. Each element represents two corresponding meridians. The energy flowing through these meridians connects to specific organs. Since the meridians run from the feet through the body and head or down the arms, a trained person can read the flows of the meridians at various pressure points along the body. Problems with an organ or part of the body can be detected by a weak or disturbed flow in the corresponding meridian. A poor flow may indicate an energy blockage or result in the disease of an organ not receiving its needed quota of energy or alternately receives too much due to a backlog of blocked energy. A list of distinct symptoms has been developed related to each meridian. Thus a trained acupuncturist or acupressurist can help locate the source of a health problem. By correcting the energy flow to an affected area, health can be restored.

On occasion when my thyroid was out of kilter, I had a session of acupuncture to redirect excess energy from one meridian to another. Qui Gong and Tai Chi Chuan have also been useful exercises to keep my meridians open and flowing.

Chinese Medicine

Natural health practices, teas, pills, and tinctures developed over the centuries using native herbs, plants, animals, and fungi have continually been used in China to restore balance and harmony to the body. When I tended to develop bronchitis easily, I was directed to take a three-dollar Chinese pill as a remedy quickly restoring my normal lung capacity and health. I have not had a recurrence of bronchitis for many years. An allopathic doctor would have prescribed drugs for my symptoms, but the Chinese remedy healed the source of the disease, a particular imbalance in my body.

On another occasion, a Chinese master herbalist and Qui Gong practitioner read my state of health by doing a pulse reading from my wrist. He said I was fine but recommended I take a kidney tonic for a month and get a massage of my neck, back, and shoulders where my energy was being partially blocked from the stress of incorrect posture while sitting at the computer.

Iridology

Iridology is the study of the body's health through noting the condition of the eyes and irises. Certain changes in the body will be illustrated in eye conditions. Iris maps have been developed identifying the parts of the eyes that represent the health of other locations of the body. These markers are also related to the Rayid personality markers as some personality tendencies identified in Rayid will correspond with ailments identified in Iridology.

My Peg Has Magnetism

I learned about the effects of magnets on the body while attending a seminar by a doctor from a research department of the University Hospital in Edmonton. The attendees were shown how magnets applied to the body charged the red blood cells. Instead of clumping and sticking together, the macrophages flowed separately in the blood stream thereby having more surface area, making the cells more effective at destroying harmful elements and preventing disease. We learned and practiced healing methods on each other. We used large bar magnets to drive a three percent mixture of hydrogen peroxide into the body tissues to oxygenate them for healing purposes. Smaller magnets were taped onto showerheads or water bottles to energize water to provide beneficial results for the body's immune system. We were also told that taping magnets over a caste on a broken leg had been demonstrated to shorten the healing time for broken bones.

I purchased a magnetic sleeping pad to put under my mattress cover. It contained a variation of a Tessla coil wire along with magnets to aid my body's recuperative powers while I slept. Nowadays magnetic bracelets are available to improve blood properties and circulation. Many water-filtering systems also come with magnets fitted to their water lines, like the Japanese Nikken water-filtration system I had built in when I renovated my kitchen.

Reflexology

Reflexology maps show the endings of the energy meridian pathways in the feet. Different parts of the sole of each foot represent different parts of the body. Thickenings or crystal-like hard areas can be softened, thereby improving the energy flow through the whole body. Thus by having periodic reflexology sessions on your feet, you can improve your overall health.

Homeopathy

"Healing occurs in consciousness. When you heal something in consciousness it can no longer live within your body. Your body is just a reflection; it is not a cause. Your consciousness is the cause of it all."

Stephen Lewis

According to George Vithoulkas, homeopathy was practiced by physicians in the United States at the beginning of the twentieth century. However, in order for the pharmaceutical companies to continue funding the medical schools, they required homeopathy be dropped from the curriculum. Consequently, homeopathy was entirely removed from the medical training curriculum.

Homeopathy is based on the knowledge that all is comprised of energy. In a state of health the whole system is maintained in a dynamic state of balance. In illness a morbific substance has disturbed this balance. Homeopathy treats the whole system. "The principle of homeopathy is disease can be cured by strengthening the body's defense mechanism using principles of energy resonance." Homeopathic remedies are prepared by dissolving a plant substance in an alcohol/water solution, then withdrawing one drop of this tincture and diluting it many times more. Each dilution increases the therapeutic power while nullifying the toxicity. No matter how many times a liquid is diluted, the energy not only remains but also becomes stronger. By treating a disease by strengthening the body's defense mechanism with certain energy-rich substances, the body can heal itself of many disease states.

Several Laws of Cure and Suppression form the backbone of homeopathic treatment. Hannemann's Law of Similars states any substance which can produce a totality of symptoms in a healthy human being can cure that totality of symptoms in a sick human being. Herring's Law of Cure states symptoms will disappear from above downward, from within outward, from most important or vital organs to least important organs and in reverse order to appearance of symptoms. The Law of Suppression states if a specific symptom is treated without treating the whole the disease is driven in deeper.

Over the years, I have used homeopathic remedies to treat several problems. In one case, a naturopath prescribed homeopathic remedies successfully to treat my overstressed adrenal glands and thyroid when I was in a state of extreme physical exhaustion. I also used homeopathic drops to help me release emotional blocks in my body.

Aromatherapy

Energy conveyed through your sense of smell can also be surprisingly healing to your body. Having learned a little about aromatherapy, I would always keep my lavender oil nearby. I use its scent to calm my mind as I go to bed if I have been too stimulated. Peppermint calms my stomach; lemon oil helps me to relieve stress, and I also use a mixture of peppermint and other aromatherapy oils to brush my teeth each day in place of toothpaste. My dentist quickly noticed the switch from using toothpaste to tooth oil as it healed my bleeding gums. Oregano oil is kept on hand for use to combat the first symptom of a cold or flu. At one time, I even tried aromatherapy pens made with scents of banana and grapefruit that were supposed to help control eating.

Flotation Tank

There are so many ways to explore our healing. I enjoyed the relaxing and nourishing experience of being supported by a practitioner and a foam roll under my neck while lying on my back in a flotation tank. I became nearly free of thought as a sense of weightlessness and deep peace filled me as I lay in the soothing warm water.

Massage

Regular massage has kept my body flexible. I recognize the importance of receiving a regular massage of my neck and upper back since that is where I tend to tighten up due to stress or sitting too long at the computer. I purchased the infrared therapy massage bed from Migun and found regular use took away my lower back pain. The jade rollers emitting infrared energy are preprogrammed to roll up and down my spine and legs.

Electromagnetic Frequency Protectors

With the onslaught of wireless telephone and communication

towers, we are exposed to electromagnetic frequencies our bodies are not used to processing. In order to protect myself, I purchased an EMF-balancing pendant, which I wear every day. I also glued small protective EMF-balancing disks to my desktop, laptop, alarm clock, and other electrical devices. I placed a plug-in unit in an electrical outlet to neutralize the frequencies traveling through the electrical wiring. I sent more disks to family members to fasten onto their cell phones. These protective disks neutralize the effect of the EMF waves. Science has demonstrated that EMFs emitted by a cell phone are harmful to the brain when a person holds the cell phone to their ear for very long.

I Am My Own Peg's Doctor

I now understand the danger of blindly trusting only my doctors and the drugs and practices they prescribed. In the past, I unreasoningly relied upon them to guide me in the health of my body. Now I am beginning to learn to listen to my body as it communicates with me what I need. Symptoms of illness are messages my body is out of balance in some area. I learned disease begins in the colon through a build-up of undigested food and resulting toxins. Sadly I have had a tendency to override and ignore my dear peg's signals.

I Am Not Sick; My Peg Is Thirsty!

"Pain means an area is acidic. Adequate rehydration should be the first step toward pain relief. Test water as a natural painkiller."

Dr. F. Batmanghelidj, M.D.

For years after my attendance of Duke University's Rice Diet Program, I believed salt was not good for me. I thought it caused my high blood pressure. Then I watched a DVD, listened to an audio tape, and scanned several books on the topic of water and salt. These sources changed my life. I added sea salt and plenty of water back into my diet. Perhaps it is too late to lengthen my life, but for you, dear reader, the information could add years to your life. This health knowledge came from Dr. Batmanghelidj's books, *You are Not Sick You are Thirsty*, *Water: For Health for Healing for Life*, and *Your Body's Many Cries for Water.*

Dr. Batmanghelidj, (Dr. B.), a medical doctor trained at London University, began his research into the healing powers of water while being held as a political prisoner in Iran. In 1979, about one thousand professionals were rounded up and put in prison under the threat of death—a very stressful situation for the inmates in the crowded environment. Dr. B. heard moans coming from a cell and found an inmate only semi-conscious, doubled in pain, and curled into a fetal position on the floor. Dr. B. checked the man thinking he may have a ruptured ulcer, but knowing it had not yet perforated. He asked the man what he had taken so far for pain. The man groaned he had taken twenty antacid pills and three prescription pills to no avail. With no drugs at his disposal, Dr. B. gave the man three glasses of water over a period of thirty minutes and the man's pain disappeared. That water could heal disease was a powerful "ah hah" moment for Dr. B; this was a realization far from what he had been taught in medical school.

As a result of that experience, Dr. B. began researching healing effects of water while still in prison. Dr. B. realized his medical training wrongly focused on disease states beginning in the solid matter of the body. He learned water does much more in the body than was recognized and the cause of disease is dehydration. The scientific foundation on which Western medicine has been structured was based on false assumptions. Over a span of three years, Dr. B was able to heal nearly 3,000 other inmates using only water.

After his release from prison and upon his arrival to the States, Dr. B. joined an organization called The Simple in Medicine where he continued his research. His first efforts to present his research papers were put off, edited, or ignored completely by the medical community and the Food & Drug Administration. Such important information was a threat to the allopathic medical system largely run by pharmaceutical companies. Dr. B. continued his research and after twenty years of data collection decided to bring his information directly to the public through books and CDs. He knew his valuable information could start a system of health without the need for much of our current elaborate health care system.

THE FOUR FALSE ASSUMPTIONS OF WESTERN MEDICINE:
(taken from Dr. Batmanghelidj's book)

1. "Dry mouth is the only sign of dehydration in the body."

   Dr. B's research indicates otherwise: The body can suffer from deep dehydration without manifesting a dry mouth. Symptoms of drought can begin in the cells without affecting blood vessels. Dehydration in the cell interiors produces life-threatening illness without dry mouth symptoms. We sometimes think we are hungry when our bodies are actually crying out for water. Waiting to get thirsty is to die prematurely and painfully. Pain is a cry for water. Water relieves pain if enough water is ingested to reverse the drought initiated by the body. A distinct marker of dehydration is the color of urine. A very light to colorless urine indicates the body is blessed with enough water. Naturally yellow urine (not because of pigments in supplements, etc.) means the body is gradually getting short of water. Consistently orange-colored urine indicates serious health problems from dehydration.

2. "Water is a simple inert substance that only dissolves, circulates different things, and ultimately fills up the empty spaces. It has no chemical role of its own in the physiological functions of the body. All chemical actions in the body are performed by the solid matter that dissolved in water."

   Dr. B's research indicates otherwise: Water is the single most complex element in nature. Water's most important function is its energy-generating actions. It manufactures hydroelectricity at the cell membranes. Perhaps its most vital function is water's adhesive properties, which bond the solid structure of the cell membranes and protect life inside the body's cells. Modern medicine recognizes only the life-sustaining properties of water. That is why doctors never understood chronic unintentional dehydration as an ultimately deadly process. With decreased intake of water, we gradually limit life processes in the body until a pattern of decay is established.

3. "The human body can regulate its water intake efficiently throughout a person's life."

   Dr. B's research indicates otherwise: As we grow older, we lose our perception of thirst and fail to drink adequately until the plum-like cells in vital organs become prune-like, no longer able to sustain life. The body is forced to rely on drought management in order to continue to live. Dr. B. describes in simple detail the body's attempts to survive drought when not enough water is available. These drought-management processes are the body's bid to survive. But they eventually result in what medicine calls disease as selective portions of the body are deprived of water to ensure the survival of vital organs like heart and brain. Lack of water can cause diseases such as asthma, arthritis, cancer, strokes, obesity, depression, back pain, ulcers, diabetes, gout, kidney stones, high blood pressure, angina, and many others.

Dr. B. has signed written testimonies in his books saying he has cured all of these diseases with only water. One testimony is the story of Dr. Day who had a fast-growing breast cancer. The cancer became the size of an orange in just three weeks. Dr. Day had normally only consumed a little water and survived on coffee. She had the cancer removed, but it metastasized to other parts of her body. She did not pursue chemotherapy or radiation because as a doctor she recognized cancer treatments kill patients not cancer.

Dr. Day gave up her career as a highly respected orthopedic physician. To aid her healing, she began to eat better nutritionally, but her health still declined. Bedridden and close to death, she was given Dr. B.'s book. By increasing her water intake to sixteen glasses of water a day until all the cancer was gone from her body eight months later, she cured herself. Dr. Day has survived seven or more years now and has a website called www.drday.com.

4. "Any fluid can meet the body's need: All manufactured beverages and fluids will serve the body in exactly the same way as water." Dr. B's research indicates otherwise: You cannot substitute any

other beverage (coffee, juice, milk, or soft drink) for water. Dr. Day's breast cancer was the symptom of serious dehydration in her body that gradually took over and ruined her health because she drank mostly coffee. Some of the manufactured beverages in common usage today do not function in the body like normal water. When we drink beverages with caffeine in them, we actually need to drink 1.5 times as much water to rid the body of caffeine poison.

Water & Salt Are Critical For My Peg

"When pain medications are used, the cause of pain is not taken away; the acidic state of the body continues to cause other symptoms and damage.

Dr. F. Batmanghelidj, M.D.

Dr. B. indicated each day our bodies expend at least six to eight glasses of water through breathing out vapor, digesting food, etc. At the very least, this water must be replenished. He said to take your body weight in pounds and divide it by two. That number equals the amount of water in ounces your body needs each day. Dr. B. recommended people start the day by drinking at least two or three glasses of water (any water except distilled, which is too acidic). Drink a glass of water thirty minutes before meals and another glass two and a half hours after meals to complete digestion. Drink a glassful thirty minutes before going to bed at night. For every ten glasses of water you take in, you also need a half teaspoon of natural salt like Celtic sea salt or rock salt. Manufactured salt has been stripped of the eighty or more trace minerals our bodies require. Taking kelp (available in pill form) or a good vitamin supplement provides the body with needed iodine.

Please take heed and help yourself to better health. I started to several years ago. I have always consumed water, perhaps not enough to prevent aging, but maybe that is why my health is better than so many of my friends. For over twenty years, I thought that I should try to be salt free and have now discovered that was wrong. When I began adding sea salt and more water to my diet, my health improved. Now that my body receives sufficient water and salt, it no longer holds onto water; the edema in my legs and feet has ceased, and my high blood pressure has dropped. I am now nearly off medication. You also can make changes now and ensure yourself a pain-free life.

Stop!! Don't Nuke My Thyroid!

"If a patient is just nutritionally deprived, as I believe most people are who are medicated, then a prescription drug is like a jail sentence. For the rest of your life, you are forced to live with the shackles of its side effects."

John Gray PhD

For seven years, my hyper (overactive) thyroid went undiagnosed by my former physician. I saw him for a litany of stress-based problems, but I did not understand stress at that time. I constantly experienced severe hot flashes, heavy sweating, a resting heart rate of eighty instead of my normal sixty beats a minute, and eventually a heart arrhythmia so strong I couldn't function for the several hours each bout lasted. A tremor in my hands prevented me from spooning soup to my mouth. Ultimately, a six-week episode of severe insomnia triggered by a vacation in a warm climate added to my symptoms. I was always so hot. I had to carry towels with me all the time to wipe up my perspiration. I was very overweight, but during one year, I spontaneously lost about forty pounds, which I attributed to constantly saying positive affirmations of being thin. My left ankle thickened and my underarm body hair disappeared.

One New Year's Eve, I spent four hours on a heart monitor in Foothills Hospital because of an arrhythmia. I was told my heart was fine, but they didn't know why it was doing what it was doing. I thought maybe my heart chakra was opening due to my meditation practices. On another occasion, my doctor sent me to a nerve specialist who said that I had a benign essential tremor and it was not Parkinson's disease.

Since I was over fifty years old when the problems began, my doctor thought I was experiencing menopausal symptoms. He prescribed some estrogen patches (without progesterone) that started my menses again, but did not solve my problems. Indeed, they caused a later problem, endometrial hyperplasia (thickening of the uterine lining) due to being prescribed estrogen without progesterone, but that's another story.

One day in desperation, I asked whether there wasn't a doctor specializing in stress disorders and was referred to another general practitioner who practices hypnotherapy. My problems were related to too much stress due to my business rather than to menopause. The hypnotherapy treatments were helpful. I changed my attitudes, but this did not relieve my symptoms.

Then a young female visitor who had been hospitalized after nearly dying from thyroid complications spotted my symptoms. She suggested I take a Thyroid Stimulating Hormone test. She thought I could have a thyroid problem. I took her advice and the test.

The T.S.H. results came back at the abnormal reading of zero. My doctor, however, said some vitamin supplement I was taking must be causing it and did nothing further.

My naturopath suggested I obtain a second opinion. She gave me the name of an open-minded doctor. He obtained the same test results, noted its abnormality, and then went on to administer T3 and T4 tests, which were also very abnormal with results of seven and seventy (if I remember rightly). He sent me for a radioactive scan of my thyroid. It indicated the whole thyroid gland was involved in over activity. Additional blood tests confirmed I had the autoimmune version of hyperthyroidism (Grave's disease).

I visited a specialist in endocrinology and internal medicine. She gave me the choice to take a specific drug for at least a year to see whether it would calm my gland down or to have my thyroid irradiated with radioactive iodine. If I chose the second option, I would need to take a thyroid supplement for the rest of my life. I elected to take the pills.

At the end of the year, I had experienced so many drug side effects I reduced the dosage, but at least my hyperthyroid symptoms were relieved and my daily life was more bearable. I continued on a lower dosage of the drug for another nine months. I valiantly fought off the rapidly increasing weight gain but eventually lost that battle. During this period, I also experienced hemorrhaging after minor surgery and dentistry, a side effect of the drug I later learned. Contraindications for the drug in a prescription book explained why my stomach bulged in tumescence. I could no longer wear belted clothing. My energy levels were low. I began to experience aching arthritic joints, also described as a side effect. When my ankles burst out with raw red splotches after I had been doing a lot of walking one day, my new doctor took me off the drug for good. Rash biopsy tests showed possible leucocytoclastic vasculitis. Now my only other option was to nuke my thyroid, but I did not feel right about killing part of my body.

I was advised to wait for two months for the chemical buildup of the drug to leave my body in order to see whether my thyroid could normalize itself. At two months, the tests were mostly normal readings. At three months, the test readings were still in the normal range but moving away from optimum levels. I resigned myself to the possibility of radiation.

At this point, I had the great fortune to be introduced to a line of nutraceutical supplements. I began taking supplements for the endocrine system based on diascorea yam, for the immune system based on the stabilized healing molecules of aloe vera gel, and a phytochemical supplement based on freeze–dried, fully ripened fruits and vegetables with aloe vera. Within three days, I noticed a marked improvement in my energy levels. At night, I also woke up fewer times. My chronic nasal drip disappeared after a few weeks. Five months after stopping the drug and two months after starting the nutraceuticals, my thyroid test results were all normal, surprising my doctor.

In the beginning, I had an occasional hot flush. However, I could feel cold for the first time in many years. My desire for sweets largely disappeared. My weight did not normalize, but I have been able to maintain my thyroid health through continuing to take nutraceutical products and other supplements. The Graves disease symptoms have subsided, but sadly my stomach still protrudes.

While I have lost some weight, I am still obese. I still have more to learn to understand my body's communication signals and am now slowly releasing my excess weight.

Thank God, I did not agree to nuke my thyroid! Thank God for nutraceuticals!

Ow!! My Feet Hurt

It's taken me twenty-eight years to finally learn what to do for sore feet. Unfortunately, I trusted in my doctors too readily to tell me what I needed to do. Little did I realize they still don't know what to do for sore feet!

In Grade 4, when I was ten, the school nurse sent me home with a note saying I had flat feet. Nothing was done about it. I assumed it was simply normal for me to have flat feet. I didn't realize until recently every foot should have some arch to allow for proper functioning. Without it, a spur of bone can be pulled out of the heel caused by the constant inflammation of the overstretched arch tendon. This condition is called plantar fasciitis.

In 1980, as part of a complete check up for the Rice Program at Duke University, my feet were x-rayed. Among other things, the doctor commented I had heel spurs. At that time, I knew nothing about heel spurs, and the doctor did not explain further. In hindsight, I should have asked more questions. Heel spurs do require attention.

Part of my assignment for the Rice program was to walk twelve miles a day. Using a pedometer, I ensured I walked at least my twelve miles for five months while I rapidly lost eighty-eight pounds of excess weight. (Unfortunately not having solved the psychological causes of my obesity, I didn't keep weight off for long.) Without any pain, I didn't realize I was compounding my heel spurs.

Years later, when I found myself limping in crippling pain with a sore right heel, I sought medical attention. My doctor sent me to a podiatrist who took x-rays. Examining the films, he pointed out the spurs came from my heel bone and down the sides of my heels. Made of bony material they looked like hooks on the x-ray. The podiatrist taped my feet in a slightly arched position to take the pressure off the fascia and made casts of my feet. These custom-fitted plastic orthotics were made to be worn inside my shoes. The orthotics raised my arch a little allowing my foot to gradually heal. I was so grateful to be able to walk again without pain although it did take a whole year for the pain to completely subside. When I changed my shoes, I would transfer my orthotics to the pair I was going to wear.

In 1999 after moving to a new city, I again began to experience discomfort and saw a new podiatrist. Casts were again made of my feet for a new set of hard-plastic orthotic inserts. Unfortunately, they didn't solve my recurring foot pain. So I made a second visit to the podiatrist who sent the orthotics to have an additional piece added to the metatarsal area. This change only made matters worse. Taking the advice of friends who ran a custom shoe store, I was directed to a local firm that made orthotics of leather and cork materials. At last, I found comfort, at least for a few years.

In the spring of 2008, when once again I began to experience pain and stiffness in my left foot and ankle, I grudgingly went back to the podiatrist. Looking at me from across the examining room and without touching my feet at all, she said my ankle was pronating (allowing my ankle to lean over slightly). With the prescription she gave for an ankle brace, I went back to the local orthotics firm. The orthotist suggested my winter boots had not provided enough support for my ankle causing the problem. However, several tries (including a new softer material) did not lead to comfort.

The orthotist offered that he had been able to eliminate his own need for orthotics by strengthening his feet and suggested I should try doing some exercises to strengthen my feet and ankles. Luckily this time I was directed to a sports medicine clinic. I learned having to wear orthotics is totally unnatural. It is the same as a person having to walk with a crutch!

The masseuse began vigorously working on my feet, right away pointing out the talus bone in my left foot was jammed up and my ankle no longer moved freely. She gave me a number of simple exercises to practice. She also worked on my legs and hip and knee alignment. Now I am still not free from pain, but there is much improvement after three months of work. My daily exercises and biweekly massage sessions strengthen the muscles in my arches. The bone in my foot has been decompressed, and my ankle now moves more freely.

Noticing improvement but not freedom from pain, I commented to the masseuse it was taking a long time. She responded with an analogy, "How many steps does it take to go down to the basement?"

I answered, "About 14."

She replied, "Then why do you expect to get up the stairs in three?"

It is true. I'd caused the heel spurs and ankle deformity to form over many years with my excess weight. I can't expect overnight relief. I certainly regret that the doctor who previously spotted the problem twenty-eight years before did not tell me what to do about it, but I suspect he didn't even know exercise to strengthen the arches of my feet was required to solve the problem—sadly the two podiatrists didn't know this either.

Undetected Sleep Apnea

"The will of God in me is health, but I must fill my heart with thoughts that produce health. The appearance of sickness is but the effect of sick thoughts."

"There is no room in me for thoughts that out-picture as dis-ease."
Jack Addington

A person performing a cranial sacral session with me pointed out I stopped breathing every so often while I lay asleep on her massage table. My consciousness was also listening to the occasional snorts and marveling my body could be asleep and my mind awake. I had been a snorer for many years. Until I began to investigate sleep apnea through my doctor's referral, I had not realized my body's struggle for breath caused other health problems. I could finally acknowledge the reason I was always slightly depressed and felt tired when I awoke each morning. For over twenty years, I slept only for brief periods at a time, getting up often to go to the bathroom.

I was directed to a company specializing in sleep apnea. They sent me home with a small computer. I slept for one night with an electrode taped to my index finger to measure my heart rate and blood oxygen levels, a microphone at my throat, and a slender hose inserted into my nostrils that measured when I stopped breathing. When I took the computer back, the respiratory therapist connected it to his computer. I could see I had stopped breathing many times during the night. The graph indicated my oxygen levels had dropped from a norm of about 95 to just over 80. At that point, my body in desperation had taken a breath again. I also saw how my heart rate changed in response to the lack of oxygen and the subsequent gasps for air.

The therapist fitted me with a sleep apnea machine and facemask. It was a real struggle to get used to wearing the mask at bedtime. After the first week of frustration, I was back again to try yet another type of mask and later two more types over the next several weeks. I had been a mouth breather at night due to occasional sinus problems. My open-mouth breathing failed to prevent the apnea (stopped breathing) and hypopnea (shallow breathing) while I wore a facemask. I was told with most new users, there is an adjustment time of three to six weeks or even longer.

I went on the Internet and considered other options like specially made dental appliances to keep my tongue or uvula from blocking my throat when they relax. Finally the therapist and I found a solution to the mask problems with a new nose pillow mask and a separate chinstrap. Oddly enough, I began to sleep for longer periods with perhaps only one nighttime bathroom trek. The therapist pointed out the filtering of the kidneys changes when a person gets deep sleep. My depression lessened; my mind became clearer. I realized I had been overworking, perhaps even harming my heart. Through not having corrected the problem years earlier, I may have caused the beginning of heart problems. Indeed a bout of atrial fibrillation may well have been caused by my heart having to overwork instead of restore itself at night.

Because I had always felt slightly tired, I likely over ate in an attempt to compensate to increase my energy. I had assumed it was just a natural response to aging and not getting enough sleep. But often obesity and sleep apnea go together.

All snoring should be monitored to see if apnea (stopped breathing) is occurring, detected by a sort of snorting sound as a person finally takes a deep breath. The situation can go undiagnosed for years and then lead to atrial fibrillation, heart attacks with possible resultant strokes.

Honoring My Peg's Physical Type

Just as some skin types are oily and others dry, each body type has different needs. We are not all the same when it comes to determining our bodies' food requirements. Certain types of activities are also better tolerated by one body type than another. Different body structures need more strenuous exercise than others do. I have come to respect my body and its uniqueness. It is the temple of my spirit.

Body & Health Lesson Keys

1. Befriend your body. Tell it you appreciate and love it.
2. Your body communicates its needs through symptoms of energy or illness.
3. Food craving often has nothing to do with body hunger.

4. Disease is a symptom of the body, which needs to be examined. Excess acidity causes illnesses.
5. Our bodies' requirements are different. One person's meat may be another person's poison.
6. Honor and respect your body. It is the Temple of the Divine.
7. Four types of dominant glands (thyroid, adrenal, gonad, and pituitary glands) create different body structures. Each type requires different foods for supporting and maintaining its energy at the best level.
8. Ayurveda identifies constitutional types by the body's relationship to energies that affect the body. Earth and water are called Kapha dosha; space (ether) and air are called Vata dosha; water and fire are called Pitta dosha. Ayurveda teaches balance through proper activities and nourishment for each type of constitution.
9. Six tastes of foods affect digestion (sweet, sour, salty, bitter, astringent, and pungent). Each dosha requires specific tastes to maintain or bring it into harmony.
10. Genetically developed over the eons, distinct blood types—O, A, B, and AB—flourish on different foods based on ancestral food choices.
11. Meridians of energy run through the body, each connecting to various organs. Acupuncture and acupressure techniques aid energy-flow patterns in the body.
12. Chinese medicines can be inexpensive and helpful.
13. Magnets have a number of healing uses for the body from energizing water to making white blood cells more effective to mending broken bones faster.
14. Reflexology work on the ends of the meridians in the feet can help restore energy to the meridians.
15. Iridology can indicate what types of illness you may be susceptible to.

16. Homeopathy treats disease by strengthening the body's defense mechanism with very diluted energy preparations.
17. EMF protector disks are available for your cell phone and electrical devices to help balance out the effect of the harmful electromagnetic waves on the body. Another device is made to plug into your house or business wiring to neutralize the harmful rays.
18. Aromatherapy essential oils are useful for many purposes. For instance, lavender can calm the mind; lemon helps relieve stress; peppermint aids digestion, and frankincense enhances meditation. Tooth oil made with peppermint, almond, and other oils makes an excellent tooth-brushing aid to reduce bacteria.
19. Symptoms of illness are messages of imbalance in the body. Don't just treat the symptom; try to find the underlying cause. Most diseases begin with bowel toxemia.
20. Take responsibility for your own health. Don't just blindly trust your doctor; get a second opinion.
21. Unrecognized dehydration is the cause of disease. Dr. Batmanghelidj recommends a person drink one ounce of water for each half pound of body weight every day.
22. Drinking sufficient water is critical to health along with taking sufficient Celtic sea or natural rock salt daily. Absent from processed salt, natural salts contain eighty to eighty-eight trace minerals, which are needed in the body.
23. Symptoms of a hyperthyroid condition can be mistaken for menopause. The symptoms can be excessive perspiration, increased body heat, nervous tremors, heart arrhythmia, hot flushes, insomnia, weight loss, or the ability to eat large portions of food over time without gaining weight.

24. Nutraceuticals (preparations made in a way that retains the enzymes and nourishing qualities from natural fruits and vegetables) can restore balance to the endocrine system. See bibliography for names and contact information.
25. Wearing orthotics to prevent heel pain is like using a crutch. The pain of plantar fasciitis (that can cause heel spurs) can be overcome by strengthening the muscles of the feet with exercise. A sports medicine massage clinic can help. The healing of the inflammation pain may take a lengthy period.
26. Snoring may mask sleep apnea or breathing problems. Sleep apnea is caused by the soft tissues of the relaxed tongue and/or uvula closing off the ability to breath for short periods of time. When the blood-oxygen level drops too low, the body takes a deep restorative breath. This constant pattern causes the heart to work harder during the night. Undetected sleep apnea can cause heart damage. Sleep apnea is often related to being overweight. The body tries to compensate with food for its shortage of energy caused from lack of sleep through constant interruption. The deep restorative sleep needed by the body is shortened.

Chapter 6

WEIGHT LOSS KEYS

Sculpting My Peg

Nourishing My Peg
Brain Nourishment
Diets Don't Work, Life Change Does
My Peg ODs on Bread & Goodies
Denial Is Not the Answer
Why Does My Peg Overeat?
The Rice Diet
My Peg Gets Mental Help
Being Thin Doesn't Last
My Peg Examines Beliefs
Hypnotism Fails My Peg
Overeaters Anonymous
Aromatherapy Pens
Affirmations failed
Raging Hormones Overcharge My Peg
Perfect Pictures
Eating Alive
Food Sensitivities
My Peg Goes to Optimum Health
My Peg Gets Bad Taste of Ketosis
My Digestive Balance Is Critical
List of Bad Activities
Nutrition Labels
The New Atkins for a New You
Many Complex Factors in Natural Foods
Weight Loss Struggles
Weight Watchers
Entering the Zone
Commitment is a Major Key
My Peg Loves the Formula 40-30-30 Plan
Planning Ahead
Finding Enjoyable Exercise for My Peg
Qui Gong, Tai Chi, Yoga, Aquasize, Dance, Walking, Cycling, Swimming &Weight Lifting
Weight Loss Lesson Keys
Excercise Keys

WEIGHT LOSS STRUGGLES

Nourishing My Peg

Nourishment takes many forms. For example, I sustain myself through creating pleasant experiences. Good feelings also nurture my body and mind. Unfortunately, many of us with weight problems have used the taste of food to nourish our feelings. We have linked a state of feeling to taste and seek to satisfy an emotional craving with food, instead of using food to nurture the cells of the body. This leads to eating more food than our bodies need because the taste of food makes us feel good.

My food choices were also formed by my patterns of self-reward, comfort, and pain avoidance until I discovered I had distorted my ability to select nourishing food. It took a lot of work to lessen the desires triggering inappropriate eating. Unfortunately, on occasion I lapse back into poor food choices not driven by what my body needs to maintain health.

Brain Nourishment

"Being overweight is a thinking disorder, not just an eating disorder"

Dr. Daniel G. Amen

Dr. Daniel G. Amen M.D.'s book *Change Your Brain Change Your Body* includes a section about how the over or under activity of certain brain regions contributes to causing obesity or preventing weight loss. When people take steps to balance their brain functions they often will lose excess weight and restore a more balanced relationship to food. Test questions in the book help you identify your pattern of the five types of brain function Dr. Amen identified that affect weight.

I discovered some of my poor food choices may have been driven by malnourishment of my brain. Dr. Amen in his studies of the brain determined there are several types of overeaters whose eating may be driven by brain chemistry needs.

One of those types, the compulsive overeater, thinks about food all the time. Their minds are too active They are better able to control their eating with serotonin and 5Http (a precursor supplement) to calm their brains. They eat a high carbohydrate diet because carbs calm the brain. They need supplements of 5Http and St. John's Wort to increase serotonin, as well as to eliminate all night eating. With night time eating compulsives will gain more weight than results from eating the same food in the daytime which is better digested.

A second type is the impulsive overeater who sees food and grabs it impulsively. They eat without thinking. They always plan to start their diet tomorrow. They experience disorganization and impulsivity. They have low activity in the prefrontal cortex of the brain and require dopamine. This is the area that helps you to decide between eating a banana split or just a banana. They also need a diet with higher protein and lower carbohydrates. This person does worse by taking serotonin and does better with support for dopamine levels from L -Tyrosine or green tea.

The third group is the combination compulsive impulsive overeater, a category that appears to be linked genetically to parents and grandparents with an alcoholic background. The combination compulsive impulsive type has too much activity in the attention region of the brain.. They have too little activity in the prefrontal cortex part of the brain. They over-think and get stuck in negative thoughts. They have trouble supervising their own behavior. They binge eat, and can move from being obsessive to being overwhelmed. Dr. Amen discovered they need to raise both their serotonin and dopamine levels with 5Http and green tea and regular exercise is a must.

Another group the doctor identified is the SAD (seasonal affective disorder) overeater who eats and gains weight in the winter when they lack sufficient vitamin D. Dr. Amen points out if we are low in vitamin D we will keep eating as our body attempts to obtain more vitamin D since low levels can make us feel hungry all the time. Vitamin D tells the brain to stop eating. It is also linked to depression, MS, diabetes, Alzheimer's, cancer and obesity. Those with SAD have too much activity in their limbic brain region. Meditation and hypnosis helps them to ease their sadness. They have low energy, low self esteem, and may suffer from depression and pain. Exercise, fish oil and SAME supplements help restore their functionality.

The Anxious type tends to medicate their anxiety with food. They have high basal ganglia area activity and low levels of GABA. Meditation, hypnosis, vitamin B6, Magnesium and GABA supplements all are of assistance

Sadly, Dr. Amnen also stated as a person's weight goes up, their brain size goes down. He thought this was likely due to the increased toxic load on the body and inflammation caused by sugary foods. Sugar and fat act on our brain's addiction center also causing overeating.

Unbalanced blood sugar is associated with cravings and making bad decisions. Dr. Amen suggests stay away from simple sugars in white bread, candy, and cookies since sweets are mood foods and act on the brain like a drug. Excess weight increases the risk of Alzheimer's, diabetes, depression, heart disease, and cancer. Dr. Amen also stated low-fat diets cause depression, which I can attest to from my personal experience.

Dr. Amen pointed out as brain health is optimized, the heart works better, the skin looks healthier, the hormones function properly, and a person will naturally lose weight. Fish oil, exercise, and sufficient vitamin D are very important for brain health. Dr. Amen recommends that everyone take multivitamins, 1 to 2 grams a day of omega 3 oil, and that it is critical to take vitamin D3 as well as do 45 minutes of exercise at least three times a week. He also recommends that we eat breakfast, reduce stress through meditation and hypnosis, outsmart our sneaky food triggers, watch out for hidden food allergies which decrease blood flow to the brain effecting judgment, and control our automatic negative thoughts. His book lists many brain healthy foods and other supplements helpful for different brain pattern types. (More about Dr. Amen is included in the Mental Keys chapter.)

Recent work with rats has described how normally fed rats when allowed unrestricted access to a high-fat diet lost control of their eating. Even though they received electrical shocks, they would not stop eating the fat-laden foods. They were fed normal rat chow before the experiment, and then they received chocolate, cheesecake, sausage, frosting, and other high-fat foods. Within forty days, the rats became fat and showed addiction by way of changes in their brain reward circuits affected the D2 receptor that responds to dopamine. When we eat food that tastes good, dopamine is the chemical the brain releases associated with feelings of reward. The addiction was so marked that when the high-fat food was removed and replaced with the standard rat chow, the rats hardly ate any at all. Even after several weeks, the rats had not returned to normal eating behavior. Junk food binge eating is hard to stop, even when a person knows he or she is suffering ill effects from binging. Susceptible people find their behavior is almost out of control.

Diets Don't Work, Life Change Does

"Instead of trying to change what you eat, change what you want to eat."

John Gray PhD

For years, I was caught in the cycle of eating breads and pastries. Carbohydrates burned too rapidly in my system causing my blood sugar to raise and then plummet quickly leaving me ravenous again. The more carbs I ate, the more I needed to eat to satisfy my raging hunger. My excessive eating of carbohydrates triggered a terrific hunger response in my body that was actually painful, leading me to eat again. Thus even though I lost weight periodically through sporadic dieting, and fasting, I grew larger and larger until at one unhappy stage I weighed 315 pounds. When I tried to complete a restrictive diet, my food desires struggled to be met. Within days, weeks, or months, I lost the battle and was fat again. In my life, I must have lost over 750 pounds only to regain most of it.

My Peg ODs On Bread & Goodies

I had been directed by my mother to eat bread and jam for snacks as a child. I loved the crusty white bread she provided. Then my competitive nature only added to my future eating problems when I was about nine years old. When a youngster living a few doors away would come out with a large chunk of buttered bread to eat, I had to best him. I was desperate to be noticed. I would take out a whole loaf of unsliced white bread, spread it with butter and jam at both ends, to eat. it. Unknowingly I began a pattern that years later became an allergy. I soon grew addicted to eating pastries and sweets made with refined white flour. I didn't realize for many years my love of these high-glycemic foods had actually become an allergy. I even overlooked the intestinal gas I experienced. So I continued to eat refined wheat products. Now of course science has uncovered the operation of insulin in the body and showed that eating a high-glycemic diet causes weight gain and a health imbalance.

During my childhood at the time of the Second World War, my mother knew little about nutrition. She was not a very good cook. Most vegetables were served cooked and in cream sauces. One day a week we had washday pie, a baked bread dish. Organ meats, canned spam, and salted cod were also served each week with potatoes in addition to porridge and homemade vegetable soups. Dessert was often bread pudding. Some foods were not readily available like fresh fish since we lived in the prairie. In my later teen years, we would sometimes go out to have fish and chips for a treat. By the time I was an adult, I had distorted my diet. Snacks of potato chips, popcorn, and soft drinks became a large part of my normal eating choices.

During the Second World War, I recall how we would line up at the Jewish center with our ration coupons to receive our allotments of sugar and butter. A neighbor lady had hoarded big slabs of chocolate at that time. For a number of years after the war ended, her daughter would bring out big chunks of chocolate for me and other friends to enjoy. I became addicted to the pleasurable taste of sweets.

Cleaning one's plate was also emphasized in my home. There was no dessert unless I ate the first course. One unpleasant day Mother served us a lunch of creamed salmon and hardboiled eggs. I didn't care for it and had trouble swallowing my food. Mother insisted I eat it all or I could not leave the table. It was getting close to the time for the school bell to ring. I was very agitated about being late to school because I loved it. I cried and retched, but my mother insisted I stay and clean my plate. When she at last relented and let me go, I was twenty-five minutes late for school. Many years later I spoke to her about the incident. She said one of our neighbor's children had suffered from malnutrition and she would be darned if her children would be malnourished.

As a young teenager, I would sometimes go to the corner confectionery store and buy several packages of Lifesaver candies. Then because I was too embarrassed to buy all the candy I wanted at one store, I would walk several blocks up the hill to a small grocery store and buy more. It took me many years to realize I equated loving myself with feeding myself sweets.

When I was pregnant, I tried hard not to gain excess weight, but with each pregnancy, I seemed to retain ten pounds. After my third pregnancy ended in a miscarriage, I was able to diet, getting as low as I had ever been to 150 pounds (which was perfect for my five-foot, ten-inch height). But within three months I discovered I was pregnant again. Even though I worked hard in the garden and on putting in the lawn at our house during my pregnancy, I kept on even more weight after my son was born. By the time of my fifth pregnancy, I was forty pounds overweight.

Later when I experienced emotional problems, I would go to the supermarket bakery counter for a strudel or donut. Because I was fat, the clerk would not think kindly of me so I had to mask wanting the donut for myself. I would buy six or a dozen so the clerk would think I was buying them for my family. But when I got to my car, I would begin to eat one after another—maybe even three at a time. This kind of overindulgence of refined carbohydrates only caused more cravings, but I didn't understand that. It also created my eventual allergy to refined wheat products. This allergy oddly enough causes a craving for the food to which I am allergic.

My continuous attempts to lose weight began. I had so much to learn about food, my body's needs, and how my emotions affected my weight. Of course drinking Pepsis and eating potato chips and cheese snacks filled with MSG did not help. The sweet drink insisted on the correcting addition of a salty snack. When I switched to no calorie Pepsi, I was no better off since scientists have determined no calorie drinks also cause weight gain.

"Forget about the consequences of failure. Failure is only a temporary change in direction to set you straight for your next success."

Dennis Waitley

Denial Is Not the Answer

My first step toward weight reduction came through a book, Diets Don't Work by Bob Schwartz. I learned denial of a desired treat only makes my desire worse. Instead of eating one piece of cake and satisfying my craving, I found if I denied myself from having a piece of cake I could easily eat half a whole cake later. The book taught me I must allow small indulgences in order to prevent major overindulgences.

I was reminded of my teenage years when I would cook a large raisin walnut spice crumb cake for my family. Of course I had to taste a piece to see whether it had turned out properly, but I found myself stuffing piece after piece into my mouth because it tasted so good. In chagrin, I would hide the remains of the half-eaten crumb cake in the basement. Then I would bake another cake for the family and slip down to the basement periodically to finish the first one.

Why Does My Peg Overeat?

"Most overweight people are subconsciously compelled to overeat to obtain their sodium and other mineral needs. Unfortunately they do not realize that they also need water to absorb these minerals."

Dr. F. Batmanghelidj, M.D.

I could always lose weight when I dieted, but the pent-up denial would kick in at the end of the diet leading me to eat myself back into an overweight condition and most times leaving me weighing more than I did to begin with. When I ate high-glycemic carbohydrates, especially snacks and meals with lots of breads and pastries, they burned so rapidly in my system I was ravenous soon after eating. But even after I realized this, my addiction to carbohydrates ruled my life.

High-glycemic foods burned too fast for my normal levels of insulin to cope with. This kind of diet not only elevated my blood sugar and blood glucose but stimulated the release of extra insulin to control the excess glucose in my blood. Insulin did this by changing blood glucose into glycogen and storing what it could in my liver and muscle cells and placing the excess into fat cells. When too much insulin tried to combat a rush of excess glucose (from rapidly burning, high-glycemic foods), it took too much glucose from the blood, causing low blood sugar. Then my brain whose preferred food is glucose was deprived of its fuel. Now the swing from high blood sugar to low blood sugar triggered strong cravings for more carbohydrates. The continuous eating of too many high-glycemic foods kept insulin levels elevated, resulting in an increase in weight. Later I learned chronic elevated insulin levels can cause other diseases such as hypoglycemia or diabetes.

When I went shopping, I would see foods I liked and buy them on an impulse even if they were not on my grocery list. Seeing food I would enjoy pulled me like a magnet to pick up the product and put it into my shopping cart. With the treat in my cupboard at home, I could too easily grab it when I was in a mood.

When I ate in a restaurant, I would "taste" my way through the menu to see what I wished to eat. I tended to take several bites of different-flavored foods together in order to enjoy the combination. Thus I ate large mouthfuls at a time. I found it difficult to slow my eating pace, by putting my fork down after every bite, because I enjoy my food hot. I also learned that people who need to fill their mouths in order to really obtain the full flavor taste of food and enjoy the food combinations may have less sensitive tongues.

My addiction to chocolate bars was also a major struggle. I was so pleased with myself when after a few years of effort I could walk past the row of chocolate bars at the check stand and not even consider buying one. I don't think it would have been possible if I hadn't reduced my cravings through a balanced diet and through work on clearing my emotional triggers.

I still had a hoarding problem. I always bought more than I needed. I attribute part of it to my days as a Brownie and Girl Guide. "Be prepared" was the motto I learned. So I never let myself run out of anything, especially food. Sometimes I even bought more of a food item that was already sitting on my pantry shelf. I would overbuy. Adding to the problem was my bargain instinct. When something was on sale, I would buy it. Sometimes my fridge and freezer were so full, I gave away food to others.

Abandoning my shopping list, I let visual cues guide me. I would buy the green vegetables I knew I should eat but then let them rot away in the crisper. Of course, I felt guilty when the rotting vegetables needed to be thrown out.

I also had a problem sticking to an eating plan. Unless I made a definite commitment to release the excess weight, I would start out full of great intentions only to watch them wane over the weeks of dieting before I reached my ultimate goal. I would always lose some weight, perhaps even twenty or thirty pounds, but often not enough for others to even notice the difference. To drop a clothing size, I had to lose over twenty pounds.

I went to weight loss and lifestyle health programs run by a hospital on two different occasions. I would attempt to follow a restricted 1,200-calorie diet based on the food pyramid prevalent at the time that emphasized carbohydrates. I would have a small amount of success each time but would eventually give up. I also investigated a number of meal replacement and therapy programs such as Jenny Craig, whose food contained too much wheat for me. But at the conclusion of the diet, I would have to learn to make my own meals again.

The Rice Diet

I thought perhaps the reason I never reached my weight-loss goal had to do with not achieving a thin-enough state. I thought if I could get all the way down to my goal weight, then there would be such pleasure in it that my diet worries would be over. I read an article in Lady's Home Journal about great results being achieved with a rice diet. I was very distraught over weighing 265 pounds. So I took a drastic step in 1980 and attended Duke University's Rice Diet program in Durham, North Carolina. It was a medically monitored, low-calorie, salt-free diet combined with a great deal of exercise. For breakfast, I ate half a grapefruit after walking for several miles. For lunch after walking again, I was given unsalted cooked rice or puffed rice with canned peaches, watermelon, or another fruit. It was the same for dinner after completing my walk. Several weeks later, some unsalted vegetables were added, followed at six weeks by the introduction of a piece of skinless baked chicken each day.

The first week I lost twenty pounds, which was largely the release of fluid retention. I also dropped a complete clothing size. For the next several weeks, I lost seven pounds a week. Then when protein was added into the diet, my weight loss slowed to four pounds a week. Every day I religiously walked my required twelve miles. In addition, I took part in Aquasize exercise classes several times a week. I managed to lose eighty-eight pounds in five and a half months.

My Peg Gets Mental Help

While the Rice Diet Program helped me lose weight, I began to realize I needed to change my thinking. I switched to Structure House and followed a 750-calorie diet with reduced exercise requirements for my last month in Durham. Since it was not a salt-free plan, I gained some weight even on such a restricted program. However, Structure House's psychological program helped me. Their program put me on an eating plan with a morning exercise routine and behavior modification classes.

The psychologists taught us portion control and the importance of finding balance in daily life. With their help, I began to see I kept me regaining weight as a protective measure. I was a perfectionist and critical of anything that wasn't done perfectly. Burdening myself with the false belief everything had to be perfect, I knew I was unable to achieve perfection. The result was I had given up even trying to be perfect. However, I was still extremely hard on myself for not being perfect, at the same time. I harmed myself with strong self-criticism. The staff taught me perfectionism is not healthy and introduced the 80-20 rule. It takes 20% of my effort to achieve 80% of my desired outcome, but 80% more effort to achieve 100% of my desired perfection outcome. They asked if it was worth that kind of extra effort when 80% achievement is good enough for most things. I began to change my beliefs.

They also taught me that attempting to exercise to the extent I had with the Rice Diet program was not sustainable in daily life. They said if I managed to exercise five out of seven days that would be good. Allowing myself to occasionally skip exercise would take the pressure off having to perform each day. It would lessen the emotional charge around "having to." Now if I miss an occasional day, it is no longer the end of the world.

Being Thin Doesn't Last

"Growth is an erratic forward movement: two steps forward, one step back. Remember that and be gentle with yourself."

Julia Cameron

While still in Durham, I was delighted when I reached 178 pounds and could at last wear a size 16 dress. I felt completely different, even sexy and attractive. I splurged on pretty clothing for only the second time in my life, buying a completely new wardrobe. I successfully dieted from 163 pounds to 150 pounds when I was twenty-two years old only to discover I was two months pregnant with my fourth pregnancy. I can still remember my pleasure at seeing myself wearing a sleeveless black top and turquoise and black striped pants. Now much later in life, I was thrilled when a customer asked a salesclerk whether I was a model as I stood viewing myself in a sleek outfit from different angles in front of a full-length mirror. That was only the second time in my life I had been thin enough to wear beautiful garments.

I tried to circumvent gradual weight gain by attending a spa in the mountains at Lake Louise for several weeks. In addition to a very low calorie diet, I walked up and down the mountain from the town each day for exercise. My slight short-term success did not last since I went back to my unhealthy way of eating yet again. Sadly within two years after the Rice Diet, I regained most of the weight. Of course not getting enough exercise was certainly one of the reasons why. My body type needs and loves regular exercise.

Many other factors such as a variety of emotional issues continued to trigger excessive eating.

My Peg Examines Beliefs

"You are as you are because that's what you made yourself to be."
Imre Vallyon

With the help of *Diets Don't Work,* I began to examine my belief systems. The book listed many of the psychological patterns adding to overweight problems, providing me with a checklist to begin to identify the emotional causes of my overeating. I recall there was a lengthy list of several hundred psychological reasons describing why people overeat. I related to many of them (for example, lack of self worth, huge rejection issues, fear of failure, boredom, and depression). I masked and compensated with food for all of this.

I used food to unwind from stress as well as to reward myself. I ate for pleasure, to replace my lack of love, to counteract rejection, to soothe loneliness and social awkwardness, to comfort myself, and to assuage my feelings. In short, I ate for many reasons having nothing to do with being hungry. Using food as an emotional soother had become buried in my sub-consciousness. I began to realize I gain weight when my level of pleasure is low because I compensate for what is missing in my life.

I began to work through the list of psychological patterns in *Diets Don't Work* and slowly modified many aspects of my behavior. With the help of many practices, I unearthed and acknowledged each emotional block and experienced just a bit more healing. It was not easy, partly because my lowered self-worth did not find suitable substitutes to fill the emotional gaps left behind when I changed my eating patterns. So many unhealthy patterns kept ruling my eating. I needed to love myself more in order to give up my behavior crutches.

Hypnotism Fails My Peg

I tried hypnotism to help control my eating. I sat in a chair with the psychologist in front of me. He would relax me and test my responses by having me move my thumb to answer his questions. Once he felt I was sufficiently receptive, he recited positive statements of behavior change. Unfortunately, it was to no avail. The psychologist and I parted ways after a few weeks of unproductive sessions.

Overeaters Anonymous

Attending meetings of Overeaters Anonymous and trying to follow the twelve steps borrowed from Alcoholics Anonymous provided brief but not lasting assistance. I wasn't ready to fully embrace the twelve steps, although I took my turn to speak at the meeting about being a foodaholic.

Aromatherapy Pens

My mother gave me a set of aromatherapy pens to use for weight loss. Sniffing them regularly was supposed to trigger my olfactory nerves to satisfy my brain's response to hunger. While I didn't get any noticeable benefit, I was told others were helped.

Affirmations Failed

For a while, I thought my affirmations (both spoken and regularly listened to) were helping me to lose weight. I was so pleased when I spontaneously lost a number of pounds. Unfortunately, the weight loss actually occurred due to my raging hyperthyroidism.

Raging Hormones Overcharge My Peg

Undiagnosed for seven or more years, I had hyperthyroidism. I could eat very large portions of food and not gain a pound.. When the condition began to be corrected with medication, I couldn't keep the pounds from creeping back on. The hyperactivity was so severe and had gone on for so many years I wasn't able to control the change in my eating habits quickly enough. My stomach seemed to balloon out overnight, which was partly the effect of the medication on my liver. I cried when I had to finally give away all my pretty belts and accept I would likely never wear a belted dress again. I can still see myself stuffing all my belts into a plastic bag for the Salvation Army.

Perfect Pictures

"The most effective and least understood food intake control mechanism is attached to the taste buds on the tongue. The taste buds register with the brain the volume and type of food that has been processed and passed through. The slow rate of chewing gives the brain time to calculate the energy value of what has passed into the stomach—the satiety mechanism takes over and possible over eating will stop."

Dr. F. Batmanghelidj, M.D.

In my struggle to understand food choices and reduce portion sizes one book, Dr. Shapiro's *Picture Perfect Weight Loss,* actually helped me. The book featured color pictures of one food choice versus another with each adding up to the same calories. For example, here are a few of the foods that were graphically pictured with calorie values:

This food choice	equals	this food choice.
3-4 oz. of assorted cookies	460 calories	Mixed salad with 1 Tbsp dressing (80 calories) Marinated palm & artichoke hearts (30 calories) 3 oz. salmon (130 calories) Asparagus (30 calories) Oven-browned potatoes (90 calories) Poached pear in red wine (100 calories)
1 egg roll	400 calories	Bowl of Chinese vegetable soup (40 calories) 4 oz. shrimp (120 calories) 1.5 cups of broccoli (60 calories) 2 Tbsp Hoisin sauce (20 calories) 2/3 cup brown rice (130 calories) Fortune cookie (30 calories)
1 fat-free, sugar-free muffin (9 oz.)	720 calories	1 pineapple (2 lbs.) (240 calories) 1/2 cantaloupe (1 lb.) (60 calories) 1/2 kiwifruit (1.5 oz.) (10 calories) 1/2 papaya (5 oz.) (40 calories) Grapes (5 oz.) (70 calories) 2 pears (6.5 oz.) (100 calories) 2 whole-wheat rolls (2.5 oz.) (200 calories)
1 cup of cashews	880 calories	10 baked potatoes with salsa
1/3 dry bagel (1.5 oz.)	140 calories	Vegetarian ham sandwich on light bread with lettuce, tomato, mustard, and pickle

The pictures helped me to become more aware of the calorie values of different foods. I review the book periodically to remind me to make lower-calorie choices. It especially helps me to remember the calories in things like nuts that I love but now eat in small measured portions. To determine the portion size, I used the small plastic 2 oz. or 4 oz. sample size cups from trying an M&M sample. I fill each portion cup with nuts or raisins and weigh it on my kitchen scale. Then using the nutrition guide on the package, I establish the caloric value and cup size to use for the portion. Now I just need to fill the right size sample cup in order to enjoy it without going overboard.

Another type of picture helped me at one point. I visualized myself in a dress I had been able to wear when I was thin. It was a classic suedine tan dress buttoning down the front with a shirt-style collar. A narrow belt encircled my slim waist with pieces of gold chain dangling on the belt ends. The dress had looked so good on me. I had felt so attractive in that dress when I returned from the Rice Diet Program. I repeated my weight loss affirmations and saw myself in the dress having achieved my goal. I had to reframe my words to say I had "released" the weight since weight I might "lose" I would likely find again. But because I had not cleared the blocks preventing me from losing weight, I struggled to really believe my visualizations and affirmations. I couldn't align myself with them, and they were soon dropped. While I lost a few pounds, I soon gave up trying to diet yet again.

Eating Alive

"A happy mind automatically thinks happy thoughts, and a healthy body automatically hungers for healthful foods."

John Gray PhD

Another book that caught my attention was *Eating Alive, Prevention Thru Good Digestion* by Dr. John Matsen N.D. The book took me on a "journey through the digestive system to find the mysterious cause of disease" accompanied by many funny cartoons. It introduced me to how the digestive system worked, how to detoxify my system, and to food combining. Dr Madsen suggested the stomach of anyone over the age of two is in a state of "shock" from food irritants. He stated, "Consider the stomach as being like a young child who has been beaten ruthlessly since birth. It's been hiding in the attic, occasionally whimpering as you continued to torment it." He suggested wrong food choices and combinations hurt the digestive system.

In order to test for food sensitivities, the book suggested I delete certain foods from my diet for a time. I wrote out the lists of foods to avoid onto an index card I could carry with me and began to eliminate groups I, II, and III from my diet for several weeks.

Group I included coffee, tea, chocolate, white sugar, alcohol, artificial sweeteners, preservatives, salt, and tobacco. These items "are used to whip the overloaded liver and/or stressed adrenals into one more round of struggle," ultimately weakening these organs.

Group II listed baking yeast, peanuts, brown sugar, cow products, and pork, which Dr. Matsen said showed up in sensitivity testing for almost everyone.

Group III contained wheat, tomatoes, brewer's yeast, and mushrooms.

Group IV contained lamb, beef, chicken, turkey, eggs, shellfish, fish, soya, lemon, oranges, grapefruit, pineapple, apples, bananas, peaches, currants, raisins, apricots, strawberries, potatoes, squash, rye, oats, rice, corn, alfalfa, eggplant, carrots, cabbage, broccoli, cauliflower, celery, cucumbers, peppers, turnips, walnuts, cashews, brazil nuts, honey, maple syrup, molasses, raw sugar, curry, garlic, vinegar, and onions.

I found it a bit difficult to avoid these foods while eating my lunch out at work but managed to choose rice and vegetables for some meals. I noticed I felt better and even lost some weight during the several weeks I managed to stay on the very restrictive regime. It became evident to me that correct food choices reduced my body's tendency toward edema and eliminated illnesses, since most illnesses begin in the digestive system with the toxic buildup of pathogens.

So enamored with the book's information, I wrote a letter to the Premier of Alberta, Ralph Klein and sent it along with a copy of the book. He passed it on to his Minister of Health and Welfare who replied. In response to my letter urging the government to establish programs of wellness instead of sickness healthcare, I received a letter saying the Government of Alberta was in the throes of outlining such a program. Sadly in the twenty elapsed years since receiving their letter, I have yet to see any type of wellness program initiated. The government chooses to fund sickness instead, paying out millions to the allopathic medical system.

Food Sensitivities

Using kinesiology, my naturopath also checked me for food sensitivities. The results indicated I could tolerate ancient grains like kamut and spelt, but my body reacted to refined wheat. These foods caused gas and sometimes digestive discomfort. Further clues came when my sister and I tried the *Birker Benner Diet.* Dr. Birker Benner's Swiss clinic started the muesli meal made of grains, nuts, and fresh apples. My sister, who was staying with me at the time, and I would eat our muesli at eight a.m. I felt ravenous by ten or ten thirty, but she was fine. The high carbohydrate content of the muesli burned too fast in my system. I needed protein at every meal to slow my digestion down.

My Peg Goes to Optimum Health

Thinking I needed to cleanse my system of toxins, I stayed several weeks in San Diego at Optimum Health. I managed to lose about seventeen pounds on their raw and fermented vegetable, fruit, and seed diet coupled with daily wheatgrass drinks and enemas. My system was also cleansed with colonics every few days. I learned about organic gardening and how to make fresh juices and seed cheeses. Each day we went for walks and did group exercises. Some very ill people restored their health through the program.

I learned the skins of fruits contain enzymes needed by the body to digest the fruit. I then understood why we were all given a slab of watermelon complete with a small glass of juiced watermelon rind each day for breakfast. Each of us would make our own fresh wheatgrass juice using commercial juicing machines. In addition to drinking wheatgrass, we also drank a fermented wheat seed drink called Rejuvalac. I didn't care for the taste of either. But I came away fired up with a new juicer and a dehydrator to make my own juices and dried fruits at home. However, the energy to do so was short-lived. I understand now why I lost interest so quickly. My body prefers and requires meat protein to be at its best.

My Peg Gets Bad Taste of Ketosis

Under a doctor's supervision, I then went on the Atkins-type diet of high protein and fat and very low carbohydrates. I experienced an unpleasant taste in my mouth due to ketosis. A too low carbohydrate diet depleted my body of glucose and glycogen stores. When glucose was not available, my body burned stored fat and muscle for energy. It also attempted to control my blood sugar in the absence of sufficient insulin since the production of insulin was not triggered by carbohydrates. In ketosis, fat can be utilized for energy, but proteins and muscle mass are broken down and converted into glucose and energy. This state was not healthy especially for my brain, which must receive regular glucose to function properly. The ketone bodies produced by incomplete fat metabolism are actually an unhealthy waste product that can accumulate in the blood.

Yes, I lost weight readily for a while but suffered the bad breath and taste from ketosis. My doctor stopped my diet before I developed ketoacidosis, which can become a serious kidney function problem.

My Digestive Balance Is Critical

I recently examined another high-protein diet from Ideal Protein, a weight loss program from France. It is specifically designed to force the body to release old fat stores by depriving the body of fat and high-glycemic carbohydrates. Their program is effective. Several friends lost weight rapidly on it, but it is very severe in its restrictions with many required food products made with synthetic sugars. Friends that tried it found they lost weight evenly over their bodies without any loss of muscle mass. But they found it too restrictive to stay on the diet plan for any length of time. I decided it was not right for me for a long-term solution, but their information was invaluable.

Ideal Protein's informational DVD presented essential information, detailing how the stomach and pancreas work to keep the blood's Ph at a safe level; poor eating habits through a misunderstanding of this process can cause illness. In the DVD, the doctor, a trained pharmacist who gave up his successful practice to become part of the company, explained what happens when we eat. He drew the stomach, esophagus, small intestine, pancreas, and parietal cells of the stomach lining.

The doctor pointed out that between meals the stomach fluid sits in the lower area of the stomach and is at a Ph of 4.0, which is weakly acidic. When we eat a meal and/or drink water, the acid level is weakened to 4.5 Ph, and along with the muscular expansion of the stomach, the change in acidity triggers the parietal cells into action. These cells begin converting salt (NaCL) (or potassium) + water + carbon dioxide into hydrochloric acid (HCL) + (Nm) + sodium bicarbonate (or other bicarbonate) (HCO3) in a one-to-one ratio. Gastrin is created. The proton pump system sends the hydrochloric acid into the stomach for digestion, but the sodium bicarbonate is sent into the arterial system (the blood stream) to maintain the acid base balance. In making this chemical conversion, the parietal cells burn many calories.

The hydrochloric acid increases the stomach's acidity to 1.5 Ph in order to digest the protein in the meal. The acidity is reduced as the protein is changed into a number of nutrients. Carbohydrates and fats are not broken down in the stomach but are passed into the small intestine. After about twenty-five minutes in the stomach, the converted food is passed into the small intestine. At this point, the pancreas (in addition to making glucagon and insulin) creates the same chemical reaction as the parietal cells, also burning more calories. As the slurry leaves the stomach, the pancreas pumps in sodium bicarbonate to prevent the acid from burning the soft tissues of the small intestine. The pancreas creates about a quart of liquid to neutralize the acid so the pancreatic enzymes can continue the digestion process in the small intestine. It sends the hydrochloric acid from its conversion into the blood stream to maintain the necessary Ph balance of 7.3-7.4 for the arterial blood flow.

Additionally, dark cola drinks are very acidic with a Ph of 2.2. When we drink a dark cola drink full of sugar (ten teaspoons of sugar to a can), the parietal cells say, "Ok we don't need to make the conversion. There is enough acid already for digestion." So no bicarbonate is pumped into the blood stream. But the pancreas still pumps bicarbonate into the small intestine and hydrochloric acid into the blood stream. However, the arterial blood doesn't receive the original sodium bicarbonate and is no longer balanced as the arterial Ph drops. Because maintaining the alkaline Ph at 7.3-7.4 is so critical, the bloodstream immediately goes to the bones and the osteoblasts to strip out alkalizing minerals like calcium and magnesium to rebalance the blood stream.

These minerals then cause crystals of uric acid to form which may become gout, of calcium chloride crystals that may form kidney stones, or phosphate salts implicated in fibromyalgia. They can also cause hardening of the arteries. Stripping the bones of minerals eventually causes osteoporosis. These reactions occur because the foods ingested did not cause the complete balancing chemical reaction. Therefore, chronic diseases equal acid conditions.

If we are insulin resistant through an overly acidic diet, we lose magnesium from our bones. Magnesium is very important and is required for insulin receptors to work. It helps to relax the arteries and to prevent high blood pressure. If our bodies do not respond to insulin, we become insulin resistant and age faster. More insulin has to be secreted to create the same activity in the body. Insulin says store fat. Apparently, a protein diet lowers insulin levels and can re-sensitize us to insulin.

List of Bad Activities

1. Feeding a baby only grains, fruits, and carbohydrates will begin to cause insulin resistance. The liver becomes resistant to insulin requiring more insulin to produce the same effect, which can also occur if we give young children soda.
2. Eating too many acidic breads and grains without sufficient alkaline foods will eventually cause overweight and disease in susceptible people.
3. Drinking acidic drinks, especially dark-colored colas can eventually cause illness because of the distortion to the acid-balancing process, making our systems too acidic.
4. Not eating sufficient alkaline foods (green vegetables) and protein or drinking sufficient amounts of water will lead to damaging high acidity in the body.
5. When we take a product to reduce digestive acid, we actually make the problem worse because the medicine distorts the body's natural reaction. It is far better to eat proteins and alkalizing foods.

NUTRITION LABELS

The founder of Ideal Protein gave some additional helpful information. When we look at nutrition labels, we need to keep the following in mind. We need half a gram of protein per pound of body weight. A large egg equals six grams of protein. A piece of cheese equals five grams. Cheese by itself is okay. But eating cheese with carbohydrates is a bad combination. When coupled with carbohydrates, the carbohydrate will be burned for energy and the fat will be stored.

Four grams of carbohydrate equals one teaspoon of sugar. The sugar in an apple, whole grain bread, or red wine can prevent weight loss. If we want to lose weight, we must suppress our ingestion of simple and complex carbohydrates and bad fats. The body burns sugar first before it burns protein or fat. If you reduce your intake of carbohydrates, your body will burn more stored fat for energy.

Obesity, hypertension, pre-diabetes, high cholesterol, and triglycerides are all interlinked. It is a question not if you will develop one of them but when you will get the others. Too much blood sugar harms our immune system. We must take care of our acid balance through our nutrition. If we cut out most carbohydrates in order to lose weight, we must drink lots of water and take calcium and magnesium supplements.

THE NEW ATKINS FOR A NEW YOU

"After a few days on a high- protein and high-fat diet, many people are released from blood sugar hell."

John Gray PhD

In 2010, three doctors released an improved version based on the original Atkins diet of protein, fat, and low or no carbohydrates. They created a plan similar to Ideal Protein's diet without the need to purchase special high-protein supplements. In addition to a variety of protein and fatty foods, *The New Atkins* plan incorporates a gradual increase in carbohydrates from a low of 20 grams to 90 grams in the maintenance phase. Since fiber slows the digestion of carbohydrates, grams are determined by deducting the grams of fiber from the carbohydrate total listed on a nutritional label. Similar to Ideal Protein's plans, each day's menu includes low glycemic foundation vegetables to provide necessary fiber and minerals. The testimonials describe very positive lasting weight-loss results without the side effects of the old Atkins eating plan. Had I not been pleased with my progress on the Formula described later, I would consider this plan.

Many Complex Factors In Natural Foods

"Processed foods are nutritionally deficient and make you hungrier than you really are."

John Gray PhD

At a Mannatech convention in Dallas, Texas, I learned a valuable lesson about the importance of choosing natural foods and supplements. Judith A. De Cava, M.S. spoke about how vitamins must only be taken with all of their naturally occurring components. When they are not, you will eventually create disease because of the shortage in the body of the missing companion elements. For example, in Judith's book *The Real Truth About Vitamins And Antioxidants*, she lists the chemical makeup of vitamin C and vitamin E. When we take a synthetic vitamin C only containing ascorbic acid, we leave out ascorbigen, bioflavonoid complexes, tyrosinase, P factor, K factor, and J factors that comprise natural vitamin C. The synthetic vitamin is therefore not complete. The continuous ingestion of only ascorbic acid actually causes disease in the body because of the overbalance of only one element and the shortage of the others. The chromatograms in Judith's book also show the distinct energy differences between synthetic ascorbic acid and an acerola cherry, the source of natural vitamin C.

The diagram of the components of natural vitamin E shows it contains not just alpha tocopherol but also delta tocopherol, gamma tocopherol, beta tocopherol, xanthine, selenium, lipositols, and four other factors. Most over-the-counter vitamin E has only d-alpha tocopherol in it. Once I understood the difference, I carefully purchased vitamin E with as many of its natural components as possible. The best multi-vitamins are those cultivated and grown in a plant or yeast base while being fed the required minerals. When the plant has matured, it is harvested and compressed into pills containing all the naturally occurring elements.

Weight Loss Struggles

As a large woman, I couldn't buy attractive clothing. For years, I had to go to a dressmaker and have my clothes made. Then I became a little smaller enabling me to shop at only one fat lady store carrying the largest sizes. I had to shop there for many years. That store did not (and still doesn't) see the beauty in a fat person and provided the ugliest of fashions. Any clothing suitable for work or that was dressier was made from polyester, which my body could not stand. It made my cells unable to breathe causing me to overheat. After all, all those additional pounds meant I was hot much of the time.

A master herbalist, Terry Willard, showed me the importance of keeping my system more alkaline when I sought help for a digestive problem. My stomach was too acidic causing pain due to my high carbohydrate diet and love of Pepsis and snack foods. *Acid & Alkaline* by Herman Aihara helped me understand which foods were alkaline when ingested. Bit by bit I learned about the foods I needed to eat and to avoid.

Early on, I also saw a physic, Narayana, who came to Calgary from Europe. He told me I would find a product not yet available called alfalfa that would be beneficial for me. He struggled to say the word *alfalfa* as he read it in his mind from something he was being shown. A few years later compressed alfalfa tablets became available. I have used them regularly, especially if I feel I am too acidic. They neutralize the acidity and keep me from developing colds or stomach upsets.

From a live blood analysis session, I learned there was an excess of phosphorous in my blood. I was warned excess phosphorous damaged the myelin sheath covering the nerves in my body. The excess phosphorous had likely resulted from drinking too many bottles of Pepsi and eating large portions of red meat.

I made the effort to drink a lot of water each day and to return salt to my diet as suggested by Dr. Batmanghelidj. Oddly enough, the re-introduction of sea salt and additional water reduced the edema I experienced in my legs and ankles for many years and actually helped to lower my blood pressure.

Weight Watchers

"Why is it one diet can work well for one person but not another? It's not because you didn't follow the diet correctly. It's because the diet didn't follow you."

Ann Louise Gittleman. M. S.

Along the way, I tried Weight Watchers but couldn't seem to get into their eating plan. I had an aversion to eating all of the vegetables. Then I tried a succession of diets from a plethora of diet books (see bibliography) as well as fasting for weeks by juice fasting or on the Master Cleanse. I would lose some weight only to gradually regain it. When they were introduced, I began to read nutrition labels, first thinking I needed to find foods only low in fat as most diets seemed to suggest.

Entering the Zone

I discovered *The Zone Diet*, an insulin controlling plan, developed by Barry Sears, PhD. Barry called the Zone "that mysterious but very real state in which your body and mind work together at their ultimate best." A partial excerpt from his book was very helpful. He pointed out:

- "Eating fat does not make you fat. It's your body's response to excess carbohydrates in your diet that makes you fat. Your body has a limited capacity to store excess carbohydrates, but it can convert those excess carbohydrates into excess fat.

- It's hard to lose weight by simply restricting calories. Eating less and losing excess body fat do not automatically go hand in hand. Low-calorie, high carbohydrate diets generate a series of biochemical signals in your body that will take you out of the Zone, making it more difficult to access stored body fat for energy. Result: you'll reach a weight-loss plateau, beyond which you simply can't lose any more weight.

- Diets based on choice restriction and calorie limits usually fail. People on restrictive diets get tired of feeling hungry and deprived. They go off their diets, put the weight back on primarily as increased body fat, and then feel bad about themselves for not having enough will power, discipline, or motivation.

- Weight loss has little to do with will power. You need information not will power. If you change what you eat, you don't have to be overly concerned about how much you eat. Adhering to a diet of Zone favorable meals, you can eat enough to feel satisfied and still wind up losing fat—without obsessively counting calories or fat grams.

- Food can be good or bad. The ratio of macronutrients—protein, carbohydrate, and fat—in the meals you eat is the key to permanent weight loss and optimal health. Unless you understand the rules controling the powerful biochemical responses generated by food, you will never reach the Zone.

- The biochemical effects of food have been constant for the last forty million years. All mammals, including man, have essentially the same responses to food. Those responses have been genetically conserved throughout evolution, and are unlikely to change in the near future."

Now I understood the importance of a balanced diet. To make it easier to understand the relationship of nutriments and their effect on the body, Dr. Sear created Zone food blocks. A Zone food block was three grams of fat, a protein food block was seven grams, and a carbohydrate block was nine grams. Dr. Sear established a table of foods and their nutritional values. Instructional information also helped each person to create his or her own unique eating plan. It took into account lean body mass and activity level. His books give the block values of many foods as well as recipes so a person can make up an individualized menu. A balanced meal required eating blocks on a 1-1-1 ratio of carbohydrates to protein to fat.

Because I was working and didn't feel like doing much cooking for one person, I didn't master the block system adequately, although I realized Dr. Sear's nutritional reasoning was sound. I searched for foods based on a 40-30-30 calorie ratio of carbohydrates to protein to fat. To achieve that balanced ratio, nutrition labels needed to be approximately 25 grams of carbohydrate to 15 grams of protein and only 6 grams of fat in a portion of about 200 calories. Most prepared foods were too high in carbohydrates and fat. Reading food labels, I did manage to find some Lean Cuisine and Weight Watcher ready-made meals that fit the formula.

At last after struggling with food blocks with the Zone Diet, I discovered the *Formula 40 -30-30 Personalized Weight Loss Program* developed by Barry Sear's nutritionists, Gene and Joyce Daoust. It was based on the same formula as the Zone Diet. The Formula provided balanced 40-30-30 recipes to follow that didn't require me to figure out food blocks or percentages. That made it easier. Because I was working long hours and didn't have much time for cooking, I hired a friend to make and freeze some of the meals. I released twenty-eight pounds, and I kept almost all of them off. But then the energy to continue dieting waned, and I stopped dieting again.

Commitment Is a Major Key

"Maybe you have spent a good part of your life on the diet merry go round. You hop on to lose some weight, then dismount as soon as you've lost it. When you regain the pounds—as most of us inevitably do—you jump back on, and so forth."

The New Atkins for a New You by Dr. Eric Westman, Dr.Stephen D. Phinney and Dr. Jeff S. Volek

For a number of years I simply gave up trying to lose weight any more. My weight hovered around 271 pounds. I had reduced my portion sizes, which enabled my metabolism to find a normal level of weight maintenance. My torso clothing size was 3x, 4x and my hips, 4x and 5x, a typical pear shape. My large rump was even too big to fit in many chair styles, causing a constant undercurrent of self-loathing.

As I grew older into my sixties my metabolism slowed down even more. Less food was required to maintain my weight. I had to learn to consume even less.

Finally several years later, I made a strong internal commitment to release my excess weight again. I allowed my commitment to come from deep within and knew I would not allow setbacks to take me away from my weight loss goals, even though I lost only 1.5 to 2 pounds a week.

I religiously followed Weight Watchers new self-designed, low-fat eating plan, recording my points each day. Starting at 269 pounds, I selected a goal only twenty pounds below my starting weight and then moved it down another ten pounds as I neared my first goal. I visualized myself thinner and saw in my mind the scale pointing to 239 pounds. I purchased Lean Cuisine and Weight Watcher meals so I did not have to cook for myself. I did not have to follow someone else's eating plan with foods requiring special ingredients, cooking, or things I didn't normally eat. I could plan my diet around what I liked to eat. This important change enabled me to stay on the diet for a number of months.

I felt so good about myself when I lost twenty pounds and reduced my clothing size. I changed my visualization down another 20 pounds and I treated myself to several new corduroy trousers when my size dropped from size 3x to 2x. My larger clothes went off to the Salvation Army.

I religiously wrote my daily weight and food choices on weekly spreadsheets. But initially I did not plan my meals ahead. As a result, I began to choose my food throughout the day. I found I overate in the early part of the day, becoming hungry after eating only the limited points left in the evening. Thus I would end up eating more points a day than I was allowed. The long-standing habit of eating in the evening was also hard to break.

I released weight slowly because every so often I would overindulge by eating a sweet or more than I should. Or I would have a high-carbohydrate meal or pastry and set myself back again. Thus for several months, my weight did not really go down.

For a while, a hidden fear sabotaged my weight loss as I approached my first goal. I would eat too much, gaining a few pounds I then had to re-lose. This pattern kept recurring. Then I realized I had a hidden emotional block, which prevented me from becoming thin. It protected me from something indefinable—perhaps from becoming promiscuous again. I also was rejecting myself.

While I slowly lost weight again over about seven months, I reached a place in November where I couldn't seem to stick to the Weight Watchers eating plan. I became depressed and noticed my hair and skin seemed excessively dry. I recognized the Weight Watcher's plan is very low in fat. Remembering my metabolic profiling and my blood and body type, I knew I needed to add fat and more protein back into my diet.

My Peg Loves the Formula 40-30-30 Plan

"By focusing so strongly on the idea that one diet will provide all the necessary nutrients for everybody, we've completely ignored a primary factor that governs all living beings. Each one of us is different."

Ann Louise Gittleman. M. S.

So I turned once again to the Formula 40-30-30 eating plan. Now that I was retired, I was able to prepare my choices from a selection of 200 excellent recipes. The authors, the Daousts, suggest picking a few recipes to enjoy and just repeating them, since that is actually how many people eat even if they are not dieting. I picked a few I like and enjoy them repeatedly. Sometimes I make family sizes to freeze ahead in the correct portions. There are even very tasty cheesecake and pudding recipes I have served to company.

The meal portions for a person my size total about 1,500 calories a day. The plan provides five different portion sizes based on weight and activity levels. In the first three weeks (the fat flush portion), meals are designed with 40% low-glycemic carbohydrates and sufficient protein and fat at 30% each to keep insulin in check.

After the first three weeks, I could elect to follow menus from the regular diet plan, still with the same caloric value and 40-30-30 ratio but including some medium and higher glycemic-index carbohydrates like potatoes and other items made with small amounts of flour. The beauty of the plan is it gives me the complete ingredient list and portions. I don't have to figure anything out, which was a problem with the similar Zone diet. If I want to create my own recipes, the Formula also provides the tools to do so.

This time I am persevering, and I still record my foods and weight daily. All cravings for sweets have disappeared. I no longer suffer from intestinal gas. I look forward to my meals because I have chosen foods I like to eat. In fact after my first experience with the Formula plan four years ago, two of their suggested breakfast meals became my mainstay meals ever since. I love oatmeal with cottage cheese and walnuts and regularly enjoy a variety of fruit, almond, and whey smoothies for breakfast.

I was thrilled to be able to purchase size 20 clothing at a regular store on sale for ridiculously low prices compared to the cost of buying my former fat lady clothing. For many years I had been able to shop at only one or two stores carrying outsize garments. The delight in my slimmer body added impetus to my commitment to continue releasing excess weight.

I began to notice when I ate a higher-glycemic carbohydrate from the regular food plan, my weight would go up perhaps as much as two pounds from one day to the next. Then it might take several days to come back down again. This was a clue that I retained fluid tied to my inability to fully digest refined carbohydrates. I learned higher glycemic carbohydrates cause increased glycogen levels, which stores four times more water per gram. For a long time I have known that when I eat strawberries or shrimp, my weight will go down more than expected the next day. When I learned shrimp is very high in protein, I realized why.

One of the difficulties with any long-term eating plan is boredom with eating the same foods all the time. A sense of being deprived adds to the boredom, which is why I would stop dieting in the past. I would also find it very hard to go back onto the same diet again. I would try yet another diet plan when I did attempt to lose weight again. Meanwhile I may have gained back a few pounds that had to be lost all over again.

However, I have not had that problem with the Formula 40-30-30 plan. To counter boredom, I began to introduce some new items from the list of suggested meals. I found new food combinations I enjoyed. Now each day I can choose from a variety of meals, some made ahead and frozen. I just need to fetch them from the freezer in the morning to defrost.

Another difficulty I still struggle to overcome is caused by seeing food commercials on television in the evening. Even though I pre-record the programs I wish to see, skipping through the commercials quickly, I still am impacted by the food ads. I have to exercise extra diligence to prevent going to the kitchen to have an un-needed snack late in the day.

"Finish every day and be done with it. You have done what you could. Some blunders and absurdities no doubt crept in; forget them as soon as you can. Tomorrow is an new day; begin it well and serenely and with too high a spirit to be cumbered with your old nonsense. This day is all that is good and fair. It is too dear, with its hopes and invitations, to waste a moment on the yesterdays."

Ralph Waldo Emerson

Planning Ahead

When I shop, I read nutrition labels carefully looking for a balanced ratio of fat, carbohydrate, and protein. Another important key was to finally train myself to write down tomorrow's meal plan at least one day ahead. Oddly enough, it seemed to reduce the emphasis on eating and has made the plan very simple to follow. I truly enjoy it and expect I can eat this way the rest of my life.

I must also plan to only shop when I am not hungry and for a definite list of the foods I need. I have a bad habit of seeing and buying things I would like to eat as I push my cart around the grocery store, especially if I am hungry. In a weak or emotional moment, I find I have eaten something not on my diet. It was far too easy to chastise myself over the lapse. A little effort at the store to resist buying unneeded food makes it easy to resist at a weak moment later when the forbidden product is not available at home.

Planning needs to include allowing myself to enjoy snacks at a social event or enjoying a meal out with friends without guilt. But I must jump right back into my program at the next meal. Occasional missteps take the pressure away from the constant dieting mode and actually allow me to stay on my diet longer with more satisfaction and less sense of deprivation. Occasionally enjoying new untried recipes has helped stave off long term diet fatigue. Acknowledging it took many years to accumulate excess weight, I gladly accept the lengthy period of time necessary to permanently change my relationship to food. Albeit it is harder to change at my advanced age, but my growing pleasure at the results sustains me making it all worthwhile.

Finding Enjoyable Exercise for My Peg

"Without enough exercise, the metabolic rate slows and we begin to store fat and become overweight."
John Gray PhD

For a person who has disliked exercise most of my life, finding a pleasurable exercise routine is a must. As I mentioned previously, I viewed exercise as a punishment, partly because I perspired so easily. I found repetitious movements boring and a waste of time. However, as my body shows the signs of advancing age, exercise is necessary to maintain the fluidity of my joints, the circulation in my legs, and the tone of my heart. I found climbing three sets of stairs up to my apartment once or more each day has been a way to exercise without relating to it as being exercise. I had to create a morning ritual including exercise or I wouldn't get around to doing it. After a while, it became a habit just like brushing my teeth or putting on lipstick.

For over a year, I regularly went to Curves on my way home from work. I completed their half-hour circuit exercise followed by their recommended stretches. It was good for me. But then my work hours changed. When I finished work at mid-day and wanted to exercise on my way home, Curves was closed. Making a special trip later in the day was too much of a bother.

I have always loved walking outdoors. There are beautiful treed walkways away from traffic near my building. But icy sidewalks in winter are too dangerous, and I am too lazy to drive to a shopping mall just to walk. For several years while I suffered with sore feet from heel spurs and pronation of my ankle, I could not walk or use the treadmill. Recently, however, our condominium upgraded our exercise equipment to include an elliptical machine, a recumbent bicycle, and a second treadmill. With the donation of a television, I am able to enjoy the news while I pedal or walk. With my mind distracted, I can exercise much longer, hardly noticing the time is going by. My body certainly loves it. A friend and I also purchased together a vibration platform machine I use every day. It acts like a mechanical rebounder to jiggle the lymph in my body and tone my muscles. It facilitated a more even weight loss. I lost two inches from my thighs and three from my hips, where on previous diets I would normally have lost weight only on my upper body.

"Your exercise routine is of little value if you don't do it."
John Gray PhD

QUI GONG

Qui Gong practices are surprisingly healing and toning as exercise routines. Chun Yi Lyn's Qui Gong techniques helped me to get in touch with the feelings within my body. Some practices are based on visualization of energy flow coupled with breath techniques. Others are focused on healing the body and improving energy flow.

Tai Chi

There is such a beautiful rhythm and fluidity in Tai Chi and in the short form Tai Chi Chuan. The long form takes a period of months to master. I needed discipline to continue over the six months of learning and practice. The short form, however, was easier to master, and I preferred it. Each day I spent fifteen minutes doing a simple series of moves.

Yoga

Stretch yoga can be relaxing and enjoyable. The more strenuous bends and twists were not my cup of tea, but the stretching movements I found enjoyable.

Aquasize

An aquasize class is good exercise if regularly practiced. The water exerts an extra drag force so my muscles work harder as I move in kicks and stretches while half-submerged.

Dance

I discovered I love the fluidity of creative dance. Just allowing my body to move in response to music is a wonderful feeling as well as energizing. When I make my exercise into a dance, I can exercise for a long time, even if I begin to perspire heavily. I found some of Richard Simmons dance party exercise programs were even enjoyable after I learned the steps. They were a good indoor exercise when the weather didn't allow me to go outside.

Walking

Nothing compares to a long walk in nature each day. In addition to stretching my leg muscles, every sense finds pleasure. Sight, sound, and smell are all stimulated. I am touched by the state of harmony and balance, which I find particularly soothing. I can choose to walk the same path each day or vary it as often as I wish to relieve boredom. In winter when the walks are too treacherous with hidden patches of ice, I turn to the treadmill instead.

Cycling

Stationery cycling indoors in the winter and outdoor summer bicycling are fine exercise. But only if I can find a comfortable position with handlebars that don't force me to lean over and thus tire my back. Bicycle seats too small for my large derriere are very uncomfortable. However, a recumbent exercise bike eliminates the strain on my back.

Swimming

My dry skin does not enjoy long dips in the chlorinated pool. Because it also means having to spend time re-curling my hair, swimming has not been my favorite exercise. However once I drag myself into the water, I can enjoy it.

Weight Lifting

Once a personal trainer showed me the movements for various muscles, I could easily use handheld weights, but it was boring unless I could do it while watching TV.

Weight Loss Lesson Keys

1. Nourishment of yourself is not restricted to food. You should also seek to nourish your feelings, filling gaps in your self-worth.
2. Overeating of carbohydrates, breads, pastries, sweets, or soda pop can cause a vicious cycle of ravenous hunger shortly after eating. Because these refined foods have a high glycemic index, they digest very rapidly. Ultimately, in my case, they triggered overweight and trended toward diabetes, disturbing my body's insulin cycle.
3. Overeating may partially be driven by poor nourishment of the brain. Getting sufficient exercise, fish oil, and vitamin D is critical to the brain's functioning.
4. Many high-glycemic foods such as soda and potato chips are unhealthy not just because of the carbohydrate cycle but because the salt in potato chips calls for the sweet taste of soda.
5. Diet soda can actually cause obesity because the body discovers it did not receive the glucose it needed and so sends the message to eat again.
6. Nowadays in addition to some Chinese food, over 5,000 foods contain monosodium glutamate (MSG) as a flavor enhancer. As an exitotoxin, MSG is harmful to most people. Sometimes I reacted badly to MSG by getting headaches. MSG hides under many names, such as hydrolized vegetable protein, autolyzed plant protein, yeast extract, textured protein, calcium caseinate, glutamic acid, glutamate, accent, aginomoto, and gelatin.
7. Overeating wheat when my body type could not tolerate it led to the development of an allergy. My allergy may also have been caused by the genetic changes in modern grains since I can tolerate ancient grains like kamut and spelt.

8. Denying myself a treat, then allowing the longing and denial to be reinforced, caused eventual overeating later. I learned it was best to enjoy small treats in moderation and return to the diet at the next meal.
9. Dieting restriction causes the body to believe it is in a famine. When food is once again available, overeating soon returns excess pounds to the body.
10. Learning to stick to a pre-planned grocery list based on your diet menu is important, especially since seeing food can easily trigger an extra purchase.
11. Preplanning meals for a minimum of at least one or more days will help you stay on your eating plan.
12. Selecting a few foods from your diet plan to prepare and freeze ahead in appropriate portion sizes also will make it easier to follow your diet plan. All you need to do is remove the food from the freezer.
13. Knowing ahead what you will eat stops you from searching through the cupboards and fridge. When I hadn't planned my meals and snacks, I would find myself searching for what to eat next. This can lead to inappropriate food choices because you may eat something that just happens to catch your eye.
14. Making a strong commitment is a major key of staying on a long-term diet plan.
15. Choosing to eat prepared foods from a packaged diet plan requires making an extra effort to create a sustainable maintenance eating plan. Unless you sufficiently change your original eating habits, you will likely either find yourself eating all those foods you were denied while on the plan or eat too large portion sizes. The first large weight loss in a diet is often water loss, which is quickly recovered if you stop controlling your diet.

16. Examining your beliefs about yourself can be a major source of healing. I uncovered many buried emotions, such as rejection, low self-esteem, perfectionism, fear of failure, stress, loneliness, social awkwardness, seeking comfort, and needing to protect myself from pain. Psychological guidance to help explore and change these emotionally based reasons for eating is also helpful.
17. Open yourself to the reason why a certain situation or feeling causes eating. Allow yourself to sit in the sensation of the uncovered feeling, resisting the feeling to eat something to satisfy the feeling. This process enables the bottled feelings to be expressed and released. Sometimes these stored feelings bring on tears. However, the negative feelings gradually dissipate as the stored energy is released.
18. Learning portion control is essential. Memorizing serving-size tips can help. For example, a small fist is about the size of a cup or 250 ml; the area of a small palm is about the size of a 3 oz. or 75 ml serving; a thumb tip is equal to 1 tsp or 5 ml, while a whole thumb is approximately equal to 1 oz. or 30 ml.
19. Super size meals include a great deal more food than your body needs even if they are a bargain in price. Request a container or bag to take excess food home.
20. Serving food on a smaller luncheon plate makes the portion look bigger.
21. Hypnotism is a tool that can help some people change eating patterns, while aromatherapy pens may also help some people control their eating through the satisfaction of olfactory senses.
22. My hyperthyroid (overactive) condition disguised my overeating because my metabolism was so stimulated.
23. Pictures of alternate lower-calorie foods help direct you to

better food choices, thus reprogramming your mind.

24. Visualization practices work only if you can fully align with the desired outcome.
25. Knowledge of how the digestive and elimination systems work will assist your diet correction efforts.
26. Test for food sensitivities by eliminating certain classes of food. Slowly reintroduce the foods and watch how your body reacts.
27. Protein is an excellent food for my thyroid and blood type O. Other foods may be best for other types.
28. While low fat diets are healthy for some body types, my body experienced dry skin and hair after a period on a low-fat diet.
29. Eating an unbalanced diet can trigger the unhealthy effects of ketosis, caused by incomplete fat metabolism that can accumulate in the blood.
30. I created diet sustainability through a balanced 40-30-30 diet with large meals that eliminated cravings and the ability to make my meals from foods I enjoyed.
31. Enjoyable diet meals became mainstay meals in my regular diet enabling me to keep off the weight I had lost.
32. It is hard to return to normal eating after a restrictive diet. Following a maintenance plan is essential.
33. Identify the foods that cause too much acid and result in heartburn and ulcers. Learn the value of alkaline foods. Bone loss damage can result from excess acidity in the blood.
34. Many fruit skins contain enzymes for the digestion of that specific fruit.
35. Nutrition labels for approximately a 200-calorie portion of a balanced diet will have approximately 23 to 25 carbohydrate grams, 6-7 fat grams, and 15-16 protein grams. The calorie values will equal 40% of carbohydrate, 30% of protein and 30% of fat when the effect on the body is included.

36. One teaspoon of sugar equals four grams of carbohydrate. A can of soda has the equivalent of at least ten spoonfuls of sugar.
37. Take supplements in as natural a form as possible in order not to create a gradual imbalance that can lead to disease later.
38. Alfalfa and green supplements may help neutralize too much acidity.
39. The body burns sugar or carbohydrates first for energy, then protein or fat. If you reduce carbohydrates, your body will burn more stored fat for energy. If sufficient protein is included, your muscle mass will not be depleted for energy.
40. Insulin resistance can be caused by eating too many carbohydrates.
41. Dr. Barry Sear says, "The Zone is the place where you feel and function your best." I found my zone by eating a balanced diet in smaller calorie portions.
42. Choosing a diet plan that allows the freedom to select foods you enjoy leads to diet satisfaction and continued enjoyment of the diet plan.
43. Long-term diet boredom can be eliminated by trying new recipes.
44. Planning your shopping from a definite list helps avoid extra foods from creeping into your cupboards.
45. Keep your cupboards free of tempting treats.
46. Plan ahead for social function eating and for getting back on track again. Due to body chemistry, I can lose more weight by eating the same caloric value of low-glycemic (slow burning) foods versus high-glycemic (fast burning) foods.

Exercise Keys

47. Sufficient exercise is important. I no longer push myself too hard and exercise every day. When I don't feel like exercising

one day, I take a rest. This occasional day off actually helps to avoid building up a resistance to exercising. I am pleased when I complete at least five sessions a week.

48. Find an exercise program you enjoy doing.
49. Indoor exercise can fly by if your mind is distracted by television. The pleasure of being out in nature also enhances your outdoor exercise experience.
50. Creating a habit of your exercise routine ensures you will exercise regularly. For example, my morning ritual of washing, bed making, dressing, and exercising enables exercise to be a regular part of my daily activities.
51. Respect and honor your body's need for movement and regular exercise.

Chapter 7

MENTAL KEYS

Mastering Being a Square Peg

SELF-UNDERSTANDING THROUGH MY MIND

Mental Key

"It's human feeling and emotion that affect the stuff our reality is made of— it's our inner language that changes the atoms, electrons, and photons of the outer world."

Gregg Braden

My self-discovery and recovery of self led me to many aspects of the mind and its function. When I began to discover myself, then I could use my God-given abilities to heal my negativity. Many years ago, I consciously directed my existence in small ways. I learned about the mental key, the creative power of the mind through a book by Jack and Cornelia Addington, which opened my awareness to other worlds. Prior to the book, I had no knowledge of creating my own life or of other dimensions of existence.

In small ways, I consciously created a convenient available parking space even when the parking lot seemed full. When I focused my mind to win, and won a door prize, I recognized I created my own existence. The full magnitude of my discovery had not struck me very deeply, however.

Realization came. Behind my thoughts is a creative force called mind, made up of many vibrational frequencies. Based on their effects on life forms and material objects, we term some of these frequencies solar, cosmic, atomic, electric, magnetic, gravity, heat, sound, light, color, and love. In small, fine frequencies beyond our conscious awareness, they interpenetrate the ether or field of stillness enveloping everything. The emanations and movements of the sun and the planets in the ether field cause these vibrational frequencies. Based on our inherited capacities and receptivity, we experience these planetary influences on our lives.

As said many centuries ago, "In the beginning was the word and the word was made flesh." All begins in stillness, the ready-to-act creative field that envelops and includes everything. Scientists in quantum physics who have recognized its presence have called this ether "the field." When I create, I put a thought or spoken word into this universal field of stillness. Once instructed by thoughts or ideas, the pliant, waiting field puts in motion the creative forces of vibrational energy material to combine into form. Thoughts are spiritual powers with which we eventually create our personal and common realities.

All creation begins in the present moment of conscious awareness. When we apply energy of thought to the underlying stillness, its malleable qualities can be materialized to take particular form. Whether my creative thoughts manifest ease and accomplishment or sadness and negativity is up to the type of thoughts I apply to the creative force of stillness. Negative vibrations have a lower creative frequency than higher positive vibrations. Regardless of whether I consciously apply thought and desire or allow careless, casual thoughts and expressions to direct this creative energy force, it will still create form—form I eventually experience in my life. The physical world is created in response to the consciousness of us all.

There is innovation to creation. Creation only occurs in the present moment, in the "now." However, my current creation will be affected by my past if I allow poor or negative thoughts to form my thinking patterns and habits. They blur my creative impulse and thus create my less-than-optimum life experience. I can change what I habitually create in my experience through conscious reflection and re-alignment with my desired outcome. Alignment with the vision of my desire requires that I believe in the outcome as if it has already occurred. My creation may take a period of time before it manifests.

"Thought is a creative energy and will automatically correlate with it object and bring it into manifestation because thought is spiritual energy or vibration."

Charles F. Haanel

My Mental Health

Sometimes I don't recognize my mind is not functioning optimally. Unless my brain is healthy, I am not in my best mental health. After completing the tests in Dr. Daniel G. Amen's book *Change Your Brain, Change Your Life*, I learned I have several weak areas of brain activity. However, I took the actions he describes to improve my memory and reduce depression. I also added supplements to my diet to improve my brain health. His information enabled me to understand the physical component of my brain used for thinking and storing memories. The following section summarizes *Change Your Brain, Change Your Life* from the book and from the PBS broadcast program.

"When man's mind is made perfect, then and then only will the body be able perfectly to express itself."

Charles F. Haanel

CHANGE MY BRAIN, CHANGE MY LIFE

Dr. Daniel G. Amen and his associates collected over 40,000 functional brain scans using radioisotopes and SPECT imaging. They determined how things affect the performance of different portions of the brain. They discovered a healthy brain looks complete, while a diseased brain appears to have a number of openings or holes where brain activity is absent. The brains of smokers, alcoholics, or drug addicts all exhibit a number of openings. The brains of Alzheimer's patients have very large openings indicating a loss of the ability to function.

Dr Amen's website (www.amenclinics.com) lists fifty beneficial foods for the brain. I've included a few of the most important and most detrimental products below:

Foods are good for the brain:

1. Blueberries (an antioxidant)
2. Avocados
3. Walnuts (have three times the Omega 3 oils than almonds)
4. Green tea
5. Fish oil

Bad for the brain:

1. Too much caffeine
2. Alcohol
3. Inhaling fumes
4. Organic solvents

Seven Principles Of Brain Function

First principle – The brain determines how you think, feel, act, and get along with others, your personality, character, and soul.

Second Principle – When the brain works right, you work right, and when it is not working right, you don't work right. When your brain is healthy, you are focused, happy, relaxed, loving, and affectionate. When your brain is not working right, you are distracted, sad, anxious, angry, and not as effective.

Third Principle – The brain is the most complicated element in the body. If you don't take care of it, you lose 85,000 brain connections a day.

Fourth Principle – The brain is very soft in a hard skull. The brain is soft like Jell-O. Brain injuries matter. Protect your brain.

Fifth Principle – Many things can hurt or help the brain.

Things that hurt:

- Drugs
- Head injuries
- Alcohol (have only one or two drinks a week)—drinkers have smaller brains.
- Lack of exercise
- Not enough sleep—less than six hours a night of sleep decreases blood flow to the brain.
- Stress
- Smoking ages the brain and dehydrates it.

- Too much caffeine. Only one or two coffees or sodas dehydrate the brain and reduce blood flow.
- Negative thinking reduces blood flow to the brain.

Things that help:

- New learning makes new connections.
- Healthy diet
- Daily vitamins and fish oil
- Exercise
- Great sleep
- Social connections of family, hobbies, etc.
- Positive thinking, especially gratitude. Your brain is more coordinated when you are grateful.
- Meditation is amazing for brain function. It activates the most thoughtful part.
- Regular sexual activity helps mood and relieves pain. Having sex three times a week reduces heart and stroke problems by 50 percent and decreases pain by 50 percent

Sixth Principle – One size does not fit everyone's diagnosis. Depression is a symptom. Its causes include:

- Chemical imbalance
- Grief
- Chronic stress
- Financial losses
- Relationship problems
- Low thyroid

Seventh Principle – You can change your brain and change your life. Only 90 out of 3,000 brains are healthy. The number one cause of strokes is smoking. Drugs damage the brain.

Brain Part Functions

Prefrontal cortex – Humans use 30 percent, chimps 14 percent, dogs 7 percent, and cats use none.

Controls:

- Focus
- Forethought
- Judgment
- Empathy
- Impulse control
- Learning from mistakes

Problems:

- Short attention span
- Inability to learn from mistakes
- Lack impulse control
- Procrastination
- Bad judgment
- Lack empathy
- ADD (low-activity version)
- Weak conscience
- Low persistence
- Low-energy depression
- Need to be upset in order to concentrate

Things that help:

- Develop and maintain clear focus.
- Focus on what you like more than what you don't like.
- Have meaning, purpose, stimulation, and excitement in your life.
- Get organized; get help when you need it.
- Consider brainwave biofeedback training.
- Try audiovisual stimulation.
- Don't be another person's stimulant.
- Consider prefrontal cortex stimulation.
- Watch your prefrontal cortex nutrition.
- Try Mozart for focus.
- Write out goals in all aspects (relationship, money, physical, spiritual).
- Exercise (intense aerobic).
- Eat a high-protein, low-carbohydrate diet.
- Take fish oil.

Cingulate brain – located at the front of the brain

Controls:

- Brain's ability to shift gears
- To be flexible and go with the flow
- Ability to recognize options
- Idea-to-idea movement
- Error detection

Problems:

- If it works too hard, serotonin gets too low
- Get stuck in thoughts, hurts, or grudges
- Argumentative
- Faultfinding
- Micromanagers
- Rigid
- Appears selfish
- Inflexible

Things that help:

- Notice when you are stuck, distract yourself, and come back to the problem later.
- Think through answers before automatically saying no.
- Write options and solutions when you feel stuck.
- Seek the counsel of others when you feel trapped.
- Memorize and recite the serenity prayer when bothered by repetitive thoughts.
- Don't try to convince someone else who is stuck; take a break and come back later.
- Try making paradoxical requests.
- Use reverse psychology.
- Consider congulate medication.
- Try nutritional interventions.
- Exercise boosts serotonin.
- Best diet is high carbohydrate and low protein.
- Carbohydrates boost serotonin.
- Eat some dark chocolate.
- Take 5http supplement.

Limbic system

Controls:

- Emotional brain
- Our bonding
- Processes pain, smell, and libido
- Drives us to love and work
- Our mood

Problems:

- Sadness, depression
- Negativity
- Automatic negative thoughts
- Deceptive thoughts
- Less interest in things

Things that help:

- Exercise is critical at least four times a week (works better than Zoloft).
- Countries with people who ate the most fish had the lowest incidences of depression.
- Write out negative thoughts and talk back to them; ask, "Is this true?"
- Natural food supplements

Deep Limbic System

Functions:

- Sets the emotional tone of the mind
- Filters external events through internal states
- Tags events as internally important
- Stores highly charged emotional memories
- Modulate motivation
- Controls appetite and sleep cycles
- Promotes bonding
- Directly processes the sense of smell
- Modulates libido

Problems:

- Moodiness, irritability, clinical depression
- Increased negative thinking and perception
- Decreased motivation
- Flood of negative emotions
- Appetite and sleep problems
- Decreased or increased sexual responsiveness
- Social isolation

Things that help:

- Kill the ANTS (automatic negative thoughts). Feed your anteater.
- Surround yourself with people who provide positive bonding.
- Protect your children with limbic bonding.
- Build people skills to enhance limbic bonds.

- Recognize the importance of physical contact.
- Surround yourself with great smells.
- Build a library of wonderful memories.
- Consider limbic medications.
- Try physical exercise.
- Watch your limbic nutrition.

Basal Ganglia

Controls:

- Integrates feeling and movement
- Shifts and soothes fine-motor behaviors
- Suppresses unwanted-motor behaviors
- Sets the body's idle speed or anxiety level
- Enhances motivation
- Mediates pleasure/ecstasy

Problems:

- Anxiety, nervousness
- Panic attacks
- Physical sensations of anxiety
- Tendency to predict the worst
- Conflict avoidance
- Tourette's syndrome/tics
- Muscle tension, soreness
- Tremors
- Fine-motor problems
- Headaches
- Low/excessive motivation

Things that help:

- Kill the fortune-telling ANTS (automatic negative thoughts).
- Use guided imagery.
- Try diaphragmatic breathing
- Try meditation or self-hypnosis.
- Think about the "18/40/60" rule.
  At eighteen, you worry about what people think of you.
  At forty, you don't give a damn what people think of you.
  At sixty, you realize nobody's been thinking of you.
- Learn how to deal with conflict.
- Consider basal ganglia medications.
- Watch your basal ganglia nutrition.

The temporal lobes

Controls:
Dominant side (usually the left)

- Understanding and processing language
- Intermediate-term memory
- Long-term memory
- Auditory learning
- Retrieval of words
- Complex memories
- Visual and auditory processing
- Emotional stability

Non-dominant side (usually the right)

- Recognizing facial expressions

- Decoding vocal intonation
- Rhythm
- Music
- Visual learning

Problems with the dominant (usually left) temporal lobe

- Aggression, internally or externally directed
- Dark or violent thoughts
- Sensitivity to slights; mild paranoia
- Word finding speech problems
- Reading difficulties
- Emotional instability

Problems with the non-dominant (usually right) temporal lobe

- Difficulty recognizing facial expression
- Difficulty decoding vocal intonation
- Social-skill struggles

Problems with either or both temporal lobes

- Memory problems
- Headaches or abdominal pain without a clear explanation
- Anxiety or fear for no particular reason
- Abnormal sensory perceptions, visual or auditory distortions
- Feelings of déjà vu (that you have previously experienced something when you haven't) or jamais vu (not recognizing familiar people or places)
- Periods of confusion
- Religious or moral preoccupation

- Hypergraphia, exercise writing
- Seizures

Things that help:

- Create a library of wonderful experiences.
- Sing whenever/wherever you can.
- Use humming and toning to tune up your brain.
- Listen to classical music.
- Learn to play a musical instrument.
- Move in rhythms.
- Consider temporal lobe medication.
- Get enough sleep.
- Eliminate caffeine and nicotine.
- Watch your nutrition.
- Try EEG biofeedback.

How To Make My Peg Brain Great

Prescriptions

- Protect the brain from head injuries—wear a helmet that fits; use your seat belt.
- Exercise, dance, or play table tennis, which is the best sport because it utilizes eyes, hands, and feet.
- Avoid toxic substances.
- Drive in safe vehicles; keep them repaired.
- Do not use too much caffeine, alcohol, drugs, nicotine, or many pain and anxiety medicines.
- Get enough sleep.
- Feed the brain right; eat right to think right. You are what you eat.

- Anything that decreases blood flow to the brain will prematurely age it.
- Work your brain by learning new and different things.
- Stop drinking diet sodas.

Best brain diet (lean protein, good complex-and low-glycemic carbohydrates)

- Green leafy vegetables and vegetables of many colors that increase antacids
- Decrease trans fats but not all fats since 60 percent of the brain is fat and especially needs omega 3 fatty acids. One hundred trillion brain cells are made of long chain fatty acids; you can get these from fish, avocados, and walnuts.
- Water is critical to the brain, so drink plenty through the day. Eighty percent of the brain is water.
- Blueberries
- Broccoli for folate
- Green tea for thinanine and to relax (Decaf green tea is better.)
- Oatmeal
- Oranges for vitamin C
- Red bell peppers for vitamin C
- Spinach
- Tuna
- Turkey
- Multivitamin supplement
- Fish oil supplement (or flax oil if vegetarian)

Dr. Amen has many detailed suggestions to assist in brain recovery with tests to determine the source of problems along with many case histories and brain scan pictures. In addition, there is an excellent "Things to do and don't do" summary at the back of the book.

Dr. Amen also has published several other books on optimizing brain function, for example, *Magnificent Mind at any Age.* He also references *Healing the Hardware of the Soul* and states spiritual life is not good unless the brain is optimized. Without proper brain function, the ability to focus and meditate will be difficult.

"Thoughts, feelings and actions all in sync equals integrity."
Bob Procter

Education Is Critical

If one is blessed with good teachers in his or her parents, neighbors, and educators, then that individual learns how to function in a state of ever-increasing knowledge. From babyhood, we learn through experience and suggestion. Interpretation of our experiences is molded by the people and environments surrounding us. For example, if my father responded negatively to a situation, I would respond negatively as well. Perceptions based on copying my father's response to situations would gradually become my habitual patterns of response to similar situations. These programmed responses ultimately become the subconscious way we view the world.

My mother used a litany of expressions, which years later I also parroted to my children without realizing it. I found myself saying, "What is worth doing is worth doing well. Were you born in a barn? Shut the door. I hope you have six kids all as horrid as you are."

My Peg Has Passion For Lifelong Learning

The love of learning was instilled in me at an early age. My parents read to me, stimulating my mind to wish to read. I was encouraged to try new physical activities and new foods. My family traveled to other countries where I expanded my awareness, learning about how other people lived. Since life constantly changes, there is always something new for me to learn.

Gathering information to share with others has become my lifelong passion—a natural drive flowing from within. A passion is a harmonious inner energy fueling a person's desire to express and create in a specific way. The clues to your passion may lie in your early childhood when you naturally were in touch with your deeper motivating interests. As a seven year old, I wrote stories and shared them with others. My mother encouraged me to submit an article to a magazine, but they didn't print it. Then my low self-esteem kept me from expressing my passion for many years. Finding your passion requires uncovering the patterns holding you back from allowing your natural passion to surface.

Creating My Reality

"Whatever you really believe about something, your brain will alter your five senses so that you actually experience it as real and true."

Sean Stephenson

In every moment, you and I create our reality, using thoughts, feelings, and our habitual patterns of responding to the world. Our perceptions and inherited programming form our realities. Every reoccurring thought begins a habitual pattern if you repeat it often enough. After a certain amount of critical mass has accumulated, the energy of thought gathers particles of form around it, eventually manifesting a physical presence and thus the experience. In some ways, the stored habits in my subconscious mind have been a curse, especially when a memory influences me to re-act instead of responding in a fresh way.

My Thoughts Are Things

Charles W. Leadbetter could see the forms made by thoughts, so Annie Besant and he wrote *Thought-Forms*, which includes pictures of the thought forms drawn by an artist. Charles' other book *Man Visible and Invisible* and *The Mental Body* by A. E. Powell also describe this phenomenon. I was fascinated by the drawings. Especially intriguing were the shapes made by angry or hurtful thoughts that would dart like lightning bolts or curl back like accusing fingers upon the speaker.

Charles could also see the egg-shaped forms the astral and mental bodies make around a person. These forms change as a person and humankind develops. In meditation one time, I experienced an egg-shaped form surrounding my body. Since I am a kinesthetic person, I did not see but only felt the finest tension or vibration, more like an intention than a movement. Since the form was egg-shaped, I believe I moved briefly into my auric body.

"Thoughts are things and things are thoughts—what one thinks materializes."

Charles F. Haanel

My brain is like a factory. I give it raw materials, and it creates my experiences. My mind stores my repeated thoughts and feelings, creating memories and habitual ways of thinking. My thoughts are the software, my brain the computer hardware. As I give my brain new software (thoughts and feelings), it melds them into my life. In order for my mind to perform at its optimum, I must keep its machinery (the brain) in good shape with the correct nourishment.

Seeing Problems As Opportunities

My most negative experiences have often actually provided my most important lessons. How I respond to problems in my life is the key. Do I laugh, accept the situation, shrug it off, and then look at its flip side for a solution? Or do I envelop the problem in painful woe-is-me negativity? Do I see the situation as a problem or as an opportunity for growth? We always have the ability to make that choice. However until I grew in my self-worth, I automatically reverted to negativity. It required real effort on my part to view problems as solution opportunities rather than distressful occurrences.

Understanding My Peg's Mind Makeup

"Belief is the basis of all action, and this being so, the belief that dominates the heart or mind is shown in the life."

James Allen (Above Life's Turmoil)

We operate from three minds: (1) conscious, (2) subconscious, and (3) unconscious. The unconscious or universal mind is the field of mind that encompasses the past and future, including all thoughts ever created. It connects me to other people's minds. It exists in the ether. The subconscious controls my body's functions. It communicates through pictures and has the unique property of not being able to differentiate between real or imagined input. It could also be called the emotional mind because it records feeling states. My conscious mind receives input from my senses and can accept or reject the input it receives. It can also originate ideas and therefore can be considered my intellectual mind. It transmits thoughts and ideas as pictures to my subconscious mind.

The body is an instrument of the mind influenced by input from the sub-conscious mind and the senses (feeling, hearing, taste, touch, smell, plus other subtle vibrations from the environment). The body's natural responses to input have already been programmed by an individual's genetic inheritance. One's environment and family provide further input as a young baby is still open to these influences. While a person is still young, a paradigm (taken from other people's habits) is impressed upon the individual and controls their behavior.

A paradigm is a multitude of habits programmed into the subconscious mind, which acts as a filter. Your paradigms control your perceptions, your effectiveness, and even the amount of money you may make. Paradigms change your desired results. Your conscious wishes are filtered through the paradigms in the subconscious mind and are influenced. The filtering of the paradigms controls your responses even though you may think and believe you desire a different outcome.

I've experienced some difficulty in life because I did not fully recognize just how many habitual paradigms distort my life. Many of these were created by my ancestors or my childhood environment. Old ways, old habits, still rule my actions today.

I must change my paradigms in order to change my outcomes in life. A drawing (perhaps from Silva mind control) showed the way to change paradigms. It illustrated a man's head filled with minus signs and another head filled with plus signs. I must put more pluses than negatives into my subconscious mind to change the outcome from negative to positive.

"Both poverty and riches are the offspring of thought."
Napoleon Hill

Bob Procter provides three excellent free videos at his website (sixminutestraining.com), which show how paradigms block results. He also includes repetitive methods to release them. After following this practice over forty years ago to increase his flow of money, Bob's income changed from $4,000 to over $125,000 in one year. *Think and Grow Rich* by Napoleon Hill strongly influenced Bob. He also recommends Wallace D. Wattle's *The Science of Getting Rich*. (Both of these books are available as free downloads on some websites).

Through taking a number of T. Harv Eker's Peak Potential courses, I learned many affirmations. In one course, there were daily practices for ninety days to help change my paradigms. While I completed the ninety days, I didn't perceive any major changes. My paradigms were too entrenched. I gradually stopped using my little affirmation reminder cards. Listening to Bob Procter recently, I understood why I did not have much success. Bob says that to change his life he repeated his affirmations thousands of times a day for at least ninety days. I had not realized just how much effort would be needed to change my paradigms.

Silva Mind Control & Memory Training Tricks

"There are no limitations to the mind except those we acknowledge"
Napoleon Hill

I began to explore the many powers of my mind by attending Silva Mind control workshops. I took part in remote mental-healing sessions and amazed myself with how well I could remember a list of items using mnemonics or memory pegs. For example, I wanted to remember a long grocery list. Using familiar pictures from the entrance to my apartment, I would see each item placed in the scene. I found it useful to start at my front door. I would see the first item as if it hung on the door, the second item on the door knob, the next item on the bookcase inside the door, the next item on the hall carpet and so on. When I reached the grocery store and wished to retrieve my shopping list, I would think of my entrance. One by one as I mentally pictured walking through the door into the room, the shopping items would return to memory; confirmation that the sub-conscious thinks in pictures.

Jose Silva, the founder of the mind-control system learned how to utilize the brain's abilities. Sadly when I took the course, I had not yet reached the complete understanding of the creative power of thought.

"Any thought other than one of good will or good wishes toward anyone is injuring others and is therefore injuring oneself—effected through the interconnection of all minds."
Lester Levenson

The Power Of Blessings, Gratitude & Prayers

"Whatsoever ye shall ask the Father in my name he will give it you. Hitherto have ye asked nothing in my name: ask and ye shall receive, that your joy may be full."

Prayers of the Cosmos, Meditations on the Aramaic Words of Jesus

Masaru Emoto first introduced me to the power of blessings in *The Hidden Messages in Water.* This book contained photographs of ice crystals frozen after blessing the water. The blessed ice crystals displayed very beautiful arrangements when compared with crystals frozen using unblessed water. I realized the power of our words and blessings. I constantly bless my food before I eat, my water before I drink, and out in nature I bless the trees, the birds, especially the robins (whom I adore hearing), and the rabbits I may startle on my morning walk. I bless and express my gratitude for the presence of each.

When I get up, I spend a few minutes sitting on the edge of my bed in gratitude for the simple things in my life: my healthy body, fresh water, a comfortable bed, shoes that fit, a sunny day, and anything else that comes to mind. Gratitude for simple pleasures opens my heart and mind and raises my vibration into a happier state.

Prayers are also powerful when filled with feeling and a heartfelt desire for another's benefit. I loved the descriptions and translations of the Aramaic prayers from the time of Jesus contained in *Prayers of the Cosmos, Meditations on the Aramaic Words of Jesus* translated by Neil Douglas-Klotz. I identified with the subtle differences in the Lord's Prayer when translated directly from the Aramaic as follows.

Oh Birther! Father Mother of the Cosmos!
Focus your light within us—make it useful:
Create your reign of unity now—
Your one desire then acts with ours,
as in all light, so in all forms.
Grant what we need each day in bread and insight.
Loose the cords of mistakes binding us,
as we release the strands we hold of others' guilt.
Don't let surface things delude us,
But free us from what holds us back.
From you is born all ruling will,
the power and the life to do,
the song that beautifies all,
from age to age it renews
Truly—power to these statements—
may they be the ground from which all
my actions grow: Amen

Gregg Braden's *Magic of Prayer* helped me to understand the simple formula for creating a prayer that brings results. The results that come may be different from my expectation, but I give up my judgment of the outcome before I even begin.

- Before you begin, feel your connection with the Cosmic Creator in your body. Sit quietly focused within in an extraordinary state of consciousness until you can sense your connection with the universal reality.

- In the salutation, greet the Cosmic Birther with reverence, acknowledging its creative power and greatness.

- Then while feeling your desire from a place without ego or judgment of the outcome, ask for what you wish, knowing your prayer is answered.

- Then close by stating you sincerely speak from truth, in faith, and trust that it will be so.

- Amen (the witness)

Possibility Thinking

"Both poverty and riches are the offspring of thought."
Napoleon Hill

In the chapter on Emotional Keys, I described how I allowed myself to be creative following the inspiration I received from Dr. Shuller's *Move Ahead with Possibility Thinking*. I surprised myself with what I could do at the time. Many books and Internet programs can inspire us to take action. We can inspire ourselves to do and be more in so many ways. The key is to move out of our own way and allow the inspiration to activate us. The biggest hurdle seems to be accepting we can do it.

As previously described in the Enneagram section, my type #3 uses feelings and intuition for thinking. I trained my ability to think using Edward de Bono's book *The Thinking Course*, which was useful to open my mind to more ways to solve problems. An IQ test I took also gave me more confidence when it indicated I was not as stupid as I had believed. A constant barrage of negative talk so often expressed by critical parents or friends can program a poor self-image. Soon, as I did, you will internalize this and believe what you are told. You acknowledge the words by calling yourself stupid. Remove these poisonous words from your mental chatter.

Hypnosis Clears My Peg's Stress

"To interrupt the mind's endless ramblings, it is necessary to seek out its hidden motives and surrender the illusory gains. Thus surrender rather than resistance may diminish the mind's seeming control."

Dr. David R. Hawkins

My occasional ill health, exhaustion, tension, and depression were emotional problems caused by stress from overworking. My doctor would prescribe tranquilizers or anti-depressants. But I preferred not to take drugs, so I asked him if someone specialized in stress disorders. He sent me to Dr. Brian J. Gorman whose sole practice was stress relief through hypnosis. In his eighties, Dr. Gorman had been doing hypnosis for so long that he slurred all his words together. Yet he and his wife in their advanced age would climb up and down Sulpher Mountain in Banff, Alberta, twice a day as they practiced to go to the Himalayas. He was amazing.

Hypnosis is a state of super relaxation. In this state, helpful suggestions can be given to the subconscious mind without being blocked by the conscious mind. For the sessions, I would sit in a comfortable chair while Dr. Gorman used his somnambulist voice to direct my mind to accept positive suggestions (with the ultimate goal being the removal of stress from my body). With his help in his office and from listening to his hypnosis tapes at home, I changed my mental attitude. These mental changes positively affected my self-image and released my body and mind from stress over a period of weeks.

Dr. Gorman wrote an interesting book on stress treatment called *Attitude Therapy for Stress Disorders,* and supplement *Fog' Em All!*.

He describes the many effects of psychological stress and the methods to modify attitudes and behavior using different relaxation techniques. He described his case histories as he helped his patients overcome a variety of stress-induced disorders. Because stress can affect parts of the body in distinctly different ways, a variety of hypnosis techniques and understandings needed to be developed. Dr. Gorman preferred to use the word relaxation for his work because the word hypnosis "held connotations of power, magic, mysticism and the occult." He learned "you only go into hypnosis if you want to. You only go as deeply into hypnosis as you want to and can, and this meant you can come out of hypnosis any time you want to."

In another type of alpha-mind training, Spectra Dynamics, I practiced techniques of self–hypnosis, directing myself into an altered state of consciousness for deep relaxation and release.

Hey Peg! Grab A Pen And Record My Dreams

"Every symbol in your dream has a special, individual connotation that belongs to you alone, just as the dream is ultimately yours alone."

Robert A. Johnson

Dreams often relay messages from the subconscious. I find it useful to record dreams immediately upon waking. I keep a notebook and pen beside my bed to record them quickly. If I roll over from my sleeping position too quickly, I often find my dream images can no longer be recalled.

If my subconscious tries to make me aware of important information, it wakens me with a sudden start at a crucial point of a dream. It wants me to recognize something significant. Every character in my dream represents a part of me in symbolic form. Even though the symbols I perceive may be of people I know, I realize each symbol actually represents an aspect of myself and my beliefs.

Many systems of dream interpretation exist, but the meaning of symbols appearing in my dreams are unique to me. While a symbol book may have some relevance, I don't just accept another person's meaning for my dream symbols. For example, someone else's experience of a symbol for a parent may be warm, loving, and caring. For another, the same image may be controlling, harsh, and abusive. If I see a mother in my dream, it will represent those qualities I associate with my mother.

Deciphering my dreams came by recognizing recurring aspects represented particular qualities. Once I understood my subconscious representations, I was able to more easily interpret my dreams. For instance, a moving vehicle and its condition represents me as well as the direction I am moving in. Water means higher levels of consciousness or spirit. Structures or houses represent my personality.

In one dream, I stood beside a rusted-out hulk of a car; I realized this image meant I needed to let go of something. Another time, my vehicle became a bicycle, which indicated a deterioration of a condition I was in. If I am in a moving vehicle and there is a turn in the road in front of me, it may signal a change in direction for my life. Houses have also represented the structure I have built around my being (in other words, my personality). If the house has big windows letting in lots of light, it seems to indicate an openness to letting in the light of spirit. If the house is derelict, it may signify needed change or outmoded habits. If I find myself in the basement of a house, I haven't mastered or realized something. Dreams of bodies of water stand for spiritual energy in my dreams.

With a little introspection, I can identify certain recurring dream symbols and what they represent. Colors also have significance. Black stands for transformation when I see it. For instance, seeing a woman with black hair will mean the transformation of my mind. Red is active; yellow is mental, and blue is passive.

Some dreams seem to be finishing or clearing out the uncompleted actions and emotions that occurred during the day. These dreams often seem to rove through many brief topics one after the other. All dreams are worth examining since they may contain helpful communications from one's subconscious. Prophetic dreams can indeed point to future occurrences.

If uncertain about a dream item, I retell my dream using other words to describe the figures. I allow my mind to correct me or provide the right version. Many dreams just seem to complete my thoughts or emotions for the day. Others have messages. Only a few may be prophetic, but my dreams have provided me with guidance and warnings.

Prophectic Dreams

"All thinking is magical, but the most magical of all thinking is no thinking at all."

Imre Vallyon

The ways in which my subconscious mind can communicate to me in my dreams is amazing, even providing glimpses of the future. In my experience, prophetic dreaming has only occurred during periods of heightened emotion and decision-making.

Two dreams came to me and foretold the future. They occurred during the emotional time surrounding my decision to leave my marriage. Both my husband and I lived in the same townhouse, and I had been wrestling with what to do. The first dream occurred in early December during the six-week period I applied The Evergreen's suggestion to praise my husband every day. (See Relationship Keys.)

In the first dream, I attended a class, studying the mind. All the participants and I are dressed in black. I stand up and tell the class I have just left my husband.

A few days later on December 7, I made my decision to leave my marriage. On that Wednesday evening, I attended a workshop on the topic of Mind Awareness. During the class, I tell others in the audience I am leaving my marriage. I am surprised as I speak to recognize my dream had been prophetic. To me, black has always represented the symbolic color of change. Everyone being dressed in black in the dream indicated we all experienced change perhaps because of the course. I especially experienced change because of my decision to divorce my husband.

Following my decision, living in the same townhouse was somewhat uneasy for both of us. We decided my husband would move out. No date was set. Then I had another prophetic dream. In this dream, my husband was dressed in a black, flowing cape. He stood at the top of a very high diving platform with a small circular pool down below. Then the scene shifted to a frozen lake. Two sledges with runners moved over the ice. On each was a sign. On the first sledge was January and the second said 21.

In reality, my husband moved out on January 21. Once again, the black cape indicated change. The high dive platform and signs told me my husband would take the plunge on January 21.

Psychic Abilities

"Thinking is no more than a tiny aspect of the totality of consciousness, the totality of who you are."
Eckhart Tolle

With psychic abilities, a person is open to receive finer input from the field of vibration we call the astral plane. It is a form of finer vibration interpenetrating our material-density field. It is not normally visible to our senses, which are attuned to receive only the material-density frequency. People with sensitivity to astral vibrations can see either the material plane or the astral plane at will.

The astral plane is the first level a person may awaken in after physical death. It contains many variations of heavenly worlds created by differing religions. The astral plane is the plane of existence we can experience when dreaming. Channeled information often originates from entities on the astral plane.

Many great books describe the unique qualities and experiences found on the astral plane, such as *The Astral Body and Other Astral Phenomena* compiled by A. E. Powell and *The Hidden Side of Things* and *The Astral Plane* both by C. W. Leadbetter. Books and courses like these encourage a person to open to their psychic abilities. However, the openness to receiving psychic impressions can lead to unwanted experiences of being taken over by entities from the astral plane. Many who open themselves believe completely in the voices speaking through them, but not all psychic messages are good. A truly high-level being would never impose himself or herself into another person's consciousness.

My friend and I used to play with an Ouji board to get messages from the astral plane. Unfortunately, my friend later experienced being taken over by a dead relative, her uncle, while she was in Florida. She found herself compelled to do as she was directed. On one such occasion, she was taking a shower when the voice of her uncle insisted she immediately visit his son. She was compelled to go to the son's house against her wishes. Eventually she went through an exorcism to become free of the voice that had taken her over.

Many people like me have undeveloped psychic abilities. As I described in Relationship Keys, I have latent psychic abilities that have not been developed out of fear of harming another through its misuse. I have also acknowledged I can tune into some type of intuition that can provide guidance. For instance, when I was a new Realtor, I was able to realize (before any construction took place) a particular area of northeast Calgary would become a very popular area for homebuyers and an adjoining area would not be popular.

I also seem to be ahead of time in seeing something I desire before it is made available to the public. For instance, I wanted to purchase a heavy oak coffee table in a square several years before they began to make such a shape in coffee tables. I had to settle for the large rectangular table.

Hearing Startles My Peg

"True intelligence is the working union of three active faculties: concrete thinking, abstract thinking, and mystical intuition."

Paul Brunton

In one unusual experience, I "heard" the birth date of one of my granddaughters. Taking part in a contest to guess the baby's birth date, I lowered my head and turned my eyes skyward for a moment. Suddenly a very masculine and sonorous voice reverberated in my mind. It said, "April 21." I was very startled. The voice had such a strong resonance my mind called it the voice of God. I wrote down the date even though the baby was thought to be due weeks earlier. I also guessed the birth weight. My granddaughter arrived on April 21, and my birth weight guess was only off by one ounce.

Since that time I have learned I can tune into the calmer alpha state of mind by turning my eyes upward. It is a slower wavelength than my usual beta wavelength. The alpha state enables me to enter meditative states. Some people tune into channelled voices from this wave frequency, but I would caution against practicing it with that goal in mind.

Listening To Holosync

For a few years, I listened to Bill Harris's progressive Holosync CDs, completing levels one through four (of twelve levels). The CDs entrained my mind to higher frequencies of vibration. Bill recognized the brain waves of spiritual adepts in meditation operate at high frequencies, which could be mimicked over time by training the mind with increasing Holosync vibrations. As part of the program, I could input and record my own affirmations to be repeated subliminally. I listened to progressive CDs and the subliminal CD in each level of the program. The goal was to release unhelpful patterns of behavior and to increase my mind's ability to enter peaceful meditative states. During the period, I did make some emotional breakthroughs, but I stopped when I felt there may be a conflict with my spiritual teacher's instructions about non-doing.

Intention & Commitment

"Life is a mirror and will reflect back to the thinker what he thinks into it."

Ernest Holmes

A clear intention is necessary in order to achieve a desired outcome. Without a clear intention coupled with a strong commitment, the energy to follow through will weaken and dissipate before the desired outcome is reached. Setting clear goals is so important to success. I expand on this further in the chapter called Actional Keys.

Mental Lesson Keys

1. There is more to life than just the day-to-day experience of living.
2. Other realities exist.
3. The mind has creative powers.
4. Your thoughts, desires, and directed intentions are the creative force that manifests your existence.
5. Alignment with your desired outcome means believing it is already present.
6. Clairvoyants can see the forms created by thought.
7. By changing your brain, you can change your life.

8. Your brain must be healthy to function at its optimum.
9. Certain foods are better for the brain than others are.
10. Seven parts of the brain perform different functions and require different healing methods.
11. Your perceptions form habits programmed at an early stage of life from your parents, teachers, and environment.
12. Your habits are formed from repeated thoughts and reactions.
13. Your habits become paradigms in your subconscious mind blocking your desired outcomes.
14. Affirmation practices can help overcome the paradigms preventing your desires from manifesting by shifting negatives to positives.
15. Life is constant change and newness.
16. Negative experiences provide important opportunities for growth.
17. Various courses can teach you how to control your mind.
18. Simple memory tricks can assist in remembering things.
19. Of the three parts of the mind (conscious, subconscious, and unconscious or universal), only the subconscious mind communicates through pictures.
20. Allow inspiration to help move you toward your desired outcome.
21. Psychics receive information from the astral plane of existence.
22. Blessings are powerful instruments of the mind.
23. Gratitude opens the heart.
24. There is a better way to pray.
25. Hypnosis can be used for relaxation and stress relief.
26. Dreams relay messages from the subconscious with symbols that can be interpreted.
27. Prophetic dreams can inform you of a future event.
28. Holosync methods teach the brain to access higher frequencies.
29. Intention and commitment is necessary to achieve a lasting goal.

Chapter 8

RELATIONSHIP KEYS

Fitting My Square Peg in with Other Pegs

SELF-ESTEEM SHAPED BY RELATIONSHIPS

Your relationships enable you to learn much about yourself. In my voyage of self-discovery, I have been helped or hindered by my relationships. I had to learn not only to relate to myself but to others. Gaining better communication skills has been an ongoing theme throughout my life.

Self-Criticism Stunts Growth Of My Peg

"For when I can love all of me, I will love all of you."
Debbie Ford

As a young person, I was clumsy, loud, easily excited, too powerful, and awkward. My hands always seemed to be wet with perspiration. My friends were gentler, sweeter, quieter, less disturbing, and much more coordinated and in control of their actions. I was like a bull in a china shop, often getting into trouble of some kind. I blurted out things embarrassing my friends and me. I was very frank and critical when I spoke. As the champion of causes, I commonly led the way in the church or community with my strongly held views. But my friends would often back down, leaving me standing alone and with egg on my face.

I soon realized others were not like me. I constantly measured myself against what I perceived in my friends. I found myself not good enough. The self-criticism only deepened until I just knew I was not good enough, not lovable enough, not worthy enough. My self-dialogue and analytical introspection damaged my self-esteem. Sadly none of my harmful comparisons with others and denigrating self-criticism was actually true.

With decided effort, I changed my perspective. One very beneficial tool was daily written gratitude for even the smallest things in my life. Daily thankfulness began to change my self-perceptions. I am so grateful for all I have from my comfortable chair to my beautiful feet that carry me everywhere, from a roof over my head to my healthy teeth. Every day I find new things to be grateful for. We are all, at heart, beautiful beings when we finally "see" and accept ourselves as we truly are.

Bonding With Other Pegs

"If we all saw every one we met as our very own Self we would all treat each other with respect, caring, and givingness. There are so many issues in this world that would be completely resolved in this way."

Hale Dwoskin

The importance of bonding between a baby and its mother and family was sadly demonstrated with parentless babies in an orphanage in Europe. The orphaned babies deprived of being held or cuddled would often die before their first birthday. Bonds are an essential part of normal development.

My earliest bonds were with my mother, father, and siblings. As I developed, I absorbed the mannerisms and ways of thinking of my parents. I mimicked them, learning how to behave as they did. What I learned through these initial relationships set in place core beliefs about my life, whether helpful, caring, and kind or harmful, negative, and unsupportive.

My mother was kept in the hospital for twelve days after I was born (as was the practice in those days). I stayed in a nursery, and the nurses periodically brought me to my mother for her to breastfeed me. Years later in one energy healing and re-birthing session I took part in, I recognized I had rejected being a woman in part because I felt abandoned by my mother at birth. This rejection along with the later loss of sight in my left eye caused problems with the female (left) side of my body. I recall during an energy-healing technique how I suddenly felt energy return to the complete left side of my body. Until that moment, I had not realized I did not feel energy on that side.

When I connect with another person, a bond forms between us. Even such a fleeting situation as giving my order to a waitress creates a connection between the server and me. From my study of Huna, I imagine these bonds as delicate spider-web filaments of energy. Reconnecting puts more energy flow through the bond's fiber, thickening it. On a conscious level, I am connected to each person with these fine filaments of energy. A reinforced or more meaningful bond develops as more energy exchanges occur. This enhanced bond conduit then provides the ability to tune in to another person. It likely explains our precognitive incidents of knowing who is going to call before the phone rings. A message was sent through the spider conduit before the actual telephone rang.

These bonding forces appear to be created within my subconscious or deeper levels to help me achieve some purpose. An attractive force may also be present drawing me to people for a shared experience. My friendships may drop away when the purpose for which they were unconsciously created is no longer present. But even if we never meet again, our bond remains.

Judging Other Pegs

"The mind is expert at creating differences and at creating the apparent separation, but if you look you will be able to find that which is the same in everything you experience. Start with the obvious similarities like, 'I am a human. He or she is a human,' and then allow yourself to be taken deeper to the deepest underlying unity."

Hale Dwoskin

As a fat person, I felt others looked down upon and discriminated against me. It made my struggle to regain my lost self-esteem harder. Even as I changed, my constant feeling I was not as good as a thin person reinforced my sense that as a fat person I was unacceptable.. Whenever I sat in a restaurant, I believed others were looking at me, judging the amount of food on my plate. Now I know they likely did not even notice, and if they did, they couldn't have cared less. They were too busy thinking about themselves.

One incident showed me that in fact I was biased toward obese people. I had just arrived in Durham at the apartment and swimming pool complex reserved for me. Since I did not yet have my own telephone, I asked an attractive young man if I could use his phone. He agreed and let me into his apartment. A 450-pound man sat in the living room on a couch. I critically thought, How could he have let himself get so very large? I judged him, even though I was also overweight. After I made my telephone call, the thin young man pointed to a photograph on the wall, which I thought was the extremely large man on the couch. But the young man said the picture was of himself a year earlier. He too had once weighed a great deal. With a shock, I recognized how I had judged each man differently. I viewed the fat man as being self-indulgent, out of control, and not worth getting to know. But I thought the attractive young man was interesting and worthwhile. Even though I was also very overweight, I allowed my preconceptions to affect my viewpoint.

Unfortunately, my experience of judging based on visual perception is not unique. Far too many people judge others without ever having walked in their shoes. We allow the media's pictures of skinny models to tell us what is good instead of listening to our own hearts.

Listening To Other Pegs

My mother didn't realize the importance of listening to a child's concerns. With the massive hormonal changes at puberty, a child needs to talk to someone about their new strange feelings and emotional upheavals. I would come into my mother's library sanctuary where she enjoyed reading and attempt to talk with her about my life. My father had already left us to be with another woman so there was no one else I could talk to. As I sat there bursting and wanting to share my information with her, Mother would keep on reading and only listen to me semi-distractedly. Eventually I would leave the room emotionally confused. Later I stopped seeking her advice, stumbling on in my awakening sexuality and relationships with people.

People have a tremendous need to be heard, to be heard and encouraged and supported or even corrected. Without the support from my parents, the seeds of low self-esteem were sown at an early age, which may have been partially fueled by the feeling my mother didn't care enough to put down the magazine to listen to me. Mother also constantly corrected my grammar in midsentence or told me to keep my loud voice down. Of course, I know now she wanted the best for me and was doing the best she could at the time.

Stop Interrupting Other Pegs

"If God had wanted us to talk more than listen, He would have given us two mouths rather than two ears."

Ken Blanchard

Along the way, I became too talkative. I began to speak too enthusiastically, adding my two cents to a conversation too soon, not allowing the speaker to finish. I constantly interrupted and finished other people's sentences. During a session with Denny Johnson of Rayid™, I learned about energy transference in conversations. When I interrupted someone, I blocked the completion of the speaker's flow of energy directed toward me. Yes, I could hear what the person said, but I did not receive the full energy of their words. By starting to speak before the other person finished, my energy was sent to meet the other person's energy flow. The flows then met in the middle. My interruption caused my energy and the speaker's energy to meet in between us instead of impacting me.

Denny pointed out the same thing occurred when I nodded my head in acknowledgement or agreement while another person still spoke. I unintentionally placed an invisible protective barrier between the speaker and me. Denny directed me to listen with my head held still until the other person concluded what they were saying.

Denny then encouraged me to practice communicating with him.

For the first time, I held my head still and did not respond until he finished. I began to cry as I felt the energy touch and enter me. My method of interrupting and head bobbing had actually built a protective barrier, preventing me from feeling sensations. If I wanted to experience true conversation with all of its nuisances, I must quietly listen without head bobbing my acknowledgement or interrupting, allowing the other to trail off into silence before responding..

Denny also advised me to not let my two hands touch for six months. This practice was to reinforce my awareness of what I was doing and focus me on the moment. For this assignment, I even mastered how to wash my hands without letting them touch.

Although I went away practicing diligently, my habit of impatient interruption was so long standing I did not completely master Denny's suggestions. My business partner also found it odd when I did not nod my head in agreement with her as she spoke. It was such a common practice between us that to her it seemed I acted strangely when I stopped doing it.

Even now in my eagerness, as a response bubbles up in my mind, I still interrupt others, seeing my mistake only after I have spoken. This may seem an odd example when related to self-esteem, but little interactions form a large part of how we see ourselves. Day by day, my little mannerisms became unconscious habitual patterns. These seemingly small ways of relating became my way of acting in the world. They thus affected and shaped my sense of self-esteem. Recognizing my actions and taking steps to change what I was doing formed a large part of the process of recovery of my sense of value.

Pegs Have Body Language

Along my path of recovery, I delved into the topic of body language communication. One of several helpful body-and face-language books having many clear diagrams was *Signals, How to Use Body Language for Power, Success and Love* by Allan Pease. Some body signals were obvious such as being closed to receiving information by crossing your arms. When someone is open and honest, they tend unconsciously to open their arms and show their palms. We signal our agreement, interest, or rejection and disagreement to others by using body language. It is an unconscious language a person can learn to be more aware of. All types of movements from hands touching the face in different ways, to crossed legs, pointed toes, tightly locked crossed ankles, or leaning forward convey subtle meanings to others. If the head is dropped forward and down, this can show disapproval. Tilting your head to one side can show interest. When a person uses a hand-to-face gesture, he expresses a negative thought such as doubt, deceit, apprehension, or outright lying. Hands clenched tightly in front of you with elbows resting on the table can signal frustration or hostility.

I learned I unconsciously mirror the other person's arm and hand position as we talk, which indicates my unconscious agreement with them. Meeting someone's gaze 60 to 70 percent of the time tells that person you like them. A person naturally distrusts someone who only holds their gaze about 30 percent of the time. I realized I telegraphed emotions I did not feel. For example, when I dropped my gaze, the other person may believe I was shy. But I really did not want to expose myself, so I avoided their eyes as a form of self-protection. I feared being truly seen out of fear of rejection. My efforts to be more open in my gaze were emotionally painful to a degree as I let myself be fully seen by another.

In North America, we also like to maintain a comfortable space around us. The space nearest to our bodies is reserved for close family and friends. We keep greater distances with others we don't know, up to twelve feet apart from others in public spaces. However, when I worked with a contractor from Czechoslovakia, he always would get too close to me when he wanted to speak to me. I felt uncomfortable, but in his country, it was the cultural norm for parties in a conversation to be close to each other.

We also judge others by the way their lips are turned up or down. Turned-down lips indicate a petulant or spoiled nature to me. I recall as a young teen riding on a transit bus one day with my mother. She told me to smile or my frown would become a permanent scowl. She was right. I often find myself with my mouth drawn in a tight downward line when I am serious or intently focused. Then I catch a glimpse of myself in a mirror and realize I do not look friendly. My expression was not at all inviting. When I am concentrating, I have to make an effort to smile occasionally. I will first grimace my mouth in order to relax it into a smile, often practicing this just before I enter a room to meet someone.

Importance Of Pegs' Names

Often I stumble over another's name or how to spell it correctly. For a long time, I disregarded the spelling and wrote to people (including my own son-in-law) using an incorrect spelling. I had no concern for how people misspelled my name, but I learned it bothered others. The other person felt I displayed a sense of superiority or lack of interest in them. When I realized this, I made an effort to spell others' names correctly. Remembering names, however, is another thing, especially as I've aged.

Pegs Have Aura Energy Fields

"The light in me is the light in every other."
Imre Vallyon

Whether I may wish to communicate personal information to others or not, it occurs beyond my conscious awareness. Not only does my body language give messages about me but my auric energy field also does. An aura is a psychic field of color energy surrounding a person's body extending outward about two feet. It indicates your mental, spiritual, and physical state as well as personality traits.

Learning about my aura colors was one more method I discovered in my quest for self-understanding. Even though I do not see auras, I react in some unconscious way to the information about others I sense on a hidden level. At a psychic fair, I had my aura photographed with a special camera and then had a reading. Although interesting, it was not as useful as information I received from the psychic Geraldine Smith Springer who can see psychic aura flows. Geraldine trained herself through lengthy research to determine the qualities represented by each color in a person's aura. She was able to tell me about the colors she saw in my aura and those of my children and other family members, which she could identify from their photographs.

The color descriptions and comments interspersed below are just a few of Geraldine Springer Smith's remarks about aura colors from the book *Slow Motion Miracles* by Sherry Sleightholm and

Geraldine's booklet *Images in Action, Human Auras* co-authored by Miki Andres. Geraldine describes how we can accumulate "blocked" energy." Often people learn very young in life to suppress very important feelings and emotions. Many people consider it a weakness to express how much they love another person. Others feel it is wrong to express their anger, so they hold it in—often to the point of explosion. Some have learned weakness should never be exposed to others "lest others use this vulnerability against them." Blocks are reinforced every time we stop ourselves from expressing a major emotion. Removing blocks is done through allowing the feelings of blocked emotion to be accepted and expressed, which may feel vulnerable and painful to experience. Removing blocks frees energy to flow, changing the qualities of our auras.

Geraldine's research enabled her to list the following aura color qualities. When a person has one or more of these colors in their aura, it will mean the person has particular natural qualities in their personalities.

White: An amalgamation of all of the primary colors. It indicates qualities of compassion, acceptance, strength, wisdom, and inner peace (seldom seen except in a highly developed spiritual being).

Black and Grey: Indicates a bodily dysfunction and in some cases impending death.

Red: Denotes extreme emotion—either anger, passion, or severe guilt triggered by lying or deceit. People in love may demonstrate shimmers of red in their auras.

Orange: Indicates unimpeded spontaneity, a refreshing absence of inhibitions. Blocked oranges will feel extreme anger but will hold it back until they explode; they can also be very childish and have sexual problems.

Gold or Yellow: Inner strength, profound sensitivity, and intuition when open. Golds have a high degree of energy. Golds have high values, standards, principles, and morals. Gold is the color of lasting relationships. They rarely have lots of friends, preferring the security and solidity of a few lasting friendships. Unblocked, they make excellent teachers, healers, professors, and counselors. Golds' love relationships are very important, and they may stay in an unhappy marriage for the sake of others, eventually losing their own identity. Golds often end up at forty or fifty saying, "Who am I? What am I here for?" Then they shoulder feelings of worthlessness and guilt. If blocked, the gold person will internalize tension until it affects their nervous system causing various illnesses. Blocked or mixed with another color like green or brown makes the person analyze too much instead of acting on their first intuition.

Green: They have a prerequisite for honest and truly candid discourse, along with natural recuperative abilities. Green is a very direct, upfront color. They may be accused of being too blunt. Greens have an absolute need for communication in all areas of life, whether in love, business, or social relationships. Greens have an incredible ability to concentrate and a "radar' making them available to all the energies around them. Green is a good health color. They do not often get sick. If blocked, they do not communicate in certain areas of their lives. They can end up manipulating people. Con artists and those selling products through deceit are often blocked greens.

Purple or Violet: They are rarely seen as first colors. Purple/violets possess an abundance of precognition and foresight; they have an inner "knowing" that extends far beyond accepted parameters. This is the psychic color. They are extremely sensitive. Blocks indicate an ignorance of their abilities to "know". Purple/violets usually dream in Technicolor with very clear imagery. They need to record their dreams. They have an incredible ability in dreaming events prior to their occurrence and in having their fantasies (daydreams) come true. Unblocked, they are very non-judgmental and understanding of situations.

Blue: Blues are innately creative and keenly sensitive, with vivid imaginations. They need to express their personalities through creative outlets. Blues are known for loyalty, sincerity, and devotion. Blues take time to commit themselves to someone or something, but when they do, it is "all or nothing." When Blues give their energy, they give 100 percent. Unfortunately, they also assume t others share this same sense of dedication. Blues may stay in a situation far too long. Blues, because of their extreme sensitivity, tend to "take things personally" more than other colors. Blues must resonate with the colors they wear or will feel uncomfortable and change garments. Blues need their sanctuary and are ideally suited to living in the country. Blues have a tendency to procrastinate. A blocked blue man will have communication problems in a personal (love) relationship although he may relate easily in business matters. Blocked, they tend to take offense at any perceived affront and may seek revenge.

Brown: Brown is the color of the analytical financier, the aggressive entrepreneur, and extremists and is associated with drive, determination, persistence, and good business sense. Browns are the "money" color, having a natural inclination towards mathematics and finance. They tend to become workaholics or extremists. They must either have their own business or be in a position where they can set their own pace. Browns cannot exist in a controlled, subordinate position. Accumulation of wealth and recognition will supersede any personal relationship. When blocked they are, judgmental and impatient.

Double colors: Two different shades of the same color strengthen and intensify that color's quality.

All colors: As people who have broadened their realm of experience beyond the average, they experience more of life's heights and depths.

Not everyone with the ability to see auras will see the colors in the same way as Geraldine since they see the auric energy through the colors of their own aura. However, they will find they can apply the same qualities to the representative colors they do see. When Geraldine signed my book, she listed my colors. She wrote I am all colors, green, a slightly blocked gold, and purple. I wonder how my aura has changed in the last twenty-five plus years of my personal growth. Perhaps I have opened my gold block. My aura taught me more about my inherent qualities. Reading from photographs, Geraldine also said my husband and several of my boys were blocked blue browns, one was a double blue, and my daughter was all colors. This information accurately described aspects of our lives.

For example, I have had a number of precognitive dreams, which must be the purple color in my aura at work. I also intuitively knew which real estate area would become popular or unpopular in the future. In addition, I once surprised myself by performing an accurate psychometry after reading a little booklet about it. In a pizza restaurant with women from the office, I had an opportunity to practice what I'd learned. Since I only recently joined the company, I knew nothing about my coworkers or their families. Holding a coworker's ring in my hand, I closed my eyes and sank into myself. In answer to the woman's questions, pictures came into my mind. Describing what I saw I was able to answer her questions. One of her questions involved her boyfriend who I had never met. I saw a dark-haired man wearing a particular quilted vest and plaid shirt, which I described to her. When I, holding their jewelry, had answered questions for several women and opened my eyes, they told me my answers to their questions were entirely accurate. I'd described the boyfriend's looks and clothing as well as certain locations. I had tapped into my psychic purple quality.

At an office party a few weeks later, one of the girls took me aside to have me answer her questions about finding a new job. I closed my eyes and held her ring but froze up out of fear of doing harm. What if my answer is wrong? I thought. I could harm someone. I was afraid to do psychometry again.

Learn To See Auras

Geraldine suggested a person could see his or her own aura by standing in a darkened room facing a mirror in almost total darkness with just the light from a candle placed directly to the right or left. If you can distinguish features or details of the body, the light is too bright and the candlewick needs to be trimmed. For four minutes, focus above the top of your head or along the line of your shoulder where it joins the neck. At first, you may begin to see a foggy haze emanating from the body. After practicing this on several occasions, colors may take shape. Geraldine cautioned not to spend over four minutes in a session since the mind can begin to hallucinate and produce optical illusions. Once while in a semi-darkened room, I saw an aura color. It was a yellow shade visible around the fingers of one hand.

My Peg Was Born With Ray Qualities

"There are seven main types of human beings, each with its outstanding natural attributes and qualities. All qualities and powers are within every human being, but in each of the seven main types there is a preponderant tendency."

Geoffrey Hodson

The Theosophical Society was founded in New York in 1875 as a group of people chosen to transmit ancient wisdom. They presented information about the seven rays or energy streams with which people incarnate. They also defined each ray or combination of rays as imparting certain inherent qualities of character temperament. Geoffrey Hodson describes a variety of aspects of rays in *The Seven Human Temperaments* including employment, achievements, and correspondences to colors, symbols, and jewels. A person's goal should be the full development of the qualities of all the rays, perhaps over a series of lives.

Studying the rays, I sought to see where I fit into the scheme of humanity. There may be some correspondence to the ray colors described by Geoffrey and the auric energy colors described by Geraldine. If so, I may have mastered and come into life with some qualities of all the rays but with more qualities of rays 2, 3, and 7. Of course, I have more to learn and integrate. A few of Geoffrey Hodson's references are listed below for comparison with the previously described aura colors of Geraldine Smith Springer.

Ray	Color	Qualities	Quest/Driving Impulse
1	White fire Electric blue Vermillion	Power Will Courage Leadership Self-reliance	To conquer To attain To find ultimate reality Often best in adversity
2	Golden yellow Azure blue	Universal love Wisdom Insight Intuition Philanthropy Sense of oneness Spiritual sympathy	To save To illumine To teach To share To serve To heal
3	Emerald green	Creative ideation Comprehension Understanding Penetrative and interpretive mental power Adaptability Tact Dignity Impartiality	Creative activity To Understand
4	Tawny bronze	Stability Harmony Balance Beauty Rhythm	To beautify

Ray	Color	Qualities	Quest/Driving Impulse
5	Lemon yellow	Analytical and logical mentality Accuracy Patience	To discover Thirst for knowledge
6	Roseate-fire	One-pointedness Ardor Fiery enthusiasm Devotion Sacrificial love Loyalty	To serve and adore To worship The cause
7	Purple	Grace Precision Ordered beauty and activity Chivalry Skill Dignity Noblebearing Careful attention to detail, order, method Military method Splendor	To harness To synthesize To make manifest

Lessons In Communicating With Other Pegs

"The person who upsets you the most is your best teacher because they bring you face to face with who you are."

Lynn Andrews

My lessons on communication (especially those in marriage) have contained many aspects—from learning how to communicate more effectively with others to learning how to communicate with my body, emotions, mind, and spiritual self. Communicating with others provides a mirror of who I am. I see myself in the responses of others and in my response or reactions to them.

If I perceive their responses to be negative, I shrink back inside. If they are positive, I open up inside. I have to recognize what I see in another is a mirror of what is within me. If I find what I see in them to be irritating or unlikable, I need to accept that those annoying qualities are mine also. They would not bother me otherwise. I would not be able to see a particular trait if I did not share that quality. Depending on what I see, I may resolve to change myself or I may choose to hide to avoid the perceived pain of being seen as less than perfect.

Through my relationships with others, I gradually built up an impression of who I am. From that impression, I determined how and where I fit into the world. In the previous discussion about the Enneagram, I spoke of how thinking I was a round peg, a wrong person, affected me. We all develop pictures of ourselves through our encounters with others. However, we can build better pictures of who we are. I can see myself as a person with worth, who contributes to a better world for all.

The following accounts of my experiences may help you to avoid similar mistakes and enhance your relationships. Seeing yourself through the accounts may aid your development toward a happier self. Don't let life rob you of your self-esteem.

Miscommunication Between Pegs

"Find the courage to ask questions and to express what you really want. Communicate with others as clearly as you can to avoid misunderstandings, sadness, and drama. With just this one agreement, you can completely transform your life."

Don Miguel Ruiz

Clearly define another person's requests to avoid misunderstandings and miscommunications. I learned to be honest with myself, even if speaking my truth did not make another person happy with me. For example, allow me to share two important commu¬nication errors.

Left with one useless arm and a partially paralyzed leg as the result of a stroke, my friend took up palette knife painting to become financially independent. I admired her loving, courageous attitude and helped her when I could. One day, I drove her to pick up some of her artwork. She presented me with an unusual oil painting, a very special gift she had just painted for me.

I was speechless. But I was also dismayed. It was not at all what I expected. When she offered to paint me a picture, I asked her to paint me a picture of dandelions. Dandelions hold a special place in my heart. Symbolically they represent me as they Dandelions are humble but indomitable, bouncing back with new flowers the day after they have been mowed down. My friend had happily agreed, and I had looked with anticipation to the day when my painting would be ready. I viewed it in my mind as a single plant with one or more, sunny-yellow flower stalks, perhaps with a stem of fluffy seeds surrounded by several jagged green curling leaves. I saw it all painted against a colorful background of varied hues.

Instead, I stood holding her labor of love for me, a beautifully framed picture. Large groupings of big, multihued boulders dominated the oil painting, fashioned boldly with her palette knife. Behind them glowered a dark gravel beach and a bit of blue ocean where I would have expected to see sky. Nestled almost hidden from view among the rocks are very tiny clumps of what might be yellow dandelions. While the rocks are interesting, the painting does not depict what I imagined. I lied and told my friend how lovely the painting is and how much I appreciate it.

We left the picture framers with my new painting stowed safely on the rear seat and drove my friend to Sears' warehouse. As I walked into the staff portion of the warehouse, I spotted a wonderful poster on the wall. The poster defined the situation perfectly. It depicted an information clerk standing behind a counter speaking to a customer on the other side. The customer wore only a bathing suit and attached with very sharp teeth to the back of the customer's shorts is a large gray shark. The information clerk is saying, "Of course I said that the beach is safe. You must have gone into the water."

My dear friend did her best to fulfill my request, but I had not made my instructions clear. I did not convey my own description to her. Thus I failed to communicate clearly, resulting in miscommunication. But this was more than miscommunication. I put on a false smile with exclamations of appreciation in order to spare her feelings, but my true feelings of disappointment churned inside me. I attempted to stifle them under a brittle smile. I was untruthful and lacked integrity, mis-communicating even with myself. I learned through this situation the importance of effective communication and of honoring and speaking the truth of your feelings.

Can you recognize any of your own experiences of miscommunication? Learning to be true to yourself is a very important part of healthy self-esteem. I moved away before I ever had the courage to tell my friend of my dishonest reaction. However, while it's still not easy to do, I make an effort to speak my true feelings. I tend to protect another's feelings at the cost of my own by telling a white lie. I now recognize the importance of being truthful. I know my remarks may cause them disquiet on occasion, but I allow myself to accept their discomfort with my words. Being open and vulnerable to the outcome of true expression is more valuable.

Missed Communication Separates Pegs

"Real, divine love, is a constant, persistent acceptance of all beings in the universe—fully, wholly, totally—as the other beings are, and in loving them because they are the way they are."

Lester Levenson

Often our hormones draw us into relationships. Even though I thought my husband and I were the best of friends and communicated well, that may or may not have been true. Looking back, I don't believe we started our relationship by being totally open and transparent with each other. Self-esteem is enhanced in an open relationship, but without genuine conversation, a relationship can rob you of self-worth as mine did.

In so many ways, my husband and I failed to communicate what we really wanted or meant. My husband was my best friend. We talked about many things. I thought we communicated well. Yes, we had our disagreements occasionally over how to raise the children or what to do with the dog. But over the years, we drifted into a comfortable communication mode. We often had a good laugh together. However, so much was not being said. So much of our discussion was only superficial. Our real feelings were unexpressed and hidden from each other.

One day my husband burst out vehemently and said, "I hate mashed potatoes!"

"But you've never told me before! I've been serving them to you for twenty years!" I replied startled.

This was the first hint we were not being open with each other. Sadly it wasn't until these last days of our twenty-nine years of marriage that I saw we had never truly communicated our deeply different buried needs. We created much misunderstanding and heartbreak as a result. You can avoid our mistake by learning from our story.

I grew up in a comfortable large home surrounded by a garden with lots of trees in one of the finer districts in the city. The main floor held the living room, dining room, sunroom, den, and kitchen. Four bedrooms, a sleeping porch, and a bathroom were upstairs. I grew up accustomed to having space around me. My proud mother kept up the outer appearance that everything was okay after she and my father divorced. We continued to live in our home, but to make ends meet, we ate a Spartan diet of canned Spam, salt cod, fried kidney, omelet, or other simple fare. We never ate out. Even before my father left, our family seldom dined at a restaurant and only to celebrate some special occasion. I grew up thinking, I am okay if I live in comfortable spacious surroundings.

My husband, however, had lived in an older part of town in the basement suite of an old six-plex with a gravel patch for a yard. When it became too crowded, several of the boys' bedrooms were moved into the other part of the basement. Access to these additional rooms was by way of a rough hole broken through the concrete firewall between two basement suites. In order to get into the other side, one walked up a wooden style of several steps and ducked through the rough opening. While their housing was not ideal, they were comfortable enough, and they ate well. My future mother-in-law would cook great meals with roasts of beef or turkey with mashed potatoes, gravy, salads, and pie or a sweet for dessert. My husband grew up thinking, I am okay if I can eat well.

After all but one of our children moved out, I agreed to my husband's wish to move from our comfortable large two-story home to a new penthouse apartment, built on a choice site overlooking the city center and mountains. The penthouse was relatively spacious, approximately 1876 square feet in size. There were two bedrooms and two bathrooms. In addition to the large living-dining room and kitchen, there was a family room with a fireplace, a bar area, and an office. A wonderfully large thirty-foot by sixty-foot rooftop deck space surrounded the penthouse. The view of the Calgary city center, river, and mountains was superb.

I went to work, putting all of my real estate income into the apartment. I customized and built it to suit me. After all, I expected to live there the rest of my life since my husband was a professional with a city practice. I was single-minded about what I wanted to create. When and if my husband would object to some of my plans, I overruled him. I continued with my own plans to create my space. I designed all of the oak cupboards for the kitchen, oak feature walls, bookcases, French doors, curtain valances, and planters. I designed the fireplace and paneling for the family room and added a bar sink and fridge. Stained glass was placed between the bathrooms sepa¬rating the six-foot Jacuzzi tub from the double-headed shower and bidet in the master bath. I went all out. The mirrored walls of the living room brought in excellent views of the downtown buildings and mountains behind them. I focused on creating my "I'm okay" space around me.

Both during construction and after we moved into the beautifully finished penthouse, my husband would take me out a number of times each week for breakfast, lunch, or dinner in the finest restaurants. My husband never told me anything about his business finances. He rebuffed all my attempts over the years to find out how our finances were. I handled only the household bills. Because we were going out to eat all the time, I assumed we must be doing really well financially. I continued to spend all of my earnings, a considerable sum, on outfitting the apartment. After all, I thought, you don't go out to dinner so often unless you have lots of extra money.

After we had to sell the apartment to solve my husband's financial problems, I began to see our communication weaknesses. While I built my dream space to feel better, his business was in trouble.

Secretly upset about it, he attempted to feel good about himself by eating out so often. The result was miscommunication that caused us both great sadness and loss.

If we access each other's true feelings by expressing ourselves openly, we will not fail to communicate clearly. In a lasting relationship, there are no secrets. There is instead shared vulnerability—an open dialogue about everything. We should have shared successes, shortcomings, and failures with total honesty, even when it was painful. Had we been open and honest with each other, we may have saved our marriage. Once I realized our communication mistakes, I spoke to my children to encourage them to be completely open and vulnerable with their spouses. They have benefitted and are in loving relationships lasting over twenty-nine years.

I value my close friendships. We speak openly of everything, allowing vulnerability. Let yourself be open. Talk about your concerns. It will enhance your self-esteem and allow your bond to grow very deep. One must work at maintaining self-esteem. The stress of busy work and home lives can add to relationship problems. Be sensitive and aware of what is occurring and take note of your communication. Are you taking steps to avoid stress? Are you communicating with total openness? Are you allowing total vulnerability?

Getting Help When My Peg Was Stuck

At several junctures in my life, I sought professional help. When I became very frustrated with my four-year-old son, I struck him on the head. He bit his tongue drawing blood. In my contrition, I realized I needed help. I didn't know how to handle young children. I sought out a Gestalt-trained therapist. She helped me to understand the growth cycles of children. She spoke of what behavior could be expected at each stage of a child's development. Having a better understanding was very helpful to me. She also directed me to several books on child development.

Sadly I didn't receive much training in how to be a good parent. I learned only from the way I was parented either following the example I received or rejecting it. My self-esteem was tested when my children were young. As a stay-at-home mom, I had no adult stimulation through the day. My mother lived overseas, and we only communicated by mail. I seldom visited with neighbors in the new area because I thought my house was too messy, not orderly enough (based on my mother's standards) to allow them to visit me in return. I was lonely and hungry for communication, which contributed to a downward spiral of further reduction in my self-esteem

Sometimes all I would have needed was to share my concerns with my mother or a friend. But being a loner and with my mother living in Spain, I had no one to talk to. If you perceive your self-esteem and sense of self-worth is threatened, get help. A psychologist helped me to see my situation from a new perspective and provided simple but valuable guidance. We are not meant to suffer by ourselves. Others are very ready to help us if they see the symptoms of trouble brewing.

Understanding The Opposite Sex

John Gray's book *Men are From Mars, Women are From Venus* goes a long way towards helping us see that the way we relate to each other is based on our different make-ups. Not understanding these differences can put pressure on our self-esteem. We may act in ways eventually leading to communication breakdowns. My story below illustrates one aspect of this difference.

Understanding Male Pegs

"One of the biggest mistakes a woman makes with a man is to offer unsolicited advice."

John Gray PhD.

Years after the incident with my son, I again sought professional help. Communicating with a psychologist was such a benefit to me. I was deeply unhappy and depressed when I finally went to see a psychologist named Glen. I wanted his help with seven items.

My words burst out: "I don't understand men. I even feared men until my mid-twenties. I am having marriage problems and want to know what to do about my marriage."

I also listed my other concerns—being selfish, being stupid, sex, and finding employment. Glen listened to me, gave me an IQ test, and talked to me over several visits.

At one of the visits, I said, "If I offer advice while my husband is doing something like changing a tire, he flies off at me. He won't listen even though my suggestion is helpful."

Glen nodded and replied with a story, "In mankind's early days, in days of early cave dwellers, men and women developed differently. In the beginning, men and women lived separately. During these times, a woman would only accept sexual advances from a man once a month at the time of her ovulation when she was sexually available. A man learned to bring gifts of food to entice a woman to have sex with him. There was a lot of competition for desirable women. Men began to regularly hunt for food so they could seek out any women who were available. The women soon learned if they wanted to have food or a piece of nice venison to eat they would have to offer sex more often. As time passed, women realized that being always sexually available, except during their monthly cycle, would enable them to attract and keep men as hunter partners. They would receive plenty to eat in exchange.

As time passed, men and women began to live as couples. Later they began to live in community groups. A pattern developed where women stayed in the camp tending their children. Men spent most days foraging or hunting game. Men learned to be intently focused and silent. It enabled them to better track and spot prey. Focus helped them to direct their clubs and arrows to successfully make a kill. As dark descended at the end of a day's hunting trip, men would gather around a fire. There they talked about their conquests. If food was plentiful, the community would stay in one place. Women could tend their children while minding the cooking fire or making clothes. They no longer needed to fend for themselves. Watching and stirring the food or turning a spit while keeping an eye out to protect their children from danger kept women busy. All the while, they would be chatting with the other women.

Over time, men developed the mental ability for one pointed focus. Women learned to be able to multitask. Specialized functions developed in men and women's brains according to skills they had learned. Men can generally only concentrate and focus on one thing at a time. They developed logical left-brain strength as a result.

Women on the other hand can pay attention to several things at once and developed right-brain intuitive skills."

As Glen spoke, I caught on immediately. I shouldn't interrupt my husband while he is doing something, but should wait until he has finished before offering my suggestions. Simple understanding of the basic differences between men and women can greatly improve your communication. It has become my second nature to wait until a man has finished what he is doing before speaking to him, especially a service man making a needed repair. Even if I have a great idea for a better way to do it, I keep silent until I can have his undivided attention.

My Peg's Choice: Marriage Or Divorce

"Human life and its relationships have become 'home' and therefore humans fear to vacate the familiar and move to the unknown."

Dr. David Hawkins

Two heads are better than one. Exchanging simple ideas can make such a difference. Glen gave me a simple tool to solve my marriage decision dilemma.

During a visit I conveyed, "I don't know what to do about my marriage. We have been married for close to thirty years. Our children are grown and gone. I haven't been happy for a long time. I was devastated and very hurt when my husband was unfaithful a number of years ago. My trust was lost. Even though I have tried to regain it, I have not been able to recover my trust in him. What can I do to help me decide which route to take? I also have never lived alone. I am afraid if I leave I will be lonely as well."

Glen replied, "Take out a sheet of paper and write down everything you would like to receive in a marriage. After completing your list, look at each item carefully. Mark down beside it whether you are receiving that quality in your marriage. See how many of your relationship desires are being met."

"Okay," I replied, and I went home to write my list. After careful thought, I was able to put down twenty-five things I would like in a relationship. As I reviewed them, I saw I was only receiving four of the items on my list. As the realization struck, I made the decision to leave my marriage. I told my husband I wanted to leave.

He replied, "If you leave, I will not be your friend."

I recognized with a shock I had never created close friendships with anyone but my husband. He and I had always been able to talk with each other about surface things, even though we had not expressed any deep vulnerability. When our relationship had begun, we spent hours sharing feelings and ideas. But over the years, sharing of any depth disappeared. Now with no one to be close to, no one to share experiences with, how could I leave?

The solution appeared on my next visit with Glen. His secretary, Lil, said she would like to get to know me. I readily agreed, and we began to meet, rapidly becoming close friends. Now I had someone to talk to and would not be lonely if I left.

The advice of another helped clear my mind. Where I can be caught up in the emotions of a situation, they can see the situation with more clarity. A simple tool like a list is also an aid to clarity. Whenever I am faced with a decision, I routinely prepare a list of pros and cons. It makes my decisions much easier. If I still feel uncertain after reviewing my list, I talk it over with a close friend or mentor.

Perfect Advice

"The key to an easy relationship with other people is not to impose your ego, nor crush the ego of others."

Swami Prajnanpad

How unbiased is the advice I give another? Often I receive advice, but truly rare is advice so unbiased it can be taken two different ways to the benefit of the hearers receiving it. On an October Thanksgiving weekend in Gabriola Island, British Columbia, I received this perfect advice. I was attending my first weekend with Michael Blake Read who channels The Evergreens. Michael would lie down in a reclining chair bidding us goodbye. Then guided by gentle statements by his wife, he would go into a deep sleeplike trance. In a few minutes, a voice vastly different from Michael's would greet her and then the audience. For the next forty-five minutes, the voice would speak to uplift the spiritual understanding of the participants.

Several sessions were held each day on a variety of subjects. The final session was a question-and-answer session. All eighty participants were given the chance to ask one question of The Evergreens. I thought about what my question would be and decided I would ask about my job and marriage.

"What do you want?" the Evergreens asked me.

"I want to know what to do about my job and my marriage." I nervously replied.

"If you want to know what to do about your marriage, find one thing about your husband and praise it every day, and in six weeks, your decision will be easy," they replied.

Upon my return, I began to apply The Evergreen's advice. I thought about how much fun my husband and I had in the morning. We often laughed and joked as we dressed. I began to praise my husband's sense of humor every day. By early December, I realized why I had such difficulty with my decision to leave my relationship. It was because my husband had many fine qualities, but they were no longer right for me. I made the decision to ask for a divorce, and by January 21, I was living on my own.

The following year I again traveled to Gabriola Island for another Thanksgiving weekend with The Evergreens. Friends I had made the previous year kindly provided me a ride to the ferry for the weekend retreat. They also invited another young woman to join us.

The young woman said she had heard a tape from the previous year's retreat. She said the answer given to one of the participant's questions changed her marriage. I was surprised to hear her repeat the advice given to me by The Evergreens. I told her that was my question. I added I had since decided to get divorced. She described how her marriage of only one year had run into great communication difficulties. She had thought of leaving, but then heard the advice given to me. She too had begun to praise her husband every day. Her husband and she had become so wonderfully close and loving toward each other that there was no more thought of ending their relationship.

The Evergreens gave such perfect advice we each benefited from the same message. Carefully considered words can provide needed healing. Each person will hear what he or she needs to hear at that specific time. I have not found occasions where I can give perfect advice. Most people really do not want to receive advice unless they ask for it specifically. Unsolicited advice will be seen as criticism. So many times, I may think of something to suggest but restrain myself from offering it.

Resonance Heals My Square Peg

Within me is my true self. I am learning to tune into my real self through resonance with what I know. When all of my actions and speech come from my heart, I am filled with natural self-esteem. I am comfortable with who I am. I know there is a spark of life, a tiny little bit of Truth within me. I know I am awareness or consciousness. Being open, like an open hand, enables a flow of good. Being closed, like a fist, shuts it off. I know I feel better when I am open, gentle, and tender with others, and when I am closed, hard, and angry, I harm myself.

As I cultivate the right relationship within myself through resonance with the openness, gentleness, and love that is my true spirit, all my concerns over self-esteem vanish. I become peaceful and serene within. One of the best ways to enhance communication with my inner being is to set aside a small space of time and sit in quiet reflection, not wanting anything in particular, not trying to still my mind or do anything, but just allowing myself to focus within and be peaceful. When I do, I immediately feel a sense of ease and a growing field of peace opening inside me.

"All humans are one family. All men are my children."
Asoka

Relationship Lesson Keys

1. Self-criticism stunts personal growth and affronts the divine loving being you are within.
2. A healthy relationship with yourself is of utmost importance. Cultivate it through gratitude.
3. Subtle bonds connect you to every person you meet. Strong bonds formed between people are an attractive force of nature for a shared experience.
4. Judge not lest ye be judged and found wanting. Judge not thyself. "Comparisons are odious" as my mother used to say.
5. Do not make judgments about a person from their looks. It is what is within that counts. Walk in the other's shoes before discriminating.
6. Other people are my mirrors. What I see in another, whether good or bad, is present in myself. If I don't like what I see, I can change myself.
7. When listening to another, give them your full attention with eye contact.
8. With perseverance and practice, you can train away your tendency to interrupt others.
9. We subconsciously read the body language of those around us. What are you projecting to others?
10. Make an effort to train yourself to smile lest your frowning mouth turn others away.
11. Respect the spelling and pronunciation of other people's names.

12. Our auric fields radiate our personalities to others' subconscious minds.
13. We can learn about ourselves from our auric personality qualities. Removing any blocks to our auric energy flow opens up our personalities and enhances self-acceptance.
14. Reading auras can be learned with practice.
15. We each came into life with certain energy qualities described as rays of color.
16. We learn about ourselves through relationships with others.
17. Be truthful in your expression. White lies are a deception.
18. Allow yourself to be completely vulnerable with your marriage partner. Do not withhold any part of yourself and your relationship will blossom and deepen.
19. Get professional help if you feel you are stuck or if your behavior is harmful to another. A professional's unbiased opinion can help you to see more clearly.
20. Learn how men and women behave and act differently.
21. From different activity requirements stemming from caveman days, men and women's brains developed differently. Do not interrupt a man while he is doing something.
22. When you need to make a serious relationship decision, make a list of pros and cons to bring clarity to the situation.
23. Perfect advice that can be taken either way is unusual. Unsolicited advice is seen as criticism. Do not give advice unless it is asked for.
24. Being open is the way to approach life. Being closed cuts you off from everything.
25. Quiet reflection can lead you to inner peace and serenity.

Chapter 9

INSTINCTUAL KEYS

Moving My Square Peg into a Square Hole Job

My Square Peg Has an Aptitude

Importance of Instinctual Drive

The Conative Index Measure of Action Modes

How the Index Describes Instinctual Drives

A Look at Others Through Conative Understanding

Finding Right Employment for Different Pegs

Change Needed for Training Different Peg Types

How to Get Yourself Tested

Instinctual Lesson Keys

SELF-EMPOWERMENT: FITTING MY SQUARE PEG INTO THE RIGHT EMPLOYMENT

Instinctual Key

"All your problems, discouragements, and heartaches are in truth opportunities in disguise."
Og Mandino

Sadly, many years went by while I worked in a variety of unfulfilling sales positions only to finally learn I had worked against my natural drives and tendencies. A simple test that measures the distribution and intensity of my Action Modes®, formerly called the Kolbe Conative Index, (now renamed and updated called the Kolbe A™ Index), showed me I would be much happier working in harmony with my in-born natural drives. When test results indicated I'd be more suited to a management role, I changed my job from real estate sales to property management. My new management role fit like a glove. I so enjoyed my work I even delayed retirement for five years until I turned seventy years of age.

My Square Peg Has An Aptitude

"Don't ask yourself what the world needs. Ask yourself what makes you come alive and go and do that because what the world needs is people who come alive."
John Eldredge

Aptitudes are natural or acquired abilities or the natural proclivity to be apt or fitting for a specialized function. They indicate categories of interest, either natural or learned, and thus the type of activity or employment a person would find pleasurable. However, aptitudes are different from instinctual drives, which are inherited inborn drives that cause a person to take action in certain ways. Working in harmony with these drives in the realm of employment led to much more success in my life.

Aptitude testing used to be performed in school at the junior and senior high level and could sometimes be arranged by unemployment offices. The tests would score an individual's ability and interest levels in a variety of topics. One test showed I would not relish being a sewing machine operator, while public speaking was a high interest on another test, and yet another said I could become an accountant. In later years, I recognized the tests given to all Realtors in my area did not measure the right qualities and could not predict who would make a good salesperson. Most of the aptitude tests I took, although interesting, did not really assist me in finding the right employment for my square peg. However, the Kolbe A™ Index, which is described in more detail below, provided different information that truly guided me.

Importance Of Instinctual Drive

"Without passion, an individual gets caught in the trap of making a living instead of designing a life."
Anthony Robbins

In-born natural abilities provide each person with combinations of instinctive methods of operating, providing ways in which they will perform. Since these innate proclivities do not change over time they will influence how a person naturally takes action. Without having discovered and then harmonized my work activities with my Conative or in-born doing nature, I would never have created the enjoyable working role and lifestyle I enjoyed. Kathy Kolbe said , "Conation is our knack for getting things done. It is separate from a person's intelligence or personality type." Successful and contented people in every type of work or endeavor are those that are working in concert with their inborn drives. Working in harmony with their inner nature enables them to outperform others. If you find yourself in a work situation that you are not happy in you may be working against your own true nature. Identifying and aligning with your innate Action Modes can dramatically change your life as it did mine.

The Conative Index Measure of Action Modes

"If we don't change our direction we are likely to end up where we are headed."
Chinese Proverb

I owe Kathy Kolbe, the author of *The Conative Connection, Acting on Instinct* a huge debt of gratitude. Her work confirmed my most harmonious Action Modes. Until I took her simple test I had not realized the importance of being in tune with my basic drives. Nor had I realized their unchanging nature would affect me throughout my life. Her test results confirmed that I worked in an area that was not natural for my preferred instinctive modes of operating. Changing my employment field, I became in harmony with my natural tendencies. My realization helped me to understand myself and others.

Unknowingly, I spent more than twenty years bucking my inborn modes to action qualities while I worked in a variety of sales positions. Over the years, I sold stationery, Avon cosmetics, jewelry, supplements, Tupperware, kitchen cabinets, and computer software, eventually progressing into selling real estate. Using my natural entrepreneurial skills, I was the top salesperson on occasion, but something kept me from truly succeeding in sales.

Indeed, I was even fired from one sales position where I had to sell low-end homes built with cheaper materials. I found it difficult to market poorer-quality structures. They did not measure up to the higher-quality standards of houses I had been selling for a previous homebuilder. I also could not ask people to sign on the dotted line until I ensured every detail was right. People wanted to buy their dream home. But I was so mired in details I confused them, letting them slip away to buy their dream from the builders down the street, where the salesperson signed them up and then worked out the details.

My "ah hah" moment came when I discovered the Kolbe A™ Index described in Kathy Kolbe's book *The Conative Connection, Acting on Instinct.* I completed the simple thirty-six-question quiz in the book (updated quiz now available online) and sent it away to the Kolbe Institute, (now Kolbe Corp.) to be analyzed by their computer. I received a report, graph, and cassette tape that made me realize I was a square peg trying to operate in a round hole!

How The Index Describes Instinctual Drives

"Everything you do is with your inner motivation and is motivated from your inner state of Beingness that you have attained."
Lester Levenson

The Conative Index is based on information that all individuals are born with. Each person has a combination of four basic patterns that do not change throughout their lifetime. These conative patterns indicate the style of doing (or mode) that drives a person's actions to strive toward a goal. When working in harmony with these patterns, the person leads a happier more fulfilling life. Importantly, the patterns form basic drives that cannot be learned. The Conative Index says each person is born with strengths in each Action Mode.

The following updated information has been provided by © 2011 Kathy Kolbe and Kolbe. Corp. All rights reserved.

> What is conation? Conation is the mental faculty that causes an individual to act, react and interact according to an innate pattern of behaviors. As one of the three elements of human behavior, its function is to convert the affective faculties, which are emotions, preferences or beliefs, and the cognitive faculties, which are learned knowledge and skills, into visible and purposeful performance. It drives us to actually do what thc other parts of the mind either make us want to do or know have to be done.
> Kolbe Action Modes are behaviors driven by your instinct- not your personality or IQ.

Four Action Modes® are universal methods of striving

All conative strengths fall into one of four Action Modes used in problem solving.

Kolbe Action Mode	Striving Behaviors
Fact Finder	Gathering and sharing information
Follow Thru	Organizing, arranging and designing
Quick Start	Dealing with unknowns, uncertainties and risks
Implementor	Handling tangibles, mechanics and space

Every person takes action in each Action Mode. We all gather information, organize, deal with unknowns and handle tangibles. But the way we approach each of those tasks is naturally different, and that's what makes up a person's conative talents. Look at a person's talents in each Action Mode and you will see the basis of the methods that will work best for them when they are striving to reach a goal.

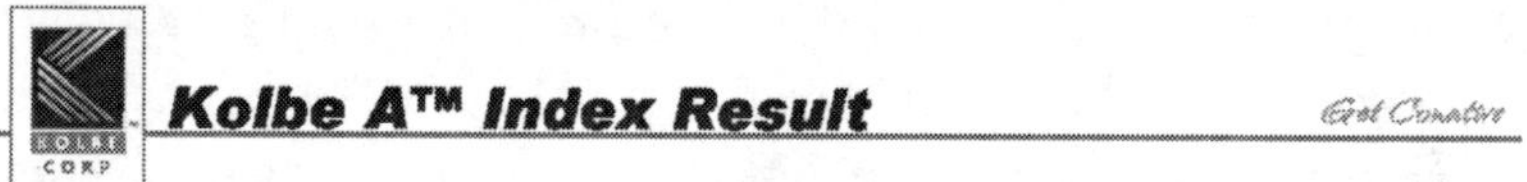

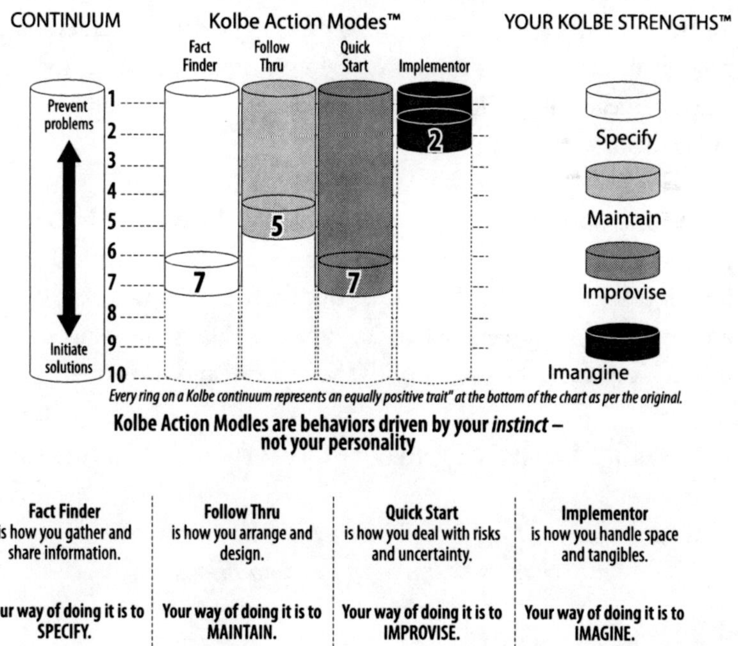

Fact Finder	Follow Thru	Quick Start	Implementor
Fact Finder is how you gather and share information.	**Follow Thru** is how you arrange and design.	**Quick Start** is how you deal with risks and uncertainty.	**Implementor** is how you handle space and tangibles.
Your way of doing it is to SPECIFY.	**Your way of doing it is to MAINTAIN.**	**Your way of doing it is to IMPROVISE.**	**Your way of doing it is to IMAGINE.**

I discovered my particular Action Mode combination combines strong drives in both **Fact Finder** qualities (7) and **Quick Start** qualities (7) called initiating with average amounts of **Follow Thru** (5) and little **Implementor** (2) called preventive. My **Fact Finder** qualities provided abilities to be detailed, and to research. My **Follow Thru** qualities provided abilities to organize, to create systems, and to complete tasks. My **Quick Start** qualities gave me the abilities to initiate, to sell, and to be entrepreneurial. My qualities in **Implementor** meant that while I could picture how things would work I would find that working in the other aspects of **Implementor** abilities such as maintaining mechanical equipment, or building and repairing things would cause me stress. I don't naturally take on that type of activity. While my combination of strengths were those of a perfect manager, they were a poor combination for the sales role I was in. My strong drive to be detail oriented held me back from closing sales until everything was perfect. My combination pattern meant I would be a much better fit as a manager than a salesperson.

When the opportunity presented itself, I changed jobs to become a property manager, and I have never been happier at work. I enjoyed it and as a result performed well. (But don't give me a screw driver or a hammer. I am useless when it comes to doing anything requiring mechanical dexterity, since I find it so stressful and unnatural.

A Look at Others Through Conative Understanding

"Everyone has been made for some particular work, and the desire for that work has been put into his heart."
Djalal ad-Din Rumi

The information enabled me to better understand instinctual striving patterns of my family and others around me. This made me much more tolerant and accepting of each one's unique ability combination patterns. I could understand, at last, the problems my ex-husband had in running his businesses. The businesses would eventually fail. He had great Quick Start abilities that helped him to start a number of business ventures, but his Follow Thru drive was preventive so he had trouble finishing jobs he started or doing invoicing and pursuing collections. He is much happier now in a job situation where he receives entrepreneurial stimulation, but someone else completes the Follow Thru steps.

I arranged for my children to be tested and found out two of my sons had a similar pattern to their father. My eldest son, Bill, enjoyed teaching school but had great difficulty marking the students' papers. He loved languages, having majored in French and Spanish at McGill University. His entrepreneurial abilities enabled him to teach at a variety of schools. He taught on an Indian reserve, then in Nigeria for several years, followed by an elite boarding school, and finally a maximum-security prison. He enjoyed renovating his home. His scores were initiative in Fact Finder and Quick Start, mid-zone in Implementor, but preventive in Follow Thru. These qualities made him an inspirational teacher. The entrepreneurial Quick Start qualities enabled him to work in a variety of jobs. But his instinctual drives did not stretch to doing the necessary Follow Thru work. His desk was piled high with unfiled papers. I coached him and my second son, who has a similar conative pattern, telling them they would need to have a strong Follow Thru person assist them in completing work.

Finding the Right Employment for Different Pegs

"Your talent is God's gift to you"
Leo Buscaglia

I began to appreciate why certain people excelled or struggled in their jobs. As a condominium property manager, I had my own company. I used to shake my head at the inability of some of my best painters or landscapers to provide a decent job quotation. They were, however, very good at performing their particular line of work. Now I realized in the same way I was low in mechanical drive (Implementor), they were likely preventive in Fact Finder language skills. Their basic instinctual drives were stronger in different areas and patterns from my own. So I began to type out their proposals for them for presentation to my boards of directors.

In my management business, one secretary excelled at organizing everything (Follow Thru); she was so strong in Follow Thru that her memos even had cover pages. I could count on her to keep up the filing and have everything prepared for meetings. However, the interruption of taking telephone messages was a source of major stress for her. She was likely preventive in Quick Start.

Another secretary tried for months to do our typing work, but we had to eventually let her go. She seemed unable to master the language skills necessary to write and proofread letters. Later another staff member told me this secretary began looking for her next job as soon as we hired her. She knew eventually she would be let go. Apparently being fired was a pattern she repeated about every nine months with each new employer. When I also had to fire her because she was not able to improve her work, my Conative understanding enabled me to suggest she consider trying a different line of employment. Perhaps a role requiring the skillful use of her hands (Implementor) would have been a better choice. She kept trying for positions requiring Fact Finder details she did not possess.

We also made the mistake of trying to fit round pegs into square holes. We attempted to put several entrepreneurial (Quick Start) types into positions where they had to do a lot of deadline clerical work. We thought once they learned the basics, they could eventually become good property managers. They likely lacked the instinctual strength in Follow Thru and Implementor skills. These skills are necessary to survive in such clerical roles. They both eventually resigned. In one case, we had the employee take the Conative Index, but the results indicated his answers had not been consistent and honest, and therefore no test result was possible. He recently contacted me through Facebook and told me how happy he was with his present employment where he has a lot of contact with people.

Another person whose test scores were 5 in Fact Finder, 6 in Follow Thru, and 4 in Quick Start and 5 in Implementor found her best role as a facilitator. She is able to work in all ability areas but found it stressful to be pushed into the forefront in any one area. When she happily became a support person to others she experienced far less stress than when she worked as a manager of a small business.

Change Needed for Training Different Peg Types

Not expressed by Kathy Kolbe or the Kolbe Corporation, but in my opinion, the Conative Index shed light on the major problem of our educational system. In addition to improving my understanding of people I gained insight about how our children are educated. Have you ever thought about why so many youngsters come out of school and have trouble finding employment they enjoy? I feel they are failed by our educational system, which does not recognize the different "peg" types. The real problem with our educational system is it does not take conative drive differences into account when educating children. This could now be remedied by the uniform testing of children using one of the Kolbe IF ™ Index tests designed for children as young as age two or the youth test called Kolbe Y ™ Index.

Persons who are initiating Fact Finders seem to dominate the ranks of teachers. To become teachers, they are required to be university graduates. Our current educational system has taught that a university degree is necessary. Unfortunately it has also taught that doing white-collar office work is the only way to happiness and fulfillment.

Teacher training often rewards initiating Fact Finder abilities to obtain a degree and excludes those who initiate with Implementor skills. (I wonder how many of them can fix their own taps or repair their automobiles?) Many teachers also come from Fact-Finder backgrounds as well, having educated Fact Finder parents. The teachers then implement teaching systems in concert with their Fact Finder qualities.

But many children do not have initiating Fact Finder qualities. Children with instinctive strengths in areas other than Fact Finder feel inferior in the school system. Unable to easily master Fact Finder language skills upon which the education system seems to be based, they fail. These children are unable to perform well in a language-skills system. They lose their self-esteem in the process of trying and failing to become something that is not natural for them. They often eventually drop out of school. Their lost self-worth sends them out in the world to lead unsatisfactory lives.

In my view, the design of our educational system needs to be changed. Unfortunately, the present system emphasizes matriculation skills (Fact Finder) over tradesmen skills (Implementor). Thus children are perceived as failures if they attend a vocational school where more emphasis is placed on hands-on skills. Each child should be tested to determine his or her conative drive pattern. Young people should be trained using the best methods for their instinctual patterns. We could then instill equal pride in being a mechanic or a teacher, a carpenter or a salesperson, a plumber or a professor. Unfortunately, we have created an unbalanced employment system. Too many unhappy people try to be square pegs in round holes, working in unnatural ways. For many, this present system will never lead to success. Their failures lower their value to society.

Is it not long overdue that we find a way to use this conative knowledge to change the educational system? We could produce happy well-adjusted workers if each child was trained in skills most suited to their natural proclivity makeup. Utilizing their particular combination drives in the best ways to reduce stress could make them much happier and successful. They could then enjoy whatever employment field was most natural to them. In suitable roles, each person could provide their best skills to create a harmonious and happy society.

How To Get Yourself Tested

"The ability to make decisions according to the purpose and potentiality of one's own Being is the most essential factor in constructive and meaningful growth."
Haridas Chaudhuri

I found being tested was simple, inexpensive, and very worthwhile. I encourage you to go to www.Kolbe.com for information on the various Kolbe Conative Index tests and their online testing. Another source for information is http://knol.google.com/k/conation. (See bibliography for more information).

Instinctual Lesson Keys

1. Your conative instinct moves you to take action.
2. Aptitude testing is different than conative testing. Aptitude tests describe interest and ability levels. Conative testing indicates inborn life-long modes of operating.
3. Each person has a combination of four natural ability drives defined by Kathy Kolbe and Kolbe. Corp. 2001 © as:

Kolbe Action Modes --	Striving Behaviors
o Fact Finder	Gathering and sharing information
o Follow Thru	Organizing, arranging and designing
o Quick Start	Dealing with unknowns, uncertainties and risks
o Implementor:	Handling tangibles, mechanics and space

4. Conative testing can lead to replacing unsatisfying employment with enjoyable fulfilling employment.
5. Conative testing of employees can lead to a better working team.

6. Our educational system could be improved if teacher's educational training requirements were designed to give equal value to different instinctual drives.
7. A better balance in society could be created by acknowledging and training children to act in their own best natural proclivities.
8. A variety of tests are available through www.Kolbe.com.

Chapter 10

ACTIONAL KEYS

Blossoming as a Square Peg in a Square Hole

SELF-DISCOVERY FOCUS TO ACHIEVE MY DREAMS

Actional Keys

No action. No accomplishment = Unfulfilled desires.
A plan + regular work toward a plan = Goal accomplished.

I had drifted in life. I didn't really know what I wanted for many years. I always moved from idea to project, then on to another idea and project with varying topics of interest. I would buy a book and begin to read it. Then as the energy waned, I'd lose interest and move on to the next topic that caught my fancy. There were always ten to twenty unread books waiting for me. I finally accepted I am a bookaholic. I will never finish reading them all. I recognized this as a lifelong pattern. So I gave myself permission to accept my tendency of buying books but often only reading a portion, sometimes only a paragraph. But I hadn't related my bookaholism to my lack of pursuing goals in other areas. Because it also meant I did not finish certain projects, I perceived this as a shortcoming.

Subduing My Peg's Inner Conflicts

"It's time to stop tiptoeing around the pool and jump into the deep end head first. It's time to think big, want more, and achieve it all!"
Mark Victor Hansen

While I might believe achieving my goals was within my conscious control, I found out that it wasn't. I discovered I needed to work in harmony with my inherent nature, my natural subconscious tendencies, if I wished to achieve anything. These programs of hidden forces controlled my efforts, not I. My goals were achievable and were only real for me if I had a strong interest or a passion to reach them. Desultory actions, hit or miss undirected actions, delayed my goal achievement.

I avoided taking necessary action to achieve a goal I thought I wanted. Examining my lack of success, I worked against my natural tendencies. I tried to force myself to achieve something my heart was not really set to achieve. I could not set goals or work toward them easily. I held myself back until Barbara Sher's book *I Could Do Anything If I Only Knew What It Was* gave me yet another perspective and new level of self-acceptance. With Barbara's book, I discovered another picture of myself, which guided me to accept what I am. In Barbara's words, the book "is designed to help you find the good life … You want a life you will love. A friend's father got it right when he said, 'The good life is when you get up in the morning and can't wait to start all over again.'"

Barbara outlines the different ways our own inner conflicts hold us back from seeing what we really want to pursue in life. For many of us, our inner conflicts have kept us from designing and achieving goals appropriate for our natures. Are we living up to our expectations? Barbara unearths many of the hindrances to setting and achieving realistic goals in our lives and defines ways to overcome these self-created limitations. She provides tools to help us accept and work with the gifts of our basic natures. Recognizing our hindrances and taking steps to release them awakens our ability to achieve our real desires in life.

My Square Peg Is A Scanner

"I would rather attempt to do something great and fail, than attempt to do nothing and succeed."

Anonymous from a church calendar

It certainly helped when I recognized my description in Barbara Sher's book. She called people whose interest flits from project to project as the energy changes, "scanners." Because of their interest in so many different things, "scanners" often have a number of projects at the same time, leaving many incomplete. Using Barbara Sher's terms, I recognized I am a scanner. What I thought was a weakness was perhaps a strength when seen from a new perspective. It was very freeing. I am a person with a tremendous love and appetite for information. I am very curious. When a topic really grabs my interest, I want to know more. I explore the topic until I can form a deep connection to the information. My delight and passion for learning many new and different things constantly leads me into new explorations. After internalizing the information, I love to communicate it to others.

Defining My Peg's Desires

"The things we want to do are usually the ones that scare us the most."

Po Bronson

Combined with the removal of hindrances, seeing myself more clearly, the right testing, and the right attitude, next I added goal setting. Setting and working effectively toward goals made a huge difference in my enjoyment of life. In order to work with goal planning, I needed to begin to get an idea of what I would like to happen in my life. What would I like to achieve? I found unless I have distinct ideas about what I want, I achieve little. Barbara's book and her earlier book, Wishcraft, written with Annie Gottlieb are filled with great ideas to help direct people to the right employment slot for their unique abilities and interests.

Passion Is Play

Passion plays an important role in finding and doing what I love. As a young child, I enjoyed writing short stories and painting in art class at school. For many years, these interests lay dormant while I tended my family and work duties. I finally recognized I have a passion to communicate. I gather information and share the knowledge with others when it moves me. I also love to paint, but my passion for painting is not as strong. What is your real passion? What is the undercurrent that drives your life? Janet Attwood has a free test that may help you find your passion at her website www.passiontest.com.

Mom's Bug Of The Week

After my children were grown and living in their own homes, we used to get together each week in a restaurant for breakfast. I always had some new discovery to share or insist my children try. Once I heard my son call my talks "Mom's bug of the week" when he thought I was out of earshot. I had such a good laugh. He was right. I was so insistent that they share in what I learned. I was too insistent. After that, I held myself back, telling them only about my most important discoveries.

Each of us has something we can be passionate about. Often if we haven't discovered it yet, we may find it by looking at our childhood interests for clues. If I identify my passion, then the saying "Do what you love and the money will follow" can come true. When I perform from my place of passion, the universe supports my efforts. When I perform from my passion, I am in touch with the flow from my divine center. I will do what I am meant to do. Find your passion and act on it. You will discover passion is play when doing work you love generates a flow of income.

My Peg Struggles With Goals

"The one battle most people lose is the battle over the fear of failure.... try...start...begin...and you will be assured you won the first round."

Robert H. Schuller

When I experienced difficulty achieving a goal, my heart was not really in the goal I had set for myself. Something held me back. Some internal pattern, perhaps hidden in my subconscious, would not allow me to really desire the outcome I thought I wanted. Unless I could accept my goal was achieved, I could not truly get the process moving. I began to delve into deep-seated patterns (some even inherited) preventing me from reaching my goals. Deeply entrenched patterns of lack of self-worth, fear of failure (so don't try), fear of success, and self-rejection (through unfavorable comparison with others) prevented my goals from materializing.

It took many years of soul searching and counseling for me to see what hindered me and then find the source of one outdated belief after another. I had added similar connecting patterns to the first one, creating a way of responding to certain trigger situations. Even though I was now a different more mature adult, I still responded from a child's perception of a need stored in my memory. By repeating the pattern, I created a habitual way of responding based on my outmoded childish beliefs to protect myself.

I needed to go within to find the source of each restrictive pattern. Core Belief Engineering, mentioned previously, was very helpful in releasing some of these obstacles. I would begin to release a pattern by asking to communicate with that part of me. I would hold a conversation with that part in my mind. I completely acknowledged each pattern's role in trying to protect me from pain. Sitting in the discomfort or even the pain of it, I re-experienced a memory as I allowed my emotions to rest in the outmoded belief pattern. Using inner dialogue, I reassured the part I was no longer a small child needing protection from the pain of strong feelings but was now an adult and could handle the emotions triggered by the old pattern. Then I would ask if it wished to let go of the old pattern. It would reply yes, or I would continue to reassure it until it did. Then going to a time before the pattern's creation (before the very first triggering incident), I released the stored energy within it. To do this, I used techniques to change the memory's location or placement in my mind. I sometimes used a visualization of an army of big- mouthed Pacmen to sweep through my body to clean out all vestiges of the pattern, or I would see the pattern lifted up to be burned up in the heat of the sun. Because all is energy, I would simply change the pattern in my mind, and my experience would change. Voice Dialogue work seems to be similar in its ability to release no longer needed protective patterns.

Lately I have been able to release limiting beliefs in another way when they surface. I allow myself to rest in the discomfort of painful feelings and tears as I recognize a limiting belief. Just sitting within the feelings and allowing them to be present is sufficient to release some of the blocked energy. This energy had been stored within the pattern of belief because at the time of first experience, I did not allow the energy to flow through me. As deeper levels of these undesirable patterns arise, I now totally rest in the painful recognition and accept them as they are, enabling the energy within them to dissipate. However, some deeper levels may remain, acting as a drag on my achievement ability.

Practical Steps Lead To Results

"The smallest of action is always better than the noblest of intentions."
Robin Sharma

It took me too long to recognize my thoughts and feelings are the creative force in my life. If I want to achieve anything, I first must put together a clearly worded concept in the present tense about what I would like to have happen and write it down. It is important my goals are written in the present tense as if I have already achieved them.

Then I must make a mental picture of each goal while adding feelings of pleasure to it as if it has already occurred. To reinforce my goal visually, I cut pictures from magazines representing what I want and paste them to a collage board. I look at each picture and add my feelings of happiness at having realized each goal. This step is a critical step, where I align myself to the goal. Placing the board where I will see it often, I infuse the picture board with my feelings of successful achievement, thereby aligning myself with the future outcome. When I revisit my mental visualization or my picture board, I think of my gratitude at having achieved my goal. I am living in my goal now. I possess an intention toward my goal and take some steps toward the goal's achievement. It can begin with any small step. Sometimes I don't know what steps will be necessary but in taking one, I will be led to succeeding action steps. I then can measure my progress regularly.

My first goal planning while working as a salesperson indicated I did not know how to set or achieve goals. I knew goal setting was important but couldn't seem to connect to making goals. I used to make written lists of big goals I wanted to achieve but didn't know what actions to take to achieve them. Consequently, most of these ideas went unrealized. Taking goal-setting courses helped me to get on track at last.

My goals to achieve certain amounts of money were only successful if they also included the systematic means to achieve the goal. It was all very good for me to write down I wanted a million dollars, but what action was I going to take to achieve it? Without action, my goal was just a pie in the sky, an imaginary taste but no real flavor on the tongue.

I broke my goal down into day-by-day and week-by-week steps. Taking these planned small actions helped the goal to materialize. Writing down my goals helped to crystallize them in my mind, give them form, and bring my goals into a sharper focus. My focused goals then began the creative process of pulling the necessary energy from the ether into form and existence. By listing my weekly activities towards reaching my goals and visualizing their successful completion, I even surprised myself when I achieved them.

There are many goal-setting and visualizing books and courses available. While they are similar, it can be hard to decide which method will work for you. Several goal-setting courses I found beneficial are listed below. Contacts for each of them are found in the bibliography.

Monthly Mentor

Thinking it was a real estate training course, I mistakenly signed up for Raymond Aaron's Monthly Mentor course. It turned out to be a very worthwhile course on goal setting with monthly meetings. Raymond's motto is "Double your income doing something you love." His system was elaborate and thorough and included the aspects of cleaning up my messes, acknowledgment, increasing my wealth, trying something new, learning something, and doing something for myself. There were monthly record sheets and mini pocket reminders of our goals. His plan included working backwards from the goal's achievement to the present while listing the steps needed to realize the goals. We also looked at our lifetime goals, writing the tombstone wording we would like to be remembered by. Each week I filled out a pocket-reminder goal card to take with me, listing my major goal reminders in the five areas. You can contact Raymond Aaron through his website (www.monthlymentor.com).

Messes Hold My Square Peg Back

"What I am today I made myself from the past. Today I make my tomorrow."

Imre Vallyon

One key for me was learning from Raymond Aaron how much my unresolved messes held me back from what I wanted. Because of my strong interest in information, I tend to collect many books and papers on topics of interest. When the energy around a topic wanes, I move on to something else, often leaving half-finished projects behind. I found I always had a number of projects waiting to be completed, whether it was a half-finished hooked rug, an embroidered clock face sitting there for twenty years, bookshelves to sort into topic categories, or articles waiting to be filed. Unfinished projects are a drag on your energy field. Not only did they clutter my mind, but they made me feel I was a failure with so many incomplete projects.

As a bookaholic, I had already recognized I often do not finish reading an entire book. I gave myself permission to be okay with reading only one paragraph in it if that is what happened. But the unread portions of the books still added to the messes I left behind me.

Dedicating time each week to completing my messes or letting them go by throwing out unfinished projects has been very important. It was surprising how it freed my mind considerably not to have these tasks cluttering my mind with "shoulds." Unfortunately, being a scanner and such a detailed person, I seem to continue to accumulate new messes.

Success Tracs Coaching Program

"You won't win if you don't begin."

Robert H. Schuller

To attend Success Tracs, I traveled to Red Deer each month to take part in the Peak Potential sessions led by Andrew Barber Starkey. They were excellent. I learned how to focus more succinctly on what I wanted to achieve. Indeed, I exceeded one of my income goals by a wide margin. Each month Andrew would provide a new idea called a Quantum Factor to focus upon and internalize (for example, cleaning up my messes or the 80-20 rule). The 80-20 rule states that eighty percent of your effort will be spent attempting to complete the last 20% of a task. how much effort is it worth to achieve perfection? I also filled in my workbook with my three priorities for the week, along with my quarterly intentions. I learned to plan freedom, production, and flex days each week. I would track my progress and successes and list what I learned and was grateful for each week. There was always an opportunity to work with a success partner to keep my focus between sessions. Time was set aside before each meeting for networking and sharing earning ideas with other attendees. Andrew advised all attendees if we kept up the system, we may not notice a lot of improvement in the first year, but by the third year, we would really see great results. Had I stayed more than the first year and a half, I could have achieved even more than I did.

Pro Coach System

Following his time spent teaching Peak Potential's Success Tracs, Andrew Barber Starkey then began his own coaching and goal-setting course under the name of ProCoach. Friends that attend speak highly of his course and are making very successful progress.

The Secret

The book and video called *The Secret* by Rhonda Byrn helped me to see the value of making a vision board of my goals. It displayed the power inherent within taking the right steps to achieve goals. When alignment with your goal is added to the Secret's information positive results happen.

My Promise & Notable Achievements

"What you get by achieving your goals is not as important as what you become by achieving your goals."
Zig Ziglar

Even after attending the above courses, goal setting remained difficult until I finally connected with Bill Bartmann's book. Having attended a number of goal-setting courses such as Monthly Mentor and Success Tracs, I had gained the basics, but none touched me with the practical realizations Bill Bartmann's book and course called *Billionaire Secrets to Success* did. His goal suggestions are succinct and simple, and they constantly built my self-esteem and willingness to try.

All my other courses taught me the importance of goals. Indeed, I had written many lists of goals over the years. I achieved many and even surpassed a few I had written down in my Success Tracs workbook. One of my big breakthroughs with Bill's book was to rename my goals as "my promise plan." As Bill suggested, I may not meet my goals, but I always keep my promises. Wow, did that get me started! As soon as I created my promise plan, events began to take over, and I began writing again.

Another incredible analogy I will never forget made me realize I didn't feel I was good enough to succeed. Bill told it in a way that I could make a moving picture of it in my mind. Bill first discussed the I Love Lucy skit in which Lucille Ball starts her first job at a chocolate factory. Her job is to take chocolates from a conveyor belt and wrap each piece. She was instructed not to let any chocolates get past her workstation. At first, she is able to keep up. But as the conveyor belt speeds up, she is unable to keep pace with the flow and begins to wrap three and put the fourth in her pocket. As the conveyor moves even faster, she wraps one and stuffs another chocolate in her uniform pocket. The conveyor continues to pick up speed. Now Lucy is not able to wrap any chocolates at all. She puts chocolates in her dress, her pockets, and even in her mouth.

Bill likened Lucy's experience to that of my mind. In my mind, I have a data clerk filing my experiences moment by moment in a file cabinet. When a data experience comes in with emotional attachment, my file clerk says to herself, "This is a priority. I had better file it where it can be recovered." She puts it into the file cabinet where it can easily be retrieved. But so many experiences enter my mind every second they overwhelm my data clerk. She is unable to file them all. Experiences lacking emotion come in on my conveyor belt and just drop off the end into a big jumbled pile of forgotten memory.

What was so illuminating about this analogy was the realization that most of my experiences filed for easy retrieval are attached to negative events. All the times I did not measure up, failed, was fired, felt I was not good enough, was embarrassed, hurt someone, felt stupid, or did something dumb I regretted were easily remembered. But my positive experiences were not given priority and were hidden in the jumbled pile. Achievements and positive experiences were in the jumble because they were not wrapped in much emotion. I discovered I had to think hard and long to recover memories of positive occurrences or even achievements.

To assist my efforts to keep my promise plan, Bill encouraged me to write a list of notable achievements. I pulled out Bill's Self-esteem Workbook and began filling in my memories of positive occurrences and achievements. In his workbook, Bill had a long list of questions to help trigger my memory. I had to search hard to find the best thing either of my parents had ever said to me and answer the question list including how it made me feel. Then I proceeded through the remaining questions on the next forty pages being as honest as I could. By the end, I compiled my private list of notable achievements. I needed to focus on and carry these with me all the time. Creating my notable achievements list was a surprisingly rewarding and uplifting tool. It enabled me to focus on the positive in moments when I might feel down. What a wonderful gift from a loving inspirational teacher!

My Peg's Daily Journal

"Not having a goal is more to be feared than not reaching a goal."
Robert H. Schuller

I keep a daily journal, even if just a few lines a day, to keep my goals at the forefront of my mind. I try to record my actions taken toward my goals. Recording even small successes and achievements can be inspiring while helping to keep up my momentum.

Each night I list five priority things I want to achieve the next day, even though I could easily have listed ten. Instead of dithering about in the morning, I am ready to get started. My mind has already entered the plan in my subconscious overnight.

What Must My Square Peg Sacrifice?

"Every adversity, every failure and every heartache carries with it the Seed of an equivalent or a greater benefit."
Napoleon Hill

Achievement of anything does not come without some kind of sacrifice. What am I willing to sacrifice to achieve my goals? Keeping track of goals and performing actions to achieve them will all take precious time. What am I willing to give up in exchange?

I was willing to get up a half hour earlier each morning. I gave up half of the time I used in the morning to read the newspaper, which I had enjoyed doing. I reduced the time I would spend reading the news to half an hour from an hour, sometimes leaving many pages unread. Instead of spending time on the computer to pay each bill as it came in, I let them accumulate paying them only once a week. I gave up some TV watching time and pleasure reading time as well. I gave up my time to attend goal-setting classes. I let go of any time-consuming activities that did not propel me toward my goals. Since I am an extremist by nature, I had to struggle to make certain I still kept some balance in my life. I had to plan timeslots in to my calendar when I would just rest and enjoy myself. Too much emphasis was placed on needing to be secure and comfortable. How much was I willing to stretch myself to take actions outside of my comfort zone?

I had to ask myself, What will I sacrifice to free the necessary time to take actions toward my goals? How will I plan for production days or enjoyment days? When will I fit in time to write my achievement progress record? What is really important to me? What do I really,

really want? Do I want it enough to sacrifice to achieve it? Based on my honest answers, I began to make daily changes.

"Once you realize that the road is the goal and that you are always on the road, not to reach a goal, but to enjoy its beauty and its wisdom, life ceases to be a task and becomes natural and simple, in itself an ecstasy."

Sri Nisargardatta Maharaj

Actional Lesson Keys

1. Work in harmony with your inherent naturakl and sub-conscious tendencies.
2. Strong interest is necessary to achieve a goal.
3. Inner conflicts can prevent goal achievement.
4. Tools to find your natural approach to work
    - Barbara Sher's books *Wishcraft* and *I Could Do Anything If I Only Knew What It Was*
    - A free test is available at www.passiontest.com
5. Define your desires to determine what you wish to achieve.
6. Passion plays an important role in doing what you love.
7. Childhood interests can provide passion clues.
8. When performing from passion you are in touch with your inner divine nature.
9. Doing what you love can lead to a flow of income.
10. Sub-conscious beliefs about yourself can prevent success.
11. Tools to help release restrictive beliefs
    - Core Belief Engineering
    - Voice Dialogue
12. Unfinished messes hold you back from achieving goals
13. Carry a pocket reminder card of your weekly goals

14. A success partner helps keep you on track toward your goal.
15. Goal setting courses (see bibliography)
    - Rhonda Byrne's The Secret
    - Bill Bartmann's Billionaire Secrets of Success
    - Raymond Aaron's Monthly Mentor
    - Harv T. Eker's Peak Potential's Success Tracs
    - Andrew Barber Starkey's ProCoach
16. Minds store memories for retrieval based on emotional content.
17. Achieve more with a promise plan in place of a goal plan
18. List and focus on your notable life time achievements to boost self-esteem.
19. Ask yourself "Do I really want this goal?" If yes, what will you sacrifice to achieve it?
20. Keep a daily journal of your achievements.

Chapter 11

SPIRITUAL KEYS

Finding My Square Peg's Innermost Self

GENUINE REBIRTH IS POSSIBLE THROUGH LIVING FROM THE HEART

After years of struggle, I increased my self-worth vibratory level to a place where spiritual development began to open up for me. I found the old saying, "When the student is ready the teacher will come," was certainly true for me. With a growing awareness of the metaphysical level and through deeper spiritual disciplines, I connected with the appropriate books and teachers for each growing level of understanding. Each day for a year, I completed the daily exercises outlined in the *Course of Miracles*. Through its guidance and the books of Dr. Jerry Jampolsky on attitudinal healing, I continued to make some positive changes in my attitudes. I was a voracious reader of astrology, *I Ching*, palmistry, Tarot, numerology, the power of the mind, lives of the saints and mystics, and a variety of spiritual topics.

I was introduced to several channels, notably Ramptha (speaking through Jayzee Knight), Lazaris (speaking through Jach Pursel), and The Evergreens (speaking through Michael Blake Read). I was fascinated by the Seth books channeled by Jane Roberts and was introduced to Edgar Cayce's channeled words. Bit by bit as my self-worth and spiritual understanding grew, I learned of yet another deeper level of awareness.

Along with attending talks and seminars given by other spiritual teachers like William David, I participated in a seminar given by Deepak Chopra in Edmonton where I was given my meditation mantra. Additionally, many lectures, books, and teachers opened me to the point where I was now ready to meet an awakened teacher. As I went deeper into the process of self-realization, I came to understand my only true spiritual goal is to set aside my life completely in full surrender to Truth.

All Is Vibration

"Quantum physics, quantum mechanics, is just another language, a way of describing the unified field, which we call spirit"
Rev. Michael Beckwith.

Growing up, my family was not particularly religious, but I attended activities at the local United church with my friends. At age sixteen, I felt a spiritual pull I did not fully understood and could not identify at the time. My inner thirst led me to join the church through baptism. To prepare for baptism, I received a small catechism booklet to read, learn, and accept some of the tenets and beliefs of the United Church. One belief was that God was everywhere, or to use their words, omnipresent. I could not understand that for many years. How can God be everywhere? God is this awesome Father figure that is somehow all powerful, I thought. He is outside me somewhere, but how can he be everywhere? That question eventually buried itself in the deep recesses of my mind.

Nearly twenty-eight years later, my self-esteem enhancement work put me in touch with people in the metaphysical movement. One of them invited me to watch some videos of Ramptha, the name given to the channeled voice that spoke through Jayzee Knight. I'd read about Ramptha in one of Shirley McLaine's books, so I was quite interested. In one of the videos, Ramptha spoke about everything being energy. That thought stuck with me, but I remained completely unaware that my subconscious mind still attempted to solve my teenage question. My subconscious mind played with thoughts about energy vibration and omnipresence.

One day I felt completely startled when a sudden understanding came to me. The realization was so momentous I will never forget it. I was instantly lifted into a state of euphoria and joy. On a sunny summer day, I walked to my office from my parking space several blocks away when the unexpected realization hit me as I looked at the sky. God is energy! Excitement filled me as the connections were made; God is light stepped down into different frequencies eventually becoming all types of matter including that of my body. Light is but a faster energy vibration of sound, which is a faster energy vibration than air or water or earth. Everything is made of one all encompassing energy moving at different speeds of vibration.

All is vibration. I looked at the sky and realized only the difference in energy frequency and amplitude separated the sky from the energy frequency of the earth around me. God is the high frequency of light but also the lower frequencies and amplitudes of matter. The difference between light and matter was only how quickly or slowly the energy particles moved or vibrated. The energy of light steps down in vibration to become that of matter but still contains the same light within it, the light of God. God can be everywhere at the same time because God is energy vibration. God as energy encompasses everything. Thus God is omnipresent!

God is omnipresent. God is both within and without. Awesome realization and joy filled me. As I walked along the street in this ecstasy, I began to talk to the parking meters, the sidewalk, and the pavement, greeting them all with great pleasure. I knew they, as well as myself, were all parts of God. My soul sang with happiness at my discovery of God's omnipresence at last. That state of joy embraced me for several more days and my life was changed forever.

Through my discoveries, I recognized I am not my body. I am spirit residing within a body. My body is actually a field of energy. I am conscious awareness. My body is not solid as my perceptions tell me. It is made of energy and moving particles with great spaces within. The sense of solidity of my body's form is derived from the limits of my perceptive abilities. A great many undetected frequencies of vibration have formed in other dimensions of existence, which I am blind to.

Dr. Bruce Lipton's broadcast analogy provides a mental picture to illustrate this. Imagine what we call spirit, consciousness, or awareness is the broadcast signal going out into the world. This signal is available everywhere. We only need a vehicle that can tune into it to obtain the message. The broadcast message can be received by a variety of instruments such as radios, televisions, or cell phones. Regardless of where they are located, if they are tuned into the frequency of the broadcast, they can receive the message. Each of these instruments represents our unique individual bodies. Even though they are not the same in form, they can all tune into the one broadcast.

My Peg Learns How Religions Begin

"To find truth or happiness, you have to go within. You have to see the Oneness, you have to see the universe as it really is, as nothing but your consciousness, which is nothing but yourself."

Hale Dwoskin

Imre Vallyon, my first spiritual teacher, taught a synthesis of all religions.

I attended a number of his month-long seminars in Edmonton and New Zealand (where he has his ashram). Imre is a an Esoteric Teacher of Synthesis. Under his guidance, we explored a number of religions by taking part in their unique rituals, chants, and meditations. Through Imre, I learned all religions sprang from and were based on the spiritual practices of one person. That person had become an illumined being living and radiating Truth.

Each illumined one found his (or her) way out of mundane existence into union with God (or higher power if you prefer). Completely awakened, these divine beings were able to live in the world but not be of the world. Because they lived with their hearts in communion with God, they emanated profound Truth while maintaining unique personalities. These emanations drew people to them who would mimic the teacher's ways in hopes of also becoming awakened into a divine relationship with God. The illuminated person's followers created the religion that sprang up around the teacher's teachings and practices and carried it on after their teacher's death.

True transmission from a living master enriches and enables people to open to the divine within themselves. Students are attracted to and pulled by the emanations of Truth permeating and surrounding their teacher. The disciples' once dormant desires for God (which I call Truth) begin to come alive. Even the mundane actions and dress of the teacher will be modeled by the students in their eagerness to become enlightened. Each religion is thus initially based and founded on Truth, openness, love, and honesty projected by the presence of an illuminated teacher.

In an effort to emulate their master, the disciples will copy his mannerisms and actions. For example, if the teacher points to a cow one day and suggests the student be as accepting as the cow is while it chews its cud, the cow may eventually become elevated as a revered and sacred animal. Years after the living teacher and his direct disciples have died, new priests or ministers arise to lead the movement. Their additional ideas will be incorporated into the original teachings until finally being formalized into distinct dogmas. The participants will cling to practices without knowing what they mean or how they originated. Without transmission of the illumined teacher's direct knowledge of Truth, the religions will become nothing but shells of what once was living Truth. Without understanding this significance, priests and ministers continue to teach what they have been taught, and people slavishly follow family traditions.

Once a living teacher dies, the direct benefit to the student from connecting with the Truth presence that permeated and emanated from the teacher is lost to the physical plane of existence. The ability to make direct contact with these Truth emanations vanishes as the teacher's energy withdraws from this plane into deeper dimensions of existence. However, the teacher may still communicate with his disciples in finer frequencies on other dimensions of existence.

Most of today's major religions have vastly changed from their origins centuries ago. The living teacher who carried the transmission energy has long since died. While present attendees may benefit in other ways, they no longer receive illuminating and transforming transmissions of Truth. Most religions are therefore no longer valid modes to enlightenment. There are, however, a few fully awakened beings of Truth living today. Sitting in their presence and following their guidance can lead to true awakening.

My Peg Receives Its Spiritual Name

One of the highlights of my stay at Imre's ashram occurred when I knelt to receive my Swami name. Imre had entered a deep state of meditation to recover the names of the attendees. I recall the vibrations I felt in my third eye (the spiritual functioning level of the pineal gland) as I lay my head down on the folded orange Tibetan monk's robe to receive my Swami name. Imre placed his hands on my head and named me Vajra Dhatu, Nityananda, Dharma Dhatu, Parem Hamsa. It means, "The diamond essence, who is eternally blissful, the essence of Truth, a supreme yogi." I have focused on my name in an effort to gradually internalize and become its meaning.

While studying at Imre's ashram in New Zealand, I was made an initiator, minister, and priest in various of Imre's very moving rituals. Another instance that strongly affected me occurred when I (as an appointed priest) gave communion to others during a Christian ritual. The energy flowing through me became so strong as I proffered the communion tablets to participants that my hands shook uncontrollably.

God's Name Is Truth

"Beneath the phenomenal experiential sequence of ordinary consciousness a primordial stillness—an undisturbable peace and silence is discovered."

Dr. David R. Hawkins

In my teenage days, I connected with the teachings of Jesus Christ through the United Church. Later I was a founding member of the

Lakeview United Church in Calgary and taught Sunday school. I accepted much of what I learned at the time, which I now believe may have been allegorical. I had learned to relate to the name God from religious descriptions, and I projected on God many of the qualities and pictures in my mind. I thus personified God and gave him various awesome and vengeful powers to wield justice. Each religion personifies God to fit its teachings. Following later understandings, I now refer to the same energy within all creation as Truth. Truth is unknowable. Truth has no personification. It just is. We reside within Truth.

Freedom From Religion

"It is important to realize it is not just a literal wording of teachings but also the entire energy field of a teacher or organization that has a subtle, unseen field effect upon students."

Dr. David R. Hawkins

How is it I was deceived for so long? I believed the Bible was true and Jesus was the Son of God. Starting with the books *Holy Blood, Holy Grail*, *Jesus and the Dead Sea Scrolls*, and *The Jesus Papers*, I discovered the Dead Sea Scrolls and Nag Hammadi Scrolls. My final understanding came painfully while reading *The Magdalene Legacy, The Jesus and Mary Bloodline Conspiracy* written by historian scholar Laurence Gardner. He details recently translated, ancient texts from *Dead Sea* and *Nag Hammadi Scrolls*, and passages attributed to many other ancient sources (including the *Old* and *New Testaments*). The historical stories that unfold include the cover up of Truth surrounding Jesus and Mary Magdalene's lives and experiences.

For seven years, as I mentioned earlier, I was under the tutelage of Imre Vallyon. I practiced chants, painted mandalas, meditated, and participated in very beautiful uplifting rituals related to many religions (for example, Buddhism, Christianity, Kabbalah, and Zen). Often profoundly moving, they filled me with reverence and deep longing for the Divine, especially the Christian rituals and chants. Meditating on my hand-painted, burning-heart mandalas of Jesus especially kindled divine longing in me. I developed a much deeper love for Jesus and a resonance I sometimes felt within my heart.

However, based on my early Christian training and the *Bible*, I had created a romanticized faith and belief that Jesus was not of this world. I believed Jesus was the Son of God come to earth to save humankind. I accepted the many biblical accounts as true, for instance, that the Angel Gabriel had foretold his birth, he was born of a virgin mother, he was never married and never had children, he raised Lazarus from the dead, and he died on the cross to save me from my sins, was entombed, and on the third day rose from the dead.

Now *The Magdalene Legacy* opened my eyes. I was engrossed as I read about Jesus and Mary Magdalene, information hidden by the Christian church for many hundreds of years. The information revealed the extent of the cover up, deceit, and power brokering that had occurred from Roman times. Page after page of *The Magdalene Legacy* revealed truths that shattered my false projection of Jesus. While I still feel a heart connection to Jesus, I now understand he was not the otherworldly God come down to earth I'd created in my projections. He was a man reborn within to be one with Truth, an ability and invitation open to us all.

From my current perspective, I believe Jesus (as an illumined being) would not be as focused on or acting out of self-interest as I still am. He would not have been attached to outcomes. He would have accepted all occurrences with an unshakable equanimity and peace, responding gently to experiences instead of reacting. Residing in serene peace within his heart, he would have embraced all men and creation recognizing them as parts of his one being. While in the world, he would truly no longer be of the world. He would have existed in states of "okayness" and total acceptance of what is—inner peace, stillness, and harmony. Truth within him would have directed his performance of daily tasks. Because of his inner rebirth into spirit, he would have fully communed with other dimensions of existence well beyond our earth.

My Peg's Journey Back To Truth

I have been drawn into the presence of a Master of Truth, an awakened being of total honesty, tenderness, and love—an illumined being. A beautiful mirror of what I can become sits before me. I respond to the gentle coaxing of emanations of Truth and love in his presence wanting to model myself after him. The bonfire of light that is my master's presence kindles a tiny flame within my heart. I feel a tender pull to awaken to my real self. I, in recognition, acknowledge deep within that Truth is my first true priority in life and give permission to begin my journey to surrender completely to Truth.

At first, I struggle against the pull, still choosing the Maya world of separation while only giving lip service to Truth as my first priority. I still insist on pushing the river to make life flow my way. Too enamored by many worldly stimulations, I am continually drawn into a shallow separative existence. I use personal power for myself.

Honesty now shows me I am not, nor have I ever been, truly in charge of my life. Now I open to seeing that my life is and always was a false creation. I have a separate self-created personality. I now see my desires to live in comfort, to become thinner or healthier, or to earn more money all stem from this false self-created way of being. I am attached to the control of my life, possessions, living in comfort, and financial security. My needing and wanting all hold me back from my desire to live in a true state of being. My thoughts and emotions have focused on myself, creating barriers cutting me off from living as an open heart. I see I hold myself apart from my real inner knowing out of fear: fear of pain, fear of loss, fear of the unknown future.

My master's guidance in stillness and gentle tenderness shows me total acceptance and total honesty are tools to develop the foundations for a new way of being. Living in humility and vulnerability and giving over control of my life to my inner being will continue the process of setting aside my unreality. To embrace Truth within, I must listen to my inner knowing and honestly accept everything in my life without any desire to change it. A still heart in the midst of the chaos and upheavals of life will develop, providing a peaceful response to experience rather than a reaction. Just as my Master lives in the world but not of the world, I could enjoy residing in inner peace and stillness by allowing myself to detach from outcomes in my surface existence. I can choose to live from a place of total "okayness" while residing in a state of gentleness, openness, and softness. The choice is mine to make.

As a child of the one creation, I am free to choose to continue living as I am or free to allow Truth within me to direct my life completely. Can I trust myself to honestly hear and respond to the divine within me? Truth in gentleness is willing to wait for my decision. My heart chooses Truth.

MEETING A MASTER OF TRUTH

"An additional assist to spiritual progress and the practices of meditation and contemplation is the high frequency energy field of the aura of the Teacher. This can be accessed through reading the writings of the teacher, visualizing the teacher's image, and most powerfully, by physically being in the presence of the teacher's aura."

Dr. David R. Hawkins

John de Ruiter is a heart master, who was born in Saskatchewan and raised by Catholic parents in Stettler, Alberta, although he was not a particularly religious child. Something was always missing in his life, and John felt a constant ache for meaning in life. At age seventeen, he had a mystical experience that led him to earnestly seek Truth and the meaning of life. His search led him to Christianity, and he attended a Bible college, which seemed to satisfy his longing for Truth for awhile. He became a Lutheran lay minister for a time, but religious practices did not fulfill his need and the ache for Truth remained.

About twenty-six years ago, John's life was irrevocably changed. He gave up struggling and searching for answers that had consumed him and went through the final process of letting go. He relinquished control of his life, through total uncompromising honesty and surrendering into Truth and by accepting all aspects of his "not okayness." In accepting himself completely, in being open, honest, and vulnerable, he awakened fully into unity with Truth. Letting go without reservation of any kind, he found himself flooded with something essential and satisfying, the Truth (God) within his heart. In releasing all of his needs, he was now given everything he had sought, and he entered into the true state of "being" and oneness with Truth.

John was taught internally on a regular basis over a period of years. He received a transference of abilities instilling in him the same qualities that resided within previous great masters. Now John is able to simply "be," providing guidance and transmitting through his presence the essence of Truth. Those of us who have been drawn from around the world to his presence resonate with the emanations of John's being, which awakens a hunger within us to become like him. The bonfire of Truth in John's heart awakens the tiniest little bit of Truth within us wooing us to go within and become reborn into a new reality.

In the beginning, I would experience unusual movements of energy, even though I normally do not sense energy within my body. During lengthy periods of gazing into John's eyes, I had a number of surprising inner experiences. One I recall was a gentle kundalini flow of energy from my feet to the top of my head with all my energy centers coming alive as if they were whirling inside my body. In one instance as I watched John connect with a young girl about eight feet from me, I experienced a sensation as if a huge room had opened in my heart. From my reading of mystical literature, I knew I had experienced the cave in the heart. On another occasion, I was bemused when a flow of energy came through my heart, moving out of my back and up to my head, where it flowed back in through the medulla oblongata at the base of my neck. It then flowed out the front of my throat, again entering into my third eye, and eventually flowing out through the crown chakra at the top of my head.

John taught us to open and soften our hearts; to be completely okay and in total acceptance; to see our false self-focused existence; to be totally open and vulnerable; to be honest to the core; and to trust and believe what we know in our hearts. Now my being needs to become quieted, gentled, and softened in order to follow his lead and even touch the much deeper levels of existence in Truth John leads us to. Only when I am focused within my heart in stillness with no wish to experience anything, do I sometimes notice an energy experience within my heart or head. However, I realize my development as an awakened spiritual being is not about having experiences, but about surrendering my outer unreal separative existence for the Truth and unity with all within my inner reality. The pull from the energy field of John's being entices and encourages me to follow his example and emulate his amazing depth of love and peace in Truth.

First Calgary Meeting

"How can we know a real Guru or Master? How can we tell the degree of one's realization? A fully realized Being has an inner peace that cannot be disturbed. He is completely selfless, and His every act is for others only. He is equal-minded toward all. He is desireless. He is fearless. He is Love that is all-givingness. He expects nothing from anyone. His every moment is oneness with God. To the degree that one has all the above qualities is the degree of one's realization."

Hale Dwoskin

John de Ruiter says as babies our original state is that of residing in "being" in Truth, but as we begin reacting to our experiences and shaping ourselves to our family's expectations, we lose our original state of innocence, which is one of trusting simplicity, of being loving and open—a way of living in the moment and being totally okay with ourselves.

I organized the first meeting for John in Calgary in January 1997. By word of mouth, my friend Peter and I attracted ninety people to meet John for the first time. As I went to dinner with John, I told him, "I don't know what Truth is."

He replied, "Then that is something you know."

As the session began, I introduced John to the assembly. As I sat down, I thought with gratitude, There is one thing I do know and that is we are receiving an incredible blessing. With such strong gratitude, tears sprang to my eyes and I experienced an opening of my heart. I was surprised when suddenly a huge rush of energy flowed from my heart toward John who sat to the right and about eight feet away. Then an energy field seemed to spread out from my heart in a wide circle extending across my chest. The energy radiated as if it was a sun. It felt like my heart burned with fire. I realized I was experiencing a mystical state often depicted on statues of Christ where his heart is shown with fiery rays shooting out around it.

John sat in silence connecting with people for an hour before the first questioner stood up and broke the silence. Curious, he asked, "What is this all about?"

John's reply broke the silence. The ensuing repartee and connecting continued until midnight. A few people at the meetings reported seeing energy and colors around John. In some cases, they saw a flow coming from his feet. For example, in her first meeting with John and after only five minutes of eye contact with grateful thoughts toward John, Marilyn had a kundalini experience that set her consciousness aside. A kundalini experience is a flow of awakened higher frequency energy flowing through the spine and energy centers of the body that can be very powerful. So powerful, Marilyn found herself in a pre-verbal place beyond language with all of her cells incredibly enlivened. This state took her beyond normal functionality lasting many hours into late the next day.

For four more hours the next morning in the same hastily arranged location to a group now numbering 150, John continued to connect with people and answer questions about Truth. My heart had been stirred. I felt a pull that drew me to want to become awakened to Truth like John. I gave permission to that pull and accepted where it would lead. I knew my life would be changed. I knew I would surrender to the Truth within my heart and start to let go of my wants and needs for worldly things. My permission would lead to experiences that would reverse my current outwardly focused life. Eventually through self-sacrifice, life would be focused from my heart in service for others. I would become oriented in unity and oneness in place of my current separative existence. My permission to surrender led me onward to continual letting go and change.

Symbols Point To Humble Beginnings

"There is a world within—a world of thought and feeling and power; of light and life and beauty and, although invisible, its forces are mighty."

Charles F. Haanel

Symbols in dreams and signs or sights I am drawn to look at have often portended insights to come. Sometimes I recognize the signposts when my subconscious communicates in this fashion. For example, many times the words I spied on the marquee of the neighborhood church would foretell an experience to come. Let me describe one such situation.

Very pleased that my right knee no longer hurt from a previous fall, I walked the last few steps to the top of the hill where the church was located. Listening to the songs of my beloved robins, this was my first try at exercise, my first climb in two months. Savoring the freshness of the spring air and the newness of the green leaves of the surrounding trees, I bathed in the morning sunlight. Reaching the top, I turned to survey the church marquee. Symbolically a message awaited me: "Humble Beginnings." My breath caught as once again the words described my experience. Little did I realize the magnitude of meaning those words held for me until the next day when I drove to Edmonton to attend sessions with John de Ruiter.

The collapsed debris of a building caught my eye as I turned onto Whyte Avenue in Edmonton the following afternoon. The structure had been standing during my last visit. What will its collapse mean for my life? I wondered since both buildings and automobiles had appeared in my dreams as symbolic representations of myself. Indeed, not long before my trip, I dreamed of peering into the numerous open windows of a large house. Window frames of old worn wood stood open. Looking through the windows, I noticed a great deal of clutter on the lower floor of papers, books, and other things. Symbolically it portrayed my need to let go of many articles I had collected through my life and many decisions that had become the building blocks of my personality, my coping mechanism with life.

John de Ruiter's sessions drew me to Edmonton. Sitting in the audience and feeling his presence within my heart, I arrived at a state of readiness to surrender some of my not "okayness" I had collected since childhood and built into a protective mask—my personality, my identity. Decisions made over the years to protect me from pain had built up a veritable barricade, gradually shutting off my access to my Real Self and the state John calls "home." I had created a false protective identity I called "me." I lived within this stronghold maintaining the barricade of walls out of habit. Some erected while I was perhaps only one or two years old no longer served me. Each judgment, reaction, and decision made for self-protection from some perceived pain, slight, or embarrassment added to my mask like bricks to a wall row upon row. A veritable fortress of impregnability had been created, obscuring the real me. Each solidified energy blockage put up as protection from pain or fear took me further away from innocence, honesty, and vulnerability, my true state of being. Each led me into a false identity of separation, even remolding my facial features and carving character lines around my mouth and eyes.

Now John's Truth brought my heart to a state of readiness to acknowledge and let go of some of the bricks in my barricade. I found myself within my heart center, acknowledging I keep people away out of fear, a need for protection that has long since been outgrown. I acknowledged my self-isolation and sexual shutdown were parts of a protective barrier between myself and a state of vulnerability I now wished to embrace, and I accepted my readiness and sat with these not "okaynesses."

A raw sense of pain and vulnerability flowed over me. Simultaneously, a vision opened up within my heart. I looked into a vast empty space of nothingness, yet it was somehow alive with life, with consciousness. Stretching back on either side of me were walls I recognized as my personality. Separating me from the state of nothingness were portions of two circular-shaped energy rings, portals, or barriers still to be crossed in my efforts to surrender. As I stood on the precipice looking into this abyss, I realized I had glimpsed Truth. I knew this Truth was my Real Self. At last, I understood where the surrender of my personality would take me. A strong sense of raw vulnerability washed over me. My being was filled with awe at the magnitude of change I hoped would someday transpire. While only a humble beginning, the process of surrendering my false identity had begun.

Spiritual Expression Of Tarot

"The value of Archetypal Images as they appear in the Tarot lies in their ability to remind the user of knowledge and understanding that is pre-existing in his consciousness."

Emily Peach

Every Tarot image depicts archetypical symbols derived from the operation of humankind's mind. The archetypes come from antiquity but still evoke responses today. As you read the following account, recognize that all Tarot images are actually pictures of yourself in an archetypical fashion. Each symbol has many layers of meaning and will evoke a response within you. An invaluable aid to my journey of discovery was the recognition that signposts to show what occurred in my life had already been laid out for me by the ancient wisdom of the Tarot Higher arcana keys.

When I internalized the stages of spiritual progression as illustrated in the Tarot tableau, I recognized what was happening to me on a spiritual level. The progression was a map of my journey to eventual union with Truth. With this knowledge, I was able to give my permission for many changes in my life. While I may not have mastered each step in order, they still provided a guide for me to follow. Indeed, I spent a long time in some of the stages, even backtracking now and again, and I have not yet embraced the final stage. Throughout my journey, I continued my restoration of self-worth. I began to become tolerant and far less critical and judgmental. My nature opened and softened.

THE TAROT TABLEAU

Imre Vallyon, The Foundation for Higher Learning

Imre Vallyon, The Foundation for Higher Learning

"We control whatever we can comprehend."
Imre Vallyon

Identifying Spiritual Progression Through Tarot

"Spiritual progress occurs in stages. In the beginning one learns of spiritual realities and studies them. Then come practices and application of the teachings in every aspect (of) life, and eventually one becomes the teachings. By dedication one's life becomes the prayer. By devotion, commitment and practice, spiritual concepts become experienced realities."
Dr. David R. Hawkins

Pictured above are the mandalas of the higher arcana Tarot keys. The higher arcana keys are part of the ancient Jewish system of Kabbalah. They are called keys because each contains universally understood cosmic archetypes; they can be the doorway to a higher state of awareness and so have been called the Royal Way, leading to knowledge, secret teaching, and powers. Through the keys, one can connect with the subconscious mind and open to Cosmic spirituality. To preserve the wisdom during the Middle Ages, the seventy-nine tarot key cards were revealed to the masses by the priesthood. Four suits totaling fifty-two cards became playing cards. The twenty-two keys picturing different states of consciousness became the higher arcana. The five hidden paths into death were not openly revealed at that time.

In the nineteenth and early twentieth century, initiated Kabbalists began to restore the pictorial representations of the higher arcana keys so communication to the universal mind was restored using symbols understood by all humankind. Each key represents as many as thirty-two levels of meaning. They each represent a Hebrew letter, an astrological sign, a sound, a numerical value, a pictorial meaning, a state of consciousness, a psychological meaning, a color meaning, as well as many other symbolic meanings incorporated into the keys. With practice at one point, I was able to tune into the meanings of the keys not only for my understanding but for those for whom I read the keys in a selected Tarot spread.

My Peg Understands My Tarot Journey

"Be your own lamp. Seek no other refuge but yourself. Let truth be your light."

Buddha

From the event I described at the start of the Calgary meeting, of my heart on fire and opening across my chest, I recognized I was experiencing a moment of the awakened heart shown in Higher Arcana Tarot Keys as Key 19, the Sun. Until that moment, I had not realized higher Arcana Tarot keys depict actual inner experiences occurring during true spiritual conversion. Through surrender and devotion to my spiritual master shown in Key 5, the Hierophant of the Mysteries (or Priest), I would go through the reversal. In place of focusing outwardly in self-interest, I would focus my life from within in dependency on the Tao (or God) within myself, which is depicted in Key 12, the Sacrifice. That key leads to Key 19, the Spiritual Sun. In Key 19, a blazing sun is depicted within a heart-shaped circle of yods. A naked boy and girl representing male and female principles hold hands while they stand within a symbol of unity, a double circle. They symbolize the union of male and female principles and the state of innocence necessary to awaken the heart. Between them and the sun stands a stone wall representing personality and five flowers (some turned toward the sun) representing the five senses. This indicates that even as my heart opens to more Christ energy and my senses become aware of the presence of that energy in my heart, a wall still needs to be dismantled. This wall is made up of belief systems and habits out of which I shaped my personality and created my life of separation from Truth. That wall of self-identity must be dismantled in order to return once again to the state of true innocence, unity, "being," and Truth.

One more understanding occurred in me. I realized the higher Arcana Tarot keys depict the steps to be completed in becoming reborn within the state of unity and oneness. The next step after Tarot Key 19 is rebirth through letting go of separate interests, wants, and needs of outer life as depicted in Death (Key 13). This step is taken through aligning the right relationship to the true spiritual direction (shown in Key 6, the Lovers). The Lovers depict the right relationship of the mind. The conscious mind looks to the subconscious mind to receive direction. The subconscious mind turns toward the universal mind or spirit for guidance. I've been preparing for this through the intuitive understanding and guidance of John de Ruiter represented in my life as surrender and devotion to Key 5, the Priest.

Arranged as Keys 1 to 7 in the first row, Keys 8 to 14 laid beneath the first row, and Keys 15 to 21 placed in the third row, the cards describe the stages an individual goes through to reach the state of Key 0, the Fool, placed above the spiritual progression. The figures in the first row (Keys 1-7) represent the conscious expression, the second row the subconscious state, and the third row the resulting material expression flowing through the subconscious from the conscious. The transition of the spiritually awakening person moves on a conscious level from Keys 1 to 7 while experiencing and drawing upon deeper subconscious levels of Keys 8 to 14 pictured in the material world in Keys 15 to 21.

KEY 0

STARTING WITH KEY 0, the Fool, we have the state of innocence, of pure being. It is both the beginning and the ending of the spiritual progression. Directed by Truth, life is ever unfolding, stepping into newness with total trust. All of the energy centers are activated, the mind has been tamed, and the desires purified. All memories are available but are no longer used to inform his movements. The figure is androgynous, embodying both male and female energies. The super-conscious figure with simultaneous awareness of all planes of existence holds the knowledge of the alpha and omega of all eternity, embodying the life breath as it stands on the peak of perfection. The Fool steps off the precipice knowing Truth guides his steps and will provide the ground underneath his feet.

Reading each row vertically from top to bottom, we have the following descriptions of their meanings. After each triplet, I describe how I experienced each stage of transition.

KEYS 1, 8, AND 15

CONSCIOUS LEVEL – KEY 1: The Magician represents self-conscious awareness. His action is observance. He is the initiative of self-expression and the transformer of experience. He has knowing, energy, and the power of concentration and attention. The tools with which he will create in life are placed on the table before him: earth, air, fire, and water. The garden represents the subconscious mind. Aspects of Truth, the lilies, face away from spirit. His desires, the roses blooming in the garden of the subconscious mind, are the powers the Magician can direct his attention to. Above him are the spiritual senses, the five roses. He holds the rod of will with which he draws down energy from above. His finger focuses the attention of creative energy. He is girded by the snake of eternal life. His spiritual nature, a white garment, is clothed in his red desire nature. The Magician is also the pineal gland, the organ of thought transference.

SUBCONSCIOUS LEVEL – KEY 8: The Daughter of Power, below the Magician, represents the subconscious energy force at the Magician's conscious command. It signifies rhythm, vibration, involution, evolution, alternation, and kundalini. The soul, the white angel, masters the energy forces of the power of suggestion. The Daughter of Power controls your animal nature. She awaits the Magician's conscious commands to control her animalistic passions and desires. When the Magician consciously directs thought through Key 8, he becomes aware of more than himself. He awakens to being more than a limited being.

MATERIAL EXPRESSION LEVEL – KEY 15: Illusion (or The Devil), below Key 8, represents the deceiver, the oppression of the self-created illusion of reality. But the loose chains contain the ability to be released from the bondage of the dark forces by our own actions. When the Magician directs his attention and thought power through his subconscious nature (Key 8), he begins to be aware the hell world he resides in is of his own making. He can remove the loose chains from around his neck binding him to his illusion and suppression.

MY EXPERIENCE OF KEYS 1, 8, AND 15. I awakened to the concept there was more to life than my every day, conscious existence. I didn't realize the magnitude of my discovery, but I started to slowly connect to the idea of creating through focused desire and thought, which would mold the energy within my subconscious (Key 8) to manifest material expression. I was still unaware, living as if I had no ability to change my existence. Other powers controlled my destiny, I believed. The chains shown in Key 15 still tied me to my negative low self-worth monster. The keys were present, however, to change my experience of life.

KEYS 2, 9, AND 16

CONSCIOUSNESS – KEY 2: The Daughter of the Silver Star (The Priestess) the spiritual level of the pituitary gland represents getting in touch with the subconscious mind, the fluidic universal wisdom out of which the Magician creates. Her power is to remember. She sits at the doorway to super-consciousness, the gateway to hidden knowledge of the collective unconscious. The veil (virginity) symbolizes the associative powers of the subconscious between the pillars of opposites. When the veil is rent and penetrated by the Magician, he releases her powers of subconscious creativity. The Priestess weaves the thoughts of the Magician into patterns and images in preparation for creation. She is instinct, wisdom, the power of recollection, the grasp of the universal principles, and the nature of all possibilities. She has the knowledge within of Truth and reality, and on a deep level, she holds all memory. The scroll is the book of the law and universal memory. The cross of matter on her breast represents lines of magnetic force upon which the material world is built. Her flowing gown is the stream of consciousness. The Priestess unites me, the Magician, with that to which I direct my attention. Her mental images direct the astral light of Key 9.

SUBCONSCIOUS – KEY 9: The Ancient of Days (The Hermit) is pure spirit, the intelligence of super-conscious will. He is the foundation of potential completion, adding potency to the images created by the Magician in the subconscious of the Priestess. He reveals the light of universal wisdom within the subconscious, providing a glimpse of the light of ultimate reality to begin our awakening to our true nature. His actions are directed and initiated by the Priestess' images. The formative and creative forces of the universe pour down through the Hermit from super-conscious realms above enabling the Priestess' images to be clothed and manifested in the material world of Key 16.

LEADS TO MATERIAL EXPRESSION – KEY 16: The Lightning-Struck Tower of Wisdom represents the first awakening that disrupts our belief structure. It knocks off the crown of power and certainty held by the illusion of the personality threatening our known existence with unknown change. The Tower begins the breakdown of our false conceptual reality. The yods (Hebraic symbols, define mere dots, divine points of energy) represent the continual downpour of God's energy and thc force and power of words. God's speech is perceived as lightning/thunder vibration. The experience is one of the sudden and direct realization of the eternal.

MY EXPERIENCE OF KEYS 2, 9, AND 16. With my sudden realization that all is vibration and all is energy, the knowledge so overwhelmed me that my personality life was forever changed. I gradually became comfortable with my new understanding of Key 2, that there is hidden from my conscious perception a field of very fine energy. In the Kabbalah, it is Binah, the great mother, the formative material out of which all creation arises. The Priestess is a field of energy substance within which my body and everything in the universe evolves and resides. Within her is memory, the Akashic record of all that has ever existed in form: all thought, all creation, all history. Unveiled she began to reveal my true potential as a human, beginning to awaken me to my God-given malleable powers of thought. My opening to the field's existence led to realization that there is another force active within my subconscious level: the creative power of light. The effect of my sudden recognition was as if I had been struck by lightning, Key 16. My self-constructed tower of ego was knocked from its contrived position of dominance in my personality. My being was fired with new understanding.

KEYS 3, 10 AND 17

CONSCIOUSNESS – KEY 3: The World Mother (The Empress) represents the universal motherhood principle. Her power is imagination. She is pregnant with the image presented through the Priestess by the Magician's focused idea into her fertile garden. The Empress clothes the image and growth of expression. She performs the outworking of the initiation of the Magician through the wisdom of the Priestess. She represents growing awareness of humankind's powerful abilities. The concrete appreciation and organizing power of the union of Key 1 and Key 2 in Key 3 now puts in motion the wheel of continuum of evolution in Key 10.

SUBCONSCIOUS – KEY 10: The Wheel of Life represents the wheel of manifestation where we reside as well as the endless cycles of life. Involution (the snake moving us downward) and evolution (the Hermanubis moving us upward) continuously drive us around the cycles of life. The symbol indicates the subconscious potential for mastery, which cycles between both perfection and periods of failure. Every phase of life is a personal manifestation of the perfectly coordinated progress of the cycles of the cosmos. The four figures represent earth, air, fire, and water, the representations of energy elements with which we manifest our reality.

LEADS TO MATERIAL EXPRESSION – KEY 17: The Blazing Star pictures our experience of becoming more aware of our spiritual potential. We become open within. We experience the enlivening of our energy centers in meditation. We begin to inwardly connect to the spiritual flow of awakening under the guidance of our higher self who continually pours out the energy of spirit. Through openness and honesty, our spirit begins to express itself through our self-consciousness.

MY EXPERIENCE OF KEYS 3, 10, AND 17. Because I had been mired in lack of self-worth, it took me a long time to realize that as a child of God I have been given natural powers. These are my powers of desire, imagination, focus, and directed thought. In small ways, I could create my existence through applying thought (Key 1) through Key 2 to incubate change by imagining an outcome in the union of Keys 1 and 2 in Key 3 to solve problems. My early directed-thought practices were to find a parking space when I needed it and concentrating my thought to win a door prize. My growing awareness of the greater self within me led to Key 17, conscious awareness of the chakras, meditation, and other practices to further develop my abilities.

KEYS 4, 11, AND 18

CONSCIOUSNESS – KEY 4: The Architect of the Universe (The Emperor) is the creating masculine force molding our existence by using our active power of mind (red mountains) and awareness. His is the power of reason. He represents the architect, the planner, and the one who pictures our reality. He sees in his mind, and the pictures become form. He has recognized the power of his thought and the responsibility that comes with it. The Emperor is in control of thoughts and desires before they turn into action. He is the physical experience of willpower and will to power. He sees the true world hidden behind appearances and seeks to purify his life through Key 11. The quality of our vision determines our progress toward liberation. The ankh in his hand represents spirit's triumph over matter. The cube he sits on is a symbol of manifestation. The Emperor's armor is his shield of reason protecting him from destructive forces as well as the still-remaining protective barrier he built through his formative years.

SUBCONSCIOUS – KEY 11: The Daughter of the Lord of Truth (Justice) seeks balance and Truth, cutting away false judgments and balancing our self-purification. She works to aid in the sublimation or elimination of undesirable natural tendencies and habits. The Architect focuses thought power to see truly. Justice brings up the patterns to be accepted in order to reduce the power within them. She uses her sword of Truth and honesty to cut away the untruth we have created, leading us to the doorway to the beyond.

LEADS TO MATERIAL EXPRESSION – KEY 18: The Door to the Beyond (The Moon) represents the evolutionary path we follow, the clearing of old genetic patterns, and moving toward the light of illumination in the future. The light of the moon illumines our animal passions to be subdued, which come from the depths of our genetically inherited nature. The lobster and other animals symbolize these hidden animalistic passions trying to surface. Voluntary change is experienced as we walk the path of liberation. We see a glimpse of the doorway through which we must enter and a roadway to the light we begin to desire to take.

MY EXPERIENCE OF KEYS 4, 11, AND 18.

I utilized more focused-thought practices to consciously direct my life (Key 4). I became aware of the powerful influence on my life of my thoughts and began to tame my mind into a natural state of stillness. I saw my restrictive patterns of behavior and my limiting habits. Using Core Belief Engineering and other self-reflective methods, I started accepting and harmonizing my patterns and the ways of being that no longer served my good (Key 11). Painful tears often accompanied these insights as I re-experienced embarrassing moments and my many perceived shortcomings. By allowing them to arise, to be fully seen, the energy within each was released. Much of this stored blocked energy was thus allowed expression and flowed freely away. While finer buried levels of inherited blockages within my subconscious still awaited further discovery, I continued to open myself to positive change. At the same time as I removed energy-inhibiting blockages, my spiritual awareness and desire grew, providing increased access to higher vibrational fields.

Through Imre Vallyon's teachings, I meditated, chanted, and experienced rituals developing more spiritual awareness. My studies with Imre of the Kabbalah gave me a map, the tree of life—of understanding the levels of development leading within to union with God or Truth. To progress from the positive energy of the material reality I inhabited, I must allow myself to become passive and negative to let the little bit of Truth within me to take over my life. The growing spiritual desire within me drew me to Imre Vallyon and then to my master teacher, John de Ruiter. In a Key-18 vision during an early session with John De Ruiter, I saw myself placed between the tower walls of my patterned self, looking through a circular portal, an opening into a vibrating energy field of darkness beyond. I saw where I must go but did not know how it might manifest.

KEYS 5, 12, AND 19

CONSCIOUSNESS – KEY 5: The Hierophant of the Mysteries represents finding our spiritual teacher, who imparts knowledge of the mysteries and the keys of transformation. He is the intuitive inner voice, the perception of Truth. We listen intently to the inner voice to follow its guidance. We approach the doorway to the mysteries through our guru (our teacher) with an open mind and hearts filled with reverence. The priests standing before the teacher on the right side consciousness and reverence and on the left the subconscious and openness. They look up to the super-conscious seated within the lotus of the heart. Once we heed the call to our master teacher (Key 5), we are led through Key 12 to Key 19.

SUBCONSCIOUS – KEY 12: The Sacrifice represents the reversal of our life from an outer focus on the personality's created material experience to living from an inner-focused reality in alignment with the Tao, Truth. This awakening takes us from a life selfishly focused outwardly with little awareness of our inner reality to an objective life of being suspended in a state of newness where we learn to follow the directive voice of the Tao within. Focused on Truth, our lives begin to unfold in newness as Truth directs our actions. The sacrifice is the surrender of control of our personally directed daily life to the inner guidance of Truth. The reversal of our life through wisdom and initiative and the beginning of illumination is our surrender to be supported by the Tau.

LEADS TO MATERIAL EXPRESSION – KEY 19: The Spiritual Sun is the return to the state of innocence, the opening of the heart, and the birth of the Christ child within. The union of opposites in the recognition of our oneness within all creation is represented by the cosmic circle the children stand in. The emanations of our teacher have awakened us to enter the reversal process of Key 12. Now we begin to radiate the energy of the sun from our hearts. We turn from the limitations of our senses, the sunflowers, to the freedom of spiritual knowing. Symbolized by the short wall, we still maintain our more purified personality and patterns. Spiritual energy, shown as the yods, is poured upon us from our opened heart centers.

MY EXPERIENCE OF KEYS 5, 12, AND 19. Key 5 indicated the relationship I must follow to become more in touch with Truth. I allowed my mind to be open as I absorbed John's teachings. John would make a fist and then open it to a flat palm to indicate we must become open, gentle, and soft within. Gradually my heart and mind became reverential to the little bit of Truth within my heart as the seeds of devotion to Truth were sown within me. Being in proximity to John's strong energy field was always a guide leading me deeper. Although I did not see light or colors as others do around John, I recognized the signs of resonance within my heart and third eye. My permission, acceptance, and awareness grew, and I thought of the sacrifice I must ultimately make to completely honor the calling and pull I felt within my heart. I allowed myself to enter the process of reversal in Key 12. Key 19, the Sun, which I had earlier experienced through a strong sense of gratitude had already given me an indication of where my sacrifice through full reversal would lead.

KEYS 6, 13, AND 20

CONSCIOUSNESS – KEY 6: Children of the Voice Divine show us the right relationship of our levels of consciousness. The consciousness, male or positive energy, must look inward for direction to the subconscious, female or receptive energy, who in turn receives direction from the super-conscious, indicated by the angel. The initiating force of the conscious is symbolized by the fiery tree and the fecundity of the subconscious by the fruitful tree. The quieted mind, the mountain, is in the background. Thus the right relationship of Key 6 leads us to Key 13.

SUBCONSCIOUS - KEY 13: The Great Transformer through disintegration, unfoldment, loss, and letting go strips away the unreal from the real. Through core-splitting honesty, the perpetual Transformer strips us to the bone removing all untruth. We can experience that we are physically dying as we release all we have known of personality life. The Transformer cuts off receipt of any directions from the past through mind and hands, symbolized by the severed head and hands. The white rose symbolizes the skeleton's purified desire. The seed of the new is present. The skeleton represents the fundamental matter that supports all life. The river of spiritual consciousness ever flows in the background. Key 13 is the clearing of the dross in the subconscious in preparation for the rebirth into new objective life leads to Key 20.

LEADS TO MATERIAL EXPRESSION - KEY 20: The Great Awakening answers the pull to the final surrender, the call to completely let go of the false self, even to die to self-identity, to be reborn in the objective world of the Real Self. We rise out of the ignorance and death of the old self-created personality into a new way of being. The sound of Gabriel's horn raises the new unified being out of the tomb of the old separation. The stilled mind is represented by the white mountains. In the newborn state, the being must begin his life in unfamiliar territory, under the watchful guidance of his master. He is shown filled with the color grey of understanding.

MY EXPERIENCE OF KEYS 6, 13, AND 20. Attuning myself to listen to Truth (shown in Key 6) has been difficult. Truth is so quiet, so still, I have confused it with my intuition. Changing my focus to become centered within when my whole life has been focused outward is a major challenge. I am learning to rest within my heart, to just believe in that little bit of Truth pulling me inward. I feel the calling as a resonance within. I begin to respond to the growing nurture of my heart. The full flowering of my heart's desire to surrender my life to Truth is still developing. Key 13 and faith lead me to continue the painful process of letting go, stripping bare of all want, need, and personal desire. Immersed in the heightened vibrational energy field of John, I am pulled to follow his lead to full surrender to Truth. He surrendered by being honest to the core. Yet my fears of loss of security, loss of comfort, and the unknown still hold me back. With no foreknowledge of what my life will be like on the other side, I face the challenges and obstacles thus far preventing me from stepping through the waiting portal of Key 20 into a new existence of rebirth. Only my deepening love for and pull of the Divine will enable my entry.

KEYS 7, 14, AND 21

CONSCIOUSNESS – KEY 7: The Chariot of God represents the perfected state of existence, all-knowing, fully resident within the body, with movement and the mind receiving their direction directly through cosmic intelligence. The one self of all is the rider in the chariot of his body. The one will is the director of his personality. The starry canopy and his girdle of the zodiac reveal all of the cosmos is open to guide the charioteer. The five, pointed stars on his crown are symbols of the perfected man open on the five levels of human endeavor: physical, Astral, Mental, Buddhic, and Nirvanic planes. The two faces of emotion on his shoulders show the dual nature of pleasure and pain/beauty and ugliness. The sphinxes (the horses) have no reins. The Charioteer lives without personal willpower directed by the will of the eternal, supported by its divine wisdom and understanding.

SUBCONSCIOUS – KEY 14: The Angel of the Presence maintains perfect balance of the opposites in harmony. The angel represents the higher self, the divine power that enshrines itself victoriously over its lower self, man, represented by the lion and eagle. The union of the infinite with the finite form is completed—illumination and God-realization, knowledge and conversation with the Holy Guardian Angel, the gold of enlightenment.

LEADS TO MATERIAL EXPRESSION – KEY 21: Cosmic Consciousness represents the attaining of perfection, the dance of being as the tiny bit in the heart expands and takes over, allowing spirit to completely enfold and direct your life while you respond to its direction. The state of the soul in the consciousness of divine vision, seeing and being in a state of total oneness with God. Admission into the eternal immovable kingdom of absolute unity; the stillness and space encompassing all. Self awareness of being the one identity that includes all manifestation. The final state of union with God. The perfected man who has entered the superhuman stream of evolution. New worlds and levels of existence beyond our limited perceptions as humans become open to him.

KEY 0

LEADS ONCE AGAIN TO KEY 0, THE FOOL, the beginning and the ending: the Alpha and the Omega.

CONTINUING EVOLUTION IN TRUTH

"Two things—walking in somebody else's shoes, growing in compassion and daily forgiveness—help one grow and mature spiritually."

Rev. Michael Beckwith

It is now fourteen years since I physically met my Master, John de Ruiter. Much has changed in John and me over the years. As mentioned, I experienced many energy occurrences in his presence in the beginning, as did other meeting attendees. With time, John's absolute honesty and depth of surrender has opened his capabilities into finer energies of greater worlds and responsibilities. As he has allowed absolute honesty to transform his life, his outer personality has changed. He has deepened remarkably, leading him into ever gentler and quieter states of being. He truly lives in the world but is not of the world.

I too am changed into a better person. I am softer, more positive, tolerant, and accepting of myself and what I have created in my life. My opening heart embraces others with far greater compassion and understanding of our unity. Gradually I let go of my will to allow inner guidance and Truth to direct my life. A major lesson of total self-acceptance deepens in me.

While I have described my spiritual progression based on my understanding of Tarot, there are as many paths to Self as there are persons. My way may not be your way of approaching your true nature as a part of God or Truth. When the time is right, each of us finds our own method to awakening. When we restore our self-esteem sufficiently to raise our vibrations to new levels of awareness of who and what we actually are, we are introduced to the steps for our own spiritual evolution. In the end, it comes down to belief—belief in the tiniest bit of Truth within your heart that begins your sacred journey.

As I look back, it is interesting to see how much I have changed. Day to day, I have no awareness of how much has shifted until I look back to see where I have come from. The consciousness of the world also changes in accordance with an evolving cosmic plan. Frequencies of vibration of the whole world are raised, drawing more and more people to explore their spiritual sides. These raised frequencies put pressure on those that are not yet willing to change, leading to ever-greater chaos as humankind transforms into a new way of being. Many seemingly insurmountable difficulties are actual harbingers of a new way of being to come.

HUMANKIND'S FUTURE

The Enneagram: Unveiling A Cosmic Mystery

"We are all waves on the bosom of the Ocean. The sea can exist without the waves, but the waves cannot exist without the sea. Similarly, spirit can exist without man, but ,man cannot exist without spirit."

Paramahansa Yogananda

While many may think the Enneagram symbol only describes personality styles, J. G. Bennett pointed out it can also be applied to any process. Bennett's book *Enneagram Studies* is based on ancient Sufi tradition and work of G.I. Gurdjieff. Understanding the steps in a process gained from Mr. Bennett's book has been of immeasurable value. I first lectured on his information in 1987, but my review of his material as I wrote this book led me to even deeper understandings.

One of many illuminating examples of Enneagram processes in *Enneagram Studies* explains our current state of existence. Mr. Bennett called it Biospheric Symbiosis, which I describe below, but first a description of how the Enneagram symbol is put together.

"*The Enneagram symbol describes every process that maintains itself by self-renewal, including of course life itself.*"
– J. G. Bennett, *Enneagram Studies*

The Enneagram, derived from the word nine in Greek, is a symbolic pattern showing how completing processes of development conform to a plan. It represents the action-structure of situations. The Enneagram describes and enables perception of our threefold reality. The symbol combines a number of laws of existence: the law of duality, law of three or trinity, law of seven or law of the octave, law of cycles and spiral, and law of numbers. The combination symbolism enabled me to see life occurrences from a dual perspective and incorporated a third dimension in keeping with my three-dimensional life in this world.

Enneagram Symbol Explanation

Start with the Absolute

Beginning at the level of the Godhead with the Absolute described symbolically as wholeness, or as one, there is no movement, no vibration, only consciousness. It is shown as a circle encompassing all. To that symbolic representation we add each of the following laws.

Law of Duality

In the law of duality, movement beings within wholeness (or one) as the movement of consciousness within the absolute. It focuses into a powerful force and withdraws energy from space around it, becoming a positive point like a bindu or a (+). It leaves remaining space, now emptied receptive to being filled or negative (-). One cannot exist without the other.

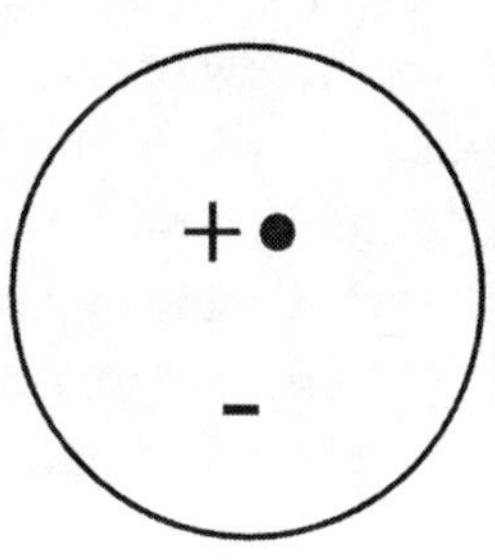

Law of Cycles or Spiral

The two forces create a flow of movement, which moves from the apex at the top of the circle, thence around its perimeter from right to left. Returning to its starting point at the apex, the flow continues but now at a higher octave since it incorporates all that has gone before. When the flow returns to its starting point at the apex, the cycle begins again, incorporating all that has gone before. Therefore, the new cycle is on a higher octave of evolution. Thus the continuing cycle becomes a type of spiral with the Enneagram representing a form of perpetual motion.

Law of Numbers

Numbers evolve from 1 to 9 and then begin again on a higher octave at 1 plus the number. The 9 point is also the original starting point 0 in the first cycle. Beginning at the apex where the 9 point of the triangle touches the circle, we add to the right by circling around the perimeter in equidistant spacing the remaining numbers 1

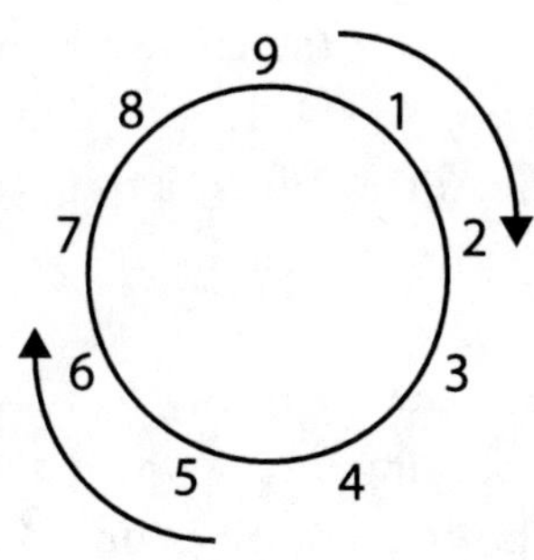

through 8. The relationship of points 1, 2, 4, 5, 7, and 8 are created from the law of seven giving us a complete cycle from 1 to 9. Point 9 is both the beginning and ending of the cycle, symbolizing the manner in which a coordinated sequence of actions sets out with the end already in view, already present though not yet in existence. An example would be a plan to achieve a goal knowing what the results will be if you follow the needed steps.

Law of Trinity

Add the law of trinity to the design by placing a triangle in the center of the circle touching the circle's outer edge. Mathematically, the circle's perimeter is divided by thirds. The one (wholeness) is divided in three parts. One divided by 1/3 equals the recurring decimal .3333. When 1 is divided by 2/3, it becomes the recurring decimal .6666, and when another 1/3 is added, the recurring decimal .9999 is obtained. "Hence we obtain a symbolism for one as an endless recurrence of the number nine." The points where the triangle intersects the circle are thus numbered 3, 6, and 9. Lines are drawn between the three points (3 to 6, to 9, to 3), creating an equilateral triangle within the circle.

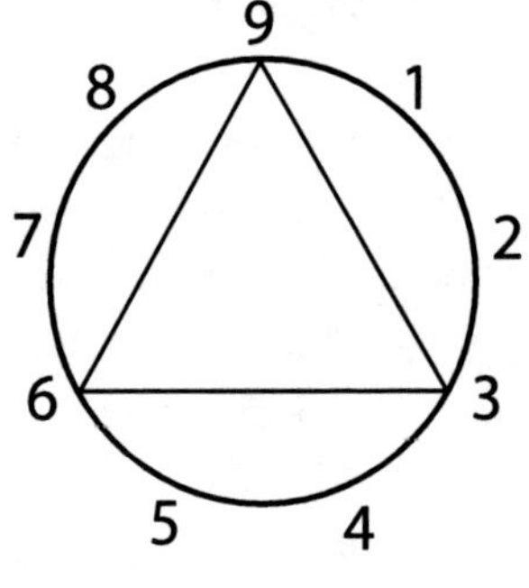

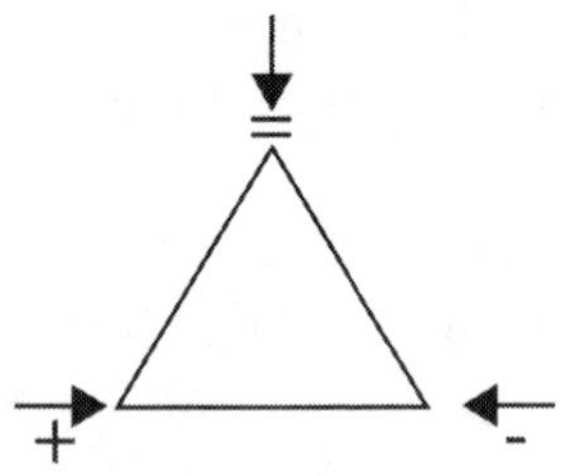

The law of trinity is a law of dynamic harmony. It contains two opposing forces where deviation and correction are applied plus a third neutralizing force. On one point, we have a negative denying force (-), on the opposite point a positive affirming force (+) and at the top between the two a neutralizing force or (=). Opposite the apex's neutralizing point is a blank space where we have a destabilizing force as the flow of energy changes from negative to positive in the cycle process.

Law of Seven and Octave

Wholeness or one (1) divided by seven also produces the recurring decimal .142857142857. The same number sequence occurs when 1 is divided by 2/7, but it now begins at the 2 position .285714285714. When 1 is divided by 3/7 again, the same sequence repeats, starting at .428571428571 and in the same manner with 5/7, 6/7, and 8/7. Lines are added to the diagram to connect numbers 1, 4, 2, 8, 5, 7, and 1 in accordance with the relationship of their recurring decimals obtained by dividing 1 by a fraction of seven. Thus a line is drawn from number 1 to 4 and then to 2, 2 to 8, 8 to 5, 5 to 7, and 7 back to 2 until all lines are connected.

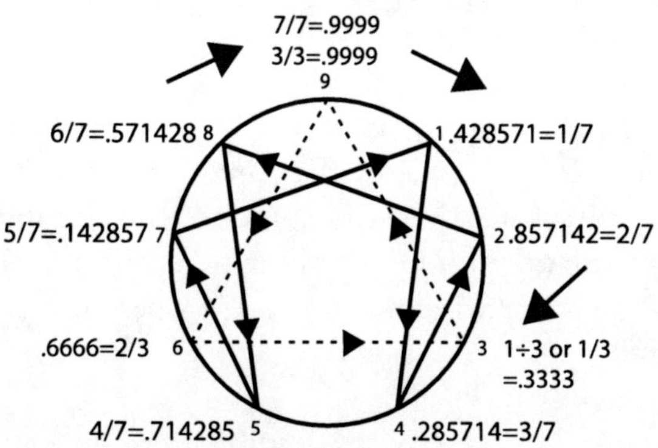

When (1) is divided by (7) the following decimal sequence results (.142857142857142857) etc. Plotting these around the perimeter of the circle indicates the direction of internal flow of energy within a self-renewing process.

These lines within the circle indicate the inner flow within a process moves from 1 to 9 around the perimeter. At the apex of 9, we have a neutralizing harmony force leading to a new beginning at 1. At base of the circle in the blank area, we have a destabilizing trauma force as direction of flow in the process changes from negative to positive. It is an opposite force to the neutralizing force of the 9 position.

Flow Direction

Imagine arrows have been added to the lines in the direction of their numerical connections. Thus the arrow on the line starting at 1 points in direction of 4, the arrow from 4 points to 2, from 2 points to 8, from 8 to 5, from 5 to 7, and from 7 to 1. Imagine arrows also connecting 9 to 6, 6 to 3, and 3 to 9 on the triangle.

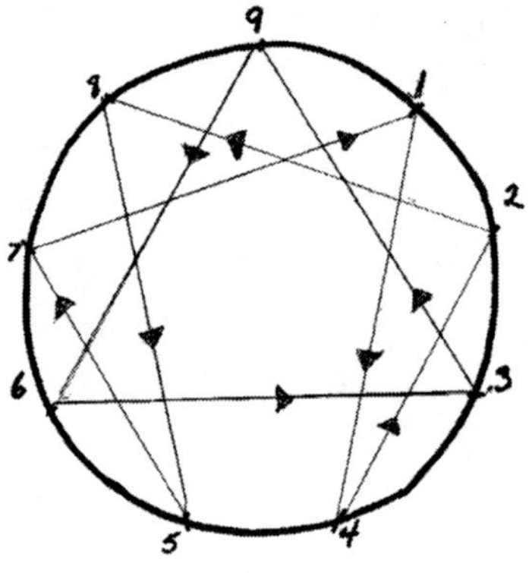

During a process from any point within the Enneagram, you may look forward along the energy-flow lines indicated by the arrows to see the future or past steps in a process. Thus for instance, at 1, you can see what the future is leading to at point 4, and at point 2, you can see what will lead to point 8 where the process nears completion.

Bennett states, "Every process, leading from an initial state A towards a final state B, must undergo deviation and distortion due to environmental disturbances." As a process progresses from point to point around the circle, the energy flow needs correction to maintain its direction from start to finish. Otherwise, it would not continue in the direction of the process. At the 3, 6, and 9 points, impulses from outside the circle are required to keep the process on track.

2 NORMAL DEVIATION OF THE CASUAL SEQUENCE

Something in the environment creates a shift and the desired effect is not achieved

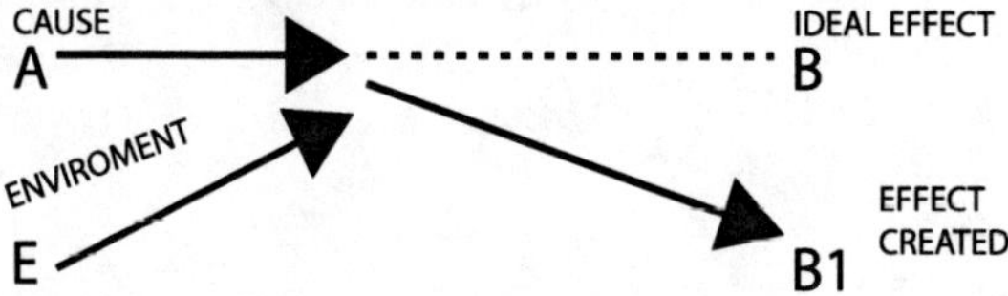

3 CORRECTION OF THE DEVIATION

The addition of a secondary correcting impulse enables the desired completion to occur

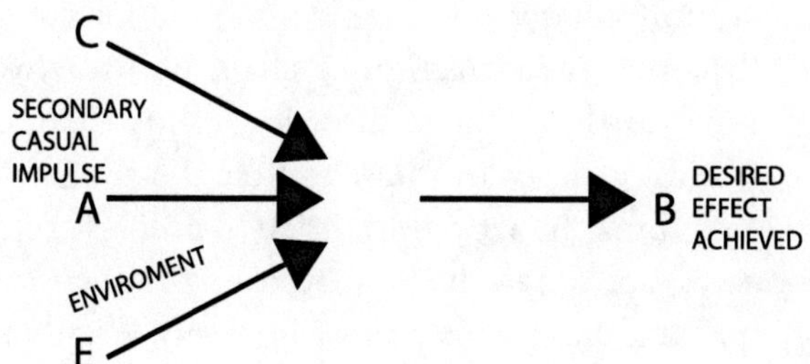

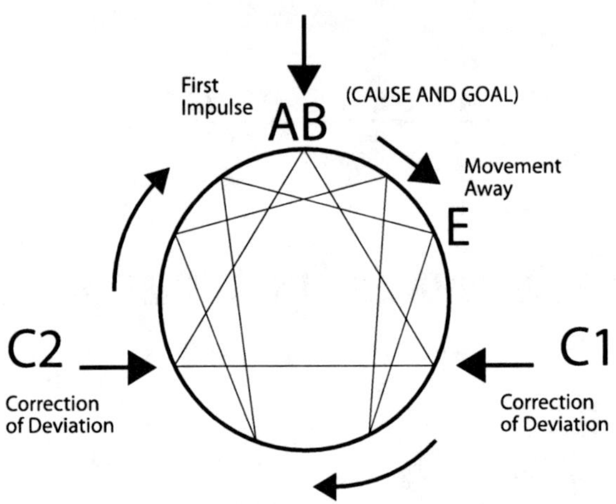

While not part of the drawing of the symbol, visualize the completed Enneagram with a dotted line drawn through it from the top (9) to the bottom between (4 and 5). Each half thus created represents opposing forces of a process. The side containing numbers from 0 to 4.5 indicates involution energy, and the side from 4.5 to 9 indicates evolution energy on route to completion at 9. Empty space at 4.5 becomes the transition or chaos point between these two energy flows as they change direction. Thus the second half expresses opposite qualities to the first after the progressing cycle passes through trauma change point. In a food process cycle example in Mr. Bennett's book, raw food on the involution side will be cooked after passing the trauma point (the oven). Another example is of a self-oriented material person moving through the abyss at the trauma point to become a spiritual other-oriented being while moving to ultimate unity with the essence of all at 9.

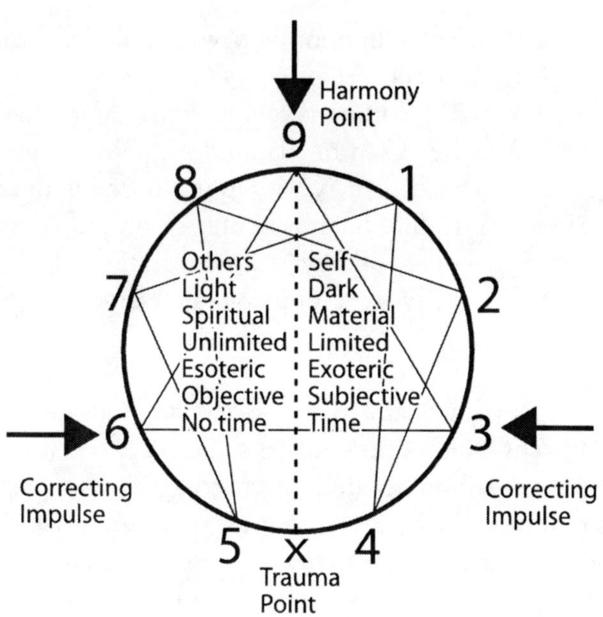

Biospheric Symbiosis

> *"Though the drama of life is governed by a cosmic plan, man may change his part by changing his center of consciousness. The Self identified with the ego is bound; the Self identified with the soul is free."*
>
> Paramahansa Yogananda

Humanity is moving into a new reality. The pull and call of our spirits propel us. It is the ultimate step of self-realization we are all moving toward. In the example of Biospheric Symbiosis, Mr. Bennett describes life on earth and the path of humanity's "process of cosmic transformation of Man himself." It represents our past and present life-process leading to the spiritualization, unity, and transformation of humankind into a new creation. It includes the involution (0 to 4.5) and evolution (4.5 to 9) we currently live in. Starting point 0 is named the "Individual Man"; point 1 is the "Family"; 2 is the "Clan or Nation." At point 3, an impulse comes in Mr. Bennett named "Civilization," meaning the material impulse of seeking to find happiness outside oneself (humankind focused with a goal of self-interest). The involution side represents humankind's growing awareness of larger and larger groups, but it is still self-oriented.

The points between 3 and 6 are society in transition. Point 4 labeled "Epochs" was world societies limited in time with specific recognizable contributions and power struggles. The space of 4-5 includes trauma and transformation (darkness, the abyss, brutality, wars, and cataclysms) as the separatist attitude begins to transform into the recognition and inclusiveness of others as it moves toward point 5 (Humanity). Another correcting impulse "Spiritualization" comes into the process at 6, including help from spiritual hierarchies beyond earth. This spiritual impulse pulls man to seek within to find his essential self and to commune with all life forms in unity.

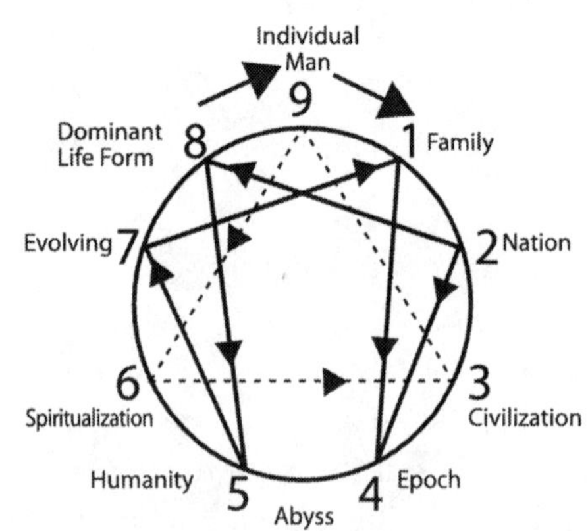

According to Bennett, Point 7 the "evolving stem" represents "The society or a particular form of life which over a major period of time is the growing point in which the significance of life on the earth is concentrated, the form in which spiritualization is concentrated." Point 8 is the "Dominant life form" representing development of an entirely new being that embodies a great new soul of the Biosphere as well as a conscious creative beingness. Point 9 is "Biospheric Symbiosis" or oneness, the totality of the great, united being including all of nature and humankind within it in an essential harmony embracing all life on our planet.

With the arrival of the Internet, I believe we have almost reached point 5 (awareness of Humanity). Humankind moves steadily closer toward Spiritualization (point 6). Great surges of remaining power struggles and wars, efforts to maintain humankind's self-interest, give way to worldwide movements of caring, compassion, and peace. There is growing recognition we are one. Spiritual help has arrived through teachers, gurus, and masters all over the world directing humankind to forget our material self-interests, asking us to turn within to live from our essence. People around the world respond, beginning to awaken to their inner calling and awareness of Truth. Instead of living only for themselves, they are being asked to live from within their hearts while embracing all life without. The increasing spiritualizing influence will keep humankind on track, eventually leading us to become a new creation united into one inclusive being. In time, we will move beyond our petty selfish differences into newness and all-embracing love.

"When your way of being is no longer full of will, mind and emotion and there is no more agenda, then all that remains is just an openness and a space for the formless reality of Truth or being, within you as consciousness, to express itself in any way it does."

John de Ruiter

In accepting this understanding, I recognize there has always been a higher purpose to life. Why did I ever wrestle control of my life from the divine to separate myself from unity only to pursue selfish interests? My journey from negative low self-worth to restoring my positive self-esteem, and now to opening to the possibility of self-realization has allowed me to be more harmonized with the greater whole of existence. I would like to surrender completely, to give up my identity to become fully awakened. Meanwhile my ability to accept what occurs in my life without emotional reaction or alarm is growing. I am far less critical and judgmental and more tolerant, gentle, and silent within. I discern the subtleties of knowing within me. I am more peaceful. I love the pull from the little bit of Truth within my heart that ever so gently invites me to surrender fully to enter a new reality. I invite you to join me.

"Be what you are! You're infinite, omniscient, omnipotent, right here and now. Be that! Stop being this limited, miserable, little ego."

Lester Levenson

Spiritual Lesson Keys

1. Recovering self-worth will open you to spiritual development.
2. Many books and teachers will be there to guide you when you are ready.
3. All is vibration. We live within a field of energy, which science is just realizing.
4. God is omnipresent, omniscient, and omnipotent: present everywhere, knowing everything, and all-powerful. We reside within God.
5. The transmission of a living Master stirs people to open themselves to their divine nature.
6. There are fully awakened beings in the world today.

7. Because it has not been personified, the word "Truth" is a better name for the ineffable. Let go of romanticized beliefs
8. Total honesty is a way to find Truth within. Be honest to your core of being.
9. Be open and soft, quieted and gentled.
10. Be okay with your present state and accept it as it is.
11. Be totally open and vulnerable to all that occurs in your life.
12. In a state of total acceptance, a person responds without emotional flare-ups or strong reactions.
13. See truly your false self-focused existence.
14. Wants and needs hold you back from surrendering to Truth.
15. Trust and believe the tiny little bit of knowing in your heart.
16. Don't focus attention on energy experiences that may be triggered by the transmissions of a Master teacher. They are often unique one-time occurrences.
17. Pay attention to symbols, signs, and your dreams as they may present significant pointers.
18. To lessen the effect of unwanted patterns, allow yourself to sit in the re-experience of a painful emotion in order to release and gradually dissipate stored energy.
19. The tiny little bit of Truth within waits in gentleness and stillness for us to give it permission to awaken us into our true nature of spiritual reality. Once permission is given it begins to ever so subtly woo us.
20. Tarot pictures are archetypes that speak to your subconscious through the symbols.
21. The Tarot tableau arrangement of higher arcana keys displays the progression of deepening spiritual development.
22. The Enneagram is a unique symbol of the progression of cycles. Applied to humankind's life on the planet, it appears to indicate our growth as we move forward in evolution to embrace our spiritual natures.

Chapter 12

LOVE & ENJOYMENT KEYS

Accepting Life as a Square Peg

SELF-CHANGE TO GROW IN LOVE AND JOY

"Loving yourself fully is a key to taking advantage of all your possibilities. It is basic to your inner joy and enthusiasm for life."

Harold H. Bloomfield, M.D. & Robert B. Kory

Change Is Painful But Worth It

"A person who accepts the force of change is already in a semi-enlightened condition."

Imre Vallyon

When I finally accepted change is normal, I embraced it instead of resisting it. Life is change. I gave myself permission to change. Letting go of my false and negative beliefs, new more positive beliefs gradually became internalized, although it has been a struggle. I became far less critical, judgmental, and far more tolerant of others. Bits of self-love and self-worth began to flower in me again. My demeanour softened. I became more quiet, calm, and peaceful. Through the power of my thoughts and desires, I was the creator of my life, so I began to police my thinking more carefully. My mind grew more still. I became conscious there was more to me than my personality. I reawakened to the knowledge I was part of a greater self within.

"The obstacles to Unconditional Love are attachment, resentments, specialness and judgmentalism."

Dr. David R. Hawkins

I released gradually my attachments to things and to family members. It didn't mean I had to give away everything I had or cut off my love and contact with my children. I could adore them, love them, and let them go. It meant not being tied to a possession. It meant not critically controlling and hanging onto my children but allowing them to live freely and independently. If something I enjoyed disappeared from my life, that was fine too. I would have no more regrets or "crying over spilt milk" as the saying goes. Before I had "pushed the river of life," insistent on having my own way, but I grew more willing to simply allow my life to flow from within. When I stopped my neediness and accepted my life, synchronicities brought me what I needed with less effort. I acknowledged my uniqueness and passions for communicating and my pleasure in painting. Mentors pointed the way to find more success in my life, and spiritual teachers reawakened me to discover who I truly am, seeing a tiny bit of the divine unity we all are a part of. As I grew in confidence and acceptance, I recognized freedom requires increasing honesty and responsibility.

There is no place to hang onto anything. Yet I (like many) still cling to the past. I keep mementos reminding me of happy past experiences, for instance. Yet the more I hold onto the past, the more I hold myself back from the freedom I desire. I should instead let myself respond to constant newness. Yes, change is painful, but hidden within it is opportunity for growth. Yes, letting go of attachments is painful, but it is worth it. The more I let the past and attachments go, the more I can embrace the fresh and new in my life. Self-acceptance continues strengthening while change takes me deeper within. As desire grows, I feel a pull to let go of my personality's control of life and to allow the divine within me to fully direct my life.

Love Heals My Peg's Misunderstanding

"Pain is inevitable, suffering is optional."
Dalai Lama

A major part of the recovery of self-worth and self-esteem is the recovery of self-love. All that time I thought I was unworthy of love was just a masquerade. I created my beliefs of low self-love, negativity, and lack of self-worth—weaving a false tale based on responses, reactions, perceptions, and concepts I built out of my experiences. Starting from a young age with the basic personality I inherited from my ancestors, I used my wants and desires to avoid pain, and along with my thoughts, and feelings, as my unrealized creative force. With them, I built the belief systems I lived by, creating a tree of personality beliefs one twig and limb at a time. Gradually the twigs and limbs of beliefs became submerged, hidden within my subconscious mind and outplayed as distinct patterns and habits. Knowing nothing else, I completely accepted my unworthy, unlovable personality tree. I was blind, having no understanding that lying within was my true reality. My way of being wasn't based on this underlying truth of who I am. I hadn't yet seen or recognized there was within me my real reality. A divinely connected part of me awaited my discovery.

"Losing an illusion makes you wiser than finding a truth."
Ludwig Bome

Love Just Is

"Love is the energizing elixir of the universe, the cause and effect of all harmonies."

Djalal ad - Din Rumi

English is woefully remiss in its description of love, perhaps because of the repression of feeling that was the legacy left by the Victorian era. Through the window of this one word, love, I attempt to communicate a vast array of feelings. But how can one word, love, possibly describe all the nuances of the range of feelings and states I experience? Sadly, this language handicap has compressed all states of love into one category. My insight into love came through the harmony of nature.

When someone says the word love, I tend to think of romantic or sexual love only. I say, "I love you" when I really mean, "I want to sex you." I say, "I love you" when I mean, "I feel pity for you." I say, "I love you" when I mean, "I feel attached or kindly disposed toward you." I lump together under one word all I feel and experience in vastly different states, adding to my confusion about what I truly feel. How can I be in touch with and express my true emotions of goodwill, affection, fondness, warm-heartedness, friendship, neighborliness, and brotherhood, when I lump them together with infatuation, yearning, attachment, intimacy, sexuality, intercourse, possession, and passion? Why do I use the same word to also describe ardor, adoration, fervor, rapture, ecstasy, agape, and devotion?

"Love....the one thing no one can take from us... the one thing we can give constantly and become increasingly rich in the giving."

Anonymous

Yet all these are states of love, and I have come to know true love does embrace and include them all. I had always thought of love from the standpoint of desiring to fill a painful void by seeking another person who could fill in my gaps. I spent a lot of time thinking, Nobody loves me, experiencing its accompanying sadness and desperate yearning. As I grew in self-love and self-acceptance, the voice in my heart changed from Nobody loves me to God loves me. I understood seeking love for myself actually denied me the experience of love. When I seek love I believe I do not possess, it eludes me, but when I can accept love is already mine (that I am already in a field of love), I discover it surrounds me and always has. Love is a state of pure harmony I open to by loving myself. Through the fullness of my self-love and self-acceptance, my selfless giving and loving flows out toward others. True love embraces me when I can "so fill myself with love that it spills into the lives of others" (The Evergreens through Michael Blake Reid). To have love, I must accept and be love.

"Love is the answer to world peace. Through love I let peace begin with me."

Jack & Cornelia Addington

I first recognized God's love as the serene peaceful state surrounding me in nature: the warmth of the sun, the breeze caressing my cheek, the earth beneath my feet, the embracing stillness, that absolute harmony nature expresses so simply and naturally, accepting me as I am and just loving me. I know God loves me when I surrender to nature's caresses and experience the sense of well-being it brings me. I acknowledge nature's total acceptance. Love just is. It surrounds me every moment wherever I may be. When I recognize myself as love, I am in a state of serenity and harmony with nature and my surroundings, a state of oneness and unity with all things is what love really is.

Opening My Heart Changes My Mind

"The moment you have in your heart this extraordinary thing called love and feel the depth, the delight, the ecstasy of it, you will discover that for you the world is transformed."

Jiddu Krishnamurti

The only thing I needed to change was my mind. As my heart opened, I began a conscious effort to uplift myself. I valued myself enough to throw away my tattered and badly worn clothing. If I truly loved myself, then I was good enough to wear nice things. Wearing nice things (even if they were hidden from view like my undergarments) enabled me to feel more love for myself.

I made an effort to smile. For so long, I'd held my mouth in a kind of frown of concentration I hadn't realized how unfriendly I looked. I began to practice a loosening grimace to relax my features into a smile. The frowning habit was so long standing I still sometimes need to remind myself I am doing it again.

Even changing my posture was important. An effort to stand straighter and taller with my head held high made improvements in my sense of self-worth. Instead of walking with downcast eyes and hunched in a slumping posture, standing straight actually lifted my spirits as well. Although with only one functional eye, I do need to watch where I am stepping since I have no depth perception.

Looking others in the eyes while speaking to them was harder to master. There was a hidden fear of being exposed as not good enough if another truly saw me. As I learned in NLP, when I am speaking and searching my memory for what to say, my eyes move to look in different quadrants. I first look down to find my feeling memories, then up for visual memories or to the right or left for hearing memories as I seek what I want to say. I still have work to do, however, as I sometimes catch myself avoiding another person's eyes.

Policing my thoughts was a necessary practice toward my recovery. It was not easy to change my negative self-deprecations. They had become habitual and inborn in my thinking. The tool I found most helpful was from Silva Mind Control. I pictured a rubber stamp with the words, "Cancel, Cancel." When I caught myself in a negative thought or statement, I would immediately tell myself, Cancel, Cancel! I pictured the rubber stamp erasing it away. Immediately I would then correct my thoughts or words with a more positive phrase. It was difficult to change my judgmental thoughts about other drivers' actions, but I had been cautioned that my attitudes held me back from inner growth. I still must challenge the habit of negatively describing situations, such as saying "that bloody something" or my tone of voice when I make a deprecating comparison between others and myself. As my mother used to say, "Comparisons are odious." Yes, Mother, I am still learning.

"End your day by privately looking directly into your eyes in the mirror and saying, 'I love you!' Do this for thirty days and watch how you transform."

Mark Victor Hansen

Looking in a mirror was another beneficial step to accepting myself as lovable. I would face my reflection while I told myself I loved myself, and I was perfect just as I am. In the beginning, it was hard to do and would bring tears because I did not believe it was true. I would find fault with what I saw. My teeth were crooked, my mouth was too thin, my hair was drab and lifeless. Eventually with practice as my self-love grew, the awareness of my perceived flaws disappeared. I could even greet myself in the mirror with a smile and a kiss of love. Real beauty is an inside job that flows from love.

Recognizing I had become insular and even shy, I saw my focus was really only on me. I'd spent so much time in internal analysis I virtually ignored others in my life. Part of developing my self-love was removing the focus from myself. I changed my center of attention to be more interested in others. I began to listen intently to others, as Denny Johnson had guided me. As a result, I have more loving friendships. I appreciate and compliment them and express my caring for my friends more often. Listening to them and opening more to others allowed greater freedom to express my natural tendency to touch and hug others. While I regret my poor memory for names and still on occasion interrupt others as they speak, I do care more for others now I love myself more.

"Judgments always have shoulds. Discernments never do."
Adyashanti

For far too long, I worried about what others thought of me. Do I look okay? Am I appropriately dressed? I kept up a barrage of "shoulds" about how I looked or appeared to others. It took many years to realize others were only really concerned about themselves. I began to see that just as I did not care what my friends might be wearing or eating, my real interest was in what my friends shared with each other. I truly related to their inner person.

"Act happy, feel happy, be happy without a reason in the world. Then you can love and do what you will."

Dan Millman

Allowing more laughter was very healing. It bubbles from me often. I remember how as a youngster of ten or eleven, my next-door friend and I had an LC club—the Laughter Club. We would find funny jokes to set us off into peals of belly-tickling laughter. Acknowledging humor is important in order to flow with what life throws at me, especially laughing often at my own foibles.

> Often we neglect ourselves the object of our love. When we realize we are created by God and we are wonderful, mental and physical instruments for living, fed from an infinite source of divine love which is God, then we realize our mistakes in overlooking loving ourselves. When we love ourselves it becomes easier to love others. (excerpted from Jack and Cornelia Addington's beautiful book *How to Love and Be Loved, Drawing the Larger Circle*)

As I recovered my self-esteem and self-love, I opened my eyes to truly see. I saw the falseness of the belief structure I had built to separate myself from my true self within. I saw that I could love and accept myself just as I am. Regardless of our thoughts about being unloving and unlovable, we have always been loved by our true selves within. Acknowledge it, then let it flower through sharing it. It is truly in giving love that we receive. The love we give away we keep.

> Start with your nearest and dearest. Draw a circle of love that includes your beloved. It is easy to love this special person. Now draw a larger circle to take in your friends and acquaintances

everywhere. Think of your love as flowing out to them, taking them into the circle. (*How to Love and Be Loved, Drawing the Larger Circle*)

Have you ever noticed the magnetism of a person who loves himself/herself? She or he exudes an attractive quality of self-love, which draws people in. They want to be with a person who radiates self-love.

We do not have to make love happen; it is within us and around us always. We just need to open to its presence within us. Give yourself permission to see and accept it. Truly accept it. Love is within you. It is true. Now I know love has always been present. My peg glows from within.

"Love radiates from us like a light from a bonfire and is denied to no one."
Deepak Chopra

Finding Balance: Key To Harmonious Life

"Happiness is when what you think, what you say, and what you do are in harmony."
Mahatma Gandhi

I lived so much of my life in an unbalanced way unbalance became my norm. Many times, I have drawn a circular pie shape and plotted each hour of my day's activities on it in wedges. Most times the imbalance in my life was evident. I did not value myself enough to allocate time in my day just for me: time for what I might wish to do, time for enjoying pleasure reading or a walk outdoors, time to attend a play or do something with a friend. I did not value myself enough to allocate space in my day or even week for myself. The old saying "All work and no play makes Jack a dull boy" is very true. My energy was pulled down into a state of boredom and light depression when I did not respect my need to balance work with play. When I work, I can work hard, but I learned the importance of balancing effort with playtime. If I don't plan for pleasure, I let other activities crowd it out of my life. Balanced daily living is a key to a less stressful and more rewarding life. In addition to outer balance, an even greater benefit comes from finding your place of inner balance.

Stepping Into Newness

"There is never a need for a different, better moment. When we see this moment as it truly is, we see something extraordinary. We don't feel the need to turn this moment into anything other than what it is, because it is extraordinary as it is. When we perceive this, we have healed the illusory split within ourselves, and we have started to heal the illusory split within the greater consciousness of humanity."

Adyshanti

Daily I am amazed at the information pouring out through the Internet and other media. I experienced little change when I was young, but now the Information Age swamps me with newness and change. Finding a balanced way to move within the overwhelming pressure of moment-by-moment change can be a challenge. We are faced with constant choices of what to do and how to be. Learning to respond to situations rather than react enables us to keep on an even keel.

Spiritual teacher, Adyashanti, provided a beautiful way to stay in the place of inner balance while performing daily functions. When a stressed attendee at Adya's retreat expressed his concerns about not meeting his girlfriend's expectations in life and feeling his need to change to please her, Adya gave a simple guidance, "What happens to you if you don't think about you?"

It was very effective. The attendee discovered a place of stillness within, which was beyond his normal self. He became relaxed with new awareness that he was okay just as he was.

When we ask ourselves the same question, we stop thinking about ourselves. We allow ourselves to drop our focus within to be simply conscious and aware, with no thought about who we are or what we think we need. We drop into a relaxed place of peaceful stillness, a place without age, gender, time, or anything other than the peaceful being we recognize within. Initially with practice, we may move in and out of this peaceful state. Gentle reminders to stop thinking about ourselves will allow us to drop into that state of stillness again. Taking action to handle our daily activities while remaining focused in this silent peacefulness enables us to remain centered in the midst of disruption and other demands. A relaxed happiness seems to flow from within that space of quiet. With love and devotion to that real Self, our lives become more balanced. They begin to flower.

Finding The Joy In Enjoyment

"Let your life be so filled with joy that it spills into the lives of others."

The Evergreens

During one of their channelled talks at Devon, when the Evergreens spoke about enjoyment, I at last recognized I did not need to suffer. My suffering was self-created. I could enjoy life instead. I bought myself a vanity license plate in 1985 that I still have on my car. It says, "ENJOY" and is a constant reminder to stop taking life so seriously and to enjoy it instead.

My curiosity has led me to explore many areas. Each new discovery or topic of interest has captured my attention and taken me to many pathways of growth and change. I shared many of these inspirations with my friends. Gradually I understood my passion is expression for the benefit of others. I enjoy sharing what many years of experience has taught me. My wish is to help younger folk find the joy of enjoyment in themselves too. Why not discover the JOY in ENJOYing life. It waits within you.

"Love and giving are two words that are synonymous. It's in the spirit of givingness that the secret to joy lies."

Lester Levenson

Success begins with self-love and giving yourself permission to do what you enjoy. No one (but yourself) needs to give you permission to choose enjoyment over suffering. Simply see what holds you back from enjoyment, then permit yourself to let go of that unproductive pattern. It will start you on the path of enjoyment.
Self-acceptance flowers out of self-love. Joy comes from loving self-acceptance. Joy comes from seeing you truly are a beautiful being. Joy comes out of loving what you are doing that is of benefit to others.

Gratitude Shines My Peg

"Gratitude is the only means of overcoming separation. Separation is the opposite of oneness."

Stephen Lewis

Daily acknowledgement of things I am grateful for has been a very positive reinforcement. It has helped me maintain a more positive outlook on life. I take a few moments at the start of each day and often again during the day to reflect and express my gratitude for the many blessings in my life. Whether my thankfulness is for something as simple as having a cup to make tea in or an opening in traffic to allow me to change lanes, I am constantly grateful and express this many times daily. Gratitude is an amazing healing tool. It enables acceptance of my peg's present bounty and good as well as reducing my negativity tendency. It adds the sheen to my life as a square peg.

Endless Blessings

"To bless a thing is to fill it with life. Life is expansion and the thing will expand and progress. To bless is to enfold it warmly in your thoughts and feeling and consciously desire its fullest and most beautiful expression. To bless is to send forth a power which is of God and therefore omnipotent. To bless is to release the hidden life in everything."

Ervin Seale

There is a simple yet beautiful technique to heal relationships with those that seem hard to love, which is described in the Addingtons' book *How to Love and Be Loved.* The authors credit Frances Wilshire who says, "Think of the person who seems hard to love and say, 'I bless you and bless you and bless you. I praise you and praise you and praise you.'" In many difficult situations, the Addingtons describe surprising healing results. I used the technique successfully to heal several difficult situations. I was actually healing myself through blessing another. I allowed them to be themselves, accepting them just as they were, as I blessed and praised them. They did not need to change; I had been reacting to my own perceptions and criticisms of them.

Blessings are a very positive beneficial energy force. Grace enfolds us in a universal field of love and tenderness. The grace of my higher self bestows never-ending showers of blessings. My higher self accepts me with no need for me to be anything other than what I presently am. Even while in turmoil, when I am aware of these constant blessings, my life becomes more peaceful and serene. I tune into my innermost being and its underlying stream of tenderness and love.

Daily I bless my food and water before eating as well as bless all those that sacrificed their lives for my well-being, wishing that their evolution be hastened. I bless my body daily. I send blessings of kindness and healing to others. Knowing I am truly blessed residing within the one universal being of love endlessly gifts my days.

Putting It All Together

"When you make the present moment, instead of the past and future, the focal point of your life, your ability to enjoy what you do—and with it the quality of your life—increases dramatically."

Eckhart Tolle

Until we awaken to who we really are, we follow the patterns established by our ancestors from which we created our personalities. We react instead of responding to life. We try to protect ourselves from perceived pain instead of being okay with our experiences. We shield our true feelings from others. As we react to protect ourselves, we build barricades to life, creating patterned ways of rejection that become habits.

Picture each habit made from moment-by-moment rejection as small pieces of lead armor. For pain avoidance, we attempt to shield ourselves by hiding behind a bit of lead. As we continue rejecting life as it presents itself, we add more and more pieces of lead to our armor. After a while, we have constructed a veritable lead suit we hide within: our personality. We become so accustomed to living from within our leaden protective shell we forget we even created it ourselves.

However, one day, a book or a word allows a little bit of light to shine through a chink in our armor. We begin to awaken. That bit of light fans a flame of a desire, a pull to awaken to the truth of our being. The shedding of that unwieldy garment begins when we acknowledge it hampers us and we give ourselves permission to change. Desire begins to lead us to return to our true selves within, providing clues to release the outmoded leaden patterns. Pieces of armor begin to loosen. Little by little, more chinks open in our plated personality, letting more rays of truth shine in. Awakening further as truth peaks in, we allow the dismantling to uncover a bit of our true being, the beginning of true change. Thus we shrug off more pieces of leaden patterns until at last we shed our lead overcoat and stand once again in the full vulnerability and beauty of life. We see our overcoat for what it truly is: a false creation built to protect us from the realities of life, a false creation blinding us to the hidden reality of our true selves within. While we may never be completely free of our old patterns, they now have shrunken to the point where they cause much less upheaval in our life. Now at last we are free.

"Habit is habit and not to be flung out of the window by any man but to be coaxed downstairs a step at a time."

Mark Twain

If you are still struggling alone with self-worth issues, don't be afraid to ask for help before your self-value plummets too far. Protect your self-esteem through openly caring for yourself in honest and truthful ways. The things you pay attention to mould you into what you are. Focusing on what you don't want will bring more of the same. Focus only on positive outcomes. To change a pattern, don't resist or fight it; that will only strengthen it, bringing you more of the same. Instead accept the pattern just as it is (as best you can). You don't need to change anything first. Self-acceptance is a major key. Turn your focus within in openness and softness while allowing the pattern to be there. Be gentle and kind with yourself. That place of openness and softness within is who you really are. Over time, you will find your patterns will gently lessen and joy will bubble up from within to find you again.

"Eventually you will come to understand that love heals everything, and love is all there is."

Gary Zukav

Our ultimate goal in life is to learn to accept what we really are: beings of goodness, love, and gentleness. We are parts of one unified reality. Living in harmony with what we truly are, we respond with openness and softness to what occurs in our lives. We are open and vulnerable, exposed to others without any covering. We make our choices from a base of being in tune with our true selves, living in freedom with responsibility.

"In the end these things matter most: How well did you love? How fully did you Love? How deeply did you learn to let go?"
Buddha

"Live well. Laugh often. Love much."
Author unknown

Love And Enjoyment Lesson Keys

1. Embrace the fresh and new by letting go of the past.
2. Change is painful, but hidden within it is opportunity for growth.
3. Give yourself permission to accept beneficial change.
4. Let the past go. Live in newness each day.
5. Let go of attachments to possessions and people. Adore them, love them, but let them go.
6. Our ancestors bequeathed us our fledgling personality
7. We build barriers called personalities to protect ourselves from perceived pain.
8. Personalities are false creations separating and blinding us to our innermost reality.
9. Your real being is a being of goodness, love, openness, and gentleness.

10. Beliefs become hidden in the subconscious mind and outplay as patterns and habits.
11. Patterns strengthen if we resist them. Accept them just as they are and they will diminish.
12. We create our lives with thought, feelings, and desires.
13. You will become like the object of your attention and awareness. What you as awareness put your attention on is a creative force.
14. Focusing on what you don't want will bring more of the same.
15. Focus only on positive speech and outcomes.
16. Making judgments and comparisons to others holds us back from Truth.
17. Suffering is self-created.
18. Respond rather than react to situations and circumstances.
19. When I seek love believing I do not possess it, it eludes me.
20. When I accept love is already mine, then I reside within love.
21. The state of harmony in nature surrounds with love.
22. Smile often and laugh at your own mistakes.
23. Allow vulnerability by looking directly into another's eyes.
24. You deserve nice things. Enhance your love of self by throwing away your tattered garments.
25. Erase habitual negative expression with the "Cancel, Cancel" rubberstamp.
26. Use mirror self-talk to erase concerns and accept you really are a beautiful person.
27. Balance work with play
28. Stop pushing the river to make things go your way. Allow the Truth within to guide your steps.
29. Success begins with self-love and giving yourself permission to do what you enjoy.
30. Synchronicities begin to draw to you what you require.

31. Mentors can help redirect your efforts.
32. Expressing and recording gratitude heals self-love.
33. Joy and love flow out of accepting yourself just as you are.
34. Self-love draws others to you from the radiance you project.
35. Blessings are a gift you give to others and yourself.
36. Focus on others instead of yourself.
37. The love we give away we keep. In giving, we receive.
38. Practice the blessing technique of blessing and praising those that are hard to love.
39. Be open and loving and your life will be filled with love.

Afterword

"Do you really want to look back on your life and see how wonderful it could have been had you not been afraid to live it?"

Caroline Myss

In the preceding pages, I have bared myself and my life to you to provide glimpses of knowledge and a variety of healing methods you can employ to enhance your true enjoyment of life. Observing your inner and outer communication to rout out all negativity lifts your vibrations. Learning to understand yourself from every point of view (physical, emotional, mental, occupational, and spiritual), you reawaken a surprising depth of self-love and self-worth. You will grow in self-understanding and self-communication skills, allowing you to see new perspectives. You will enjoy improved relationships with all parts of yourself. You will begin seeing more clearly the marvel of who you really are. Your self-love and self-worth truly flower as your critical judgements and intolerance of others drops away. Love and tolerance for all humanity become your natural expression. With full acceptance of your strengths and weaknesses, you recognize the uniqueness, the beauty, of being who you truly are. You begin to open to even greater realities within. The more you are in touch with the true center of your being, the more a new quietly calm acceptance in the midst of difficulty begins to pervade your life. Fresh newness opens in your life.

Embrace total acceptance of the magnificence of who you really are with this affirmation:

I am a wonderful worthy and lovable person.
I appreciate that about myself.
No one has ever been or ever will be quite like me.
I am an individual, an original.
And all those things that make me uniquely me
are deserving of love and praise.

You are a part of me. I pour much love and many blessing within these pages for you, dear reader. May your life be enhanced through having shared in mine.

Acknowledgement

Much gratitude goes to all those that supported me in the writing of this guide book. They enabled my dream to turn into these pages to help others recover from lack of self worth. I could not have completed this work without the generous assistance of many people including the many book authors, mentors, teachers and trainers who provided inspiration for positive change in my life; Bill Bartmann for his Promise Plan that returned me to my writing passion; Shellie Hunt, of Success is by Design, who provided expert guidance and encouragement as I began to learn about being an author; Imre Vallyon, esoteric teacher of synthesis, for approval to use his earlier Tarot pictures; Lisa Fishkind and the Kolbe Corporation for providing updated information on the conative index testing they provide; Pamela Guerreri, of Proofed to Perfection, for her go ahead appraisal and excellent detailed editing expertise; Fredrick Fluker, of Rising Ambitions Media Group, his valued efforts to design, put my words into publishable form, and for his colourful cover design, many graphic drawings and painstaking completion of the interior design set up; and Amanda Parsons, Valerie Deem, Brandon Drake, and staff at Balboa Press for completing the steps of publishing and guiding the marketing of this book. Many thanks to you all. Your efforts have been indispensible, invaluable and so greatly appreciated.

Helen
Nana Wisewoman

Bibliography

CHAPTER 1 ANCESTRAL KEYS

• Denny Ray Johnson: *What the Eye Reveals, An Introduction to the Rayid Method of Iris Interpretation* published 1984
ISBN 0-917197-00-3

• *Touch Starvation In America, a Call to Arms* published 1985
ISBN: 0-917197-02-X

• Denny Ray Johnson with J. Erik Ness: *What the Eye Reveals* published 1995. ISBN 0-917197-04-6 An updated version with many color photographs.

• Denny Johnson and Edith Cuffe : *The Nature of Birth Order in the Family Tree* published 2002. ISBN 0-917197-05-4
Eye and relationship charts available from www.rayid.com
The Unitree Foundation and Rayid International.

CHAPTER 2 PERSONALITY KEYS

• Robert J. Nogosek, Maria Beesing and Patrick H. O'Leary: *The Enneagram, a Journey of Self Discovery* Published 1984.
ISBN 0-87193-214-8

• Claudio Naranjo, M.D: *Ennea-Type Structures, Self-Analysis for the Seeker.* Published 1990 ISBN: 0-89556-063-1

• J. G. Bennett *Enneagram Studies* 1974 (Edition 1983)
Library of Congress Catalogue number 82 -60166

• Don Richard Riso: *Personality types: Using the Enneagram for Self-Discovery.* Published 1987. ISBN 0-395-44484-5 and
ISBN 0-395-40575-0

• *Understanding the Enneagram, The Practical Guide to Personality Types* published 1990. ISBN 0-395-52026-6 and
ISBN 0-395-52148-3

• Helen Palmer: *The Enneagram, the Definitive Guide to the Ancient System for Understanding Yourself and the Others in Your Life.* Published 1988 ISBN 0-06-250673-0

• *The Enneagram in Love & Work, Understanding your Intimate & Business Relationships.* Published 1995 ISBN 0-06-250721-4

• Margaret Frings Keyes: *Emotions and the Enneagram, Working Through Your Shadow Life Script.* Published 1988
ISBN 1-882042-04-2
• Richard Rohr and Andreas Ebert: *Discovering the Enneagram, An Ancient Tool for a New Spiritual Journey.* Published 1990 ISBN: 0-8245-1017-8

CHAPTER 3 PERSONALITY KEYS CONTINUED

• Shirley MacLaine, published 1983 *Out on a Limb.* ISBN 9780553050356
• H. Spencer Lewis: F.R.C.,Ph.D. *Self Mastery and Fate with the Cycles of Life* published 1929 -1979 Rosicrucian Press
• Hans J. Wernli: *Biorhythm, A scientific Exploration into the Life Cycles of the Individual* published 1960 Library of Congress # 60-15391
• Dane Rudyar: *The Astrological Houses, The Spectrum of Individual Experience* Published 1972 Library of Congress number 74-180105
• *An Astrological Mandala: The Cycle of Transformations and Its 360 Symbolic Phases* published 1974 ISBN 0-394-71992-1
• Charles F. Haanel: *You* written early in the 20th century. Reprinted ISBN 10: 1-60459-351-2 and ISBN 13: 978-1-60459-351-8
• A. T. Mann: *The Round Art, the Astrology of Time and Space* published 1979 ISBN 0-905895-18-5
• Derek and Julia Parker: *The Compleat Astrologer* published 1971- 1975 ISBN 0-55301066-2
• Hilarion: *Astrology Plus, The Hidden Meaning of the Foot, Leg, Internal Organs, Vertebrae ... plus a Complete Course in Esoteric Palmistry* published 1982
• Omraam Mikhael Aivanhov; *The Zodiac, Key to Man and to the Universe* published 1986 ISBN 2-85566-369-5
• Alice A. Bailey: *Esoteric Astrology* published by Lucis Trust 1951 No ISBN
• Will Parfitt: *The Living Qabalah, A Practical and Experiential Guide to Understanding the Tree of Life* published 1988 ISBN: 1-85230-041-8
• Dion Fortune: *The Mystical Qabalah* published 1935 and 1984 ISBN: 0-87728-596-9
• Charles Ponce: *Kabbalah, An Introduction and Illumination for the World Today* published 1973. ISBN: 0-8356-0510-8
• Faith Javane and Dusty Bunker: *Numerology and the Divine Triangle* published in 1980. ISBN: 0-914918-10-9
• Dusty Bunker: *Numerology and Your future* first published in 1980. ISBN 0-914918-18-4

• Florence Campbell: *Your Days Are Numbered, A Manual of Numerology for Everybody* published 1931- 19581982 ISBN: 0-87516-422-6

• Sandor Konraad *Numerology Key to the Tarot* published 1983 ISBN: 0-914918-45-1

• Dan Millman: *The Life You Were Born to Live , a Guide to Finding Your Life Purpose* published 1993 ISBN 0915811-60-X

• *Everyday Enlightenment, the Twelve Gateways to Personal Growth* published 1998 ISBN 0-446-52279-1

• A. E., Powell; *A Theosophical compilation The Solar System* published 1930 No ISBN

• Richard Heinberg: *Resonance* published 1977
ISBN: 0-920242-08-1

CHANNELS

• Ramptha speaks through J. Z. Knight - web site www.ramptha.com - books and CD's and MP3s available

• Lazaris speaks through Jach Pursel - web site www.lazaris.com - books and CDs available

• Michael Blake Read/ Phillippa M. Lee: I*he Evergreens Gentle Book of Practical Living*

• *Pointers, verbatim transcripts from a trance psychic* published 1977 ISBN: 0-920242-00-6

• The Evergreens spoke through trance psychic Michael Blake Read for 30 years

CHAPTER 4 EMOTIONAL KEYS

• Gerald G. Jampolsky M.D.: *Love is Letting Go of Fear* published 1979-1981 ISBN: 0-553-20796-2

• *Good bye to Guilt, Releasing Fear Through Forgiveness* published 1985 ISBN: 0-553-44182-0

• *Teach Only Love* published 1983 ISBN: 0-553-34007-7

• *Out of the Darkness into The Light, a Journey of Inner Healing* published 1989 ISBN: 0-553-34791-8

• Jerry Jampolsky founded the International Center for Attitudinal Healing.

www.jerryjampolskyanddianecirincione.com

• Anonymous: *The Course in Miracles* published 1975 -1983 by The Foundation for Inner Peace Course in Miracles Volume two Workbook for Students Course in

Miracles A Manual for Teachers
• Richard Bandler and John Grinder *Frogs into Princes, Neuro Linguistic Programming*
Published 1979 ISBN: 0-911226-18-4 or ISBN: 0-911226-18-2
• *ReFraming, Neuro-Linguistic Programming and the Transformation of Meaning* published 1982 ISBN 0-911226-24-9
• Robert H Schuller: *Move Ahead with Possibility Thinking* published 1967 ISBN: 0-515-07935-9
• *Tough times Never last but Tough People Do!* published 1983 ISBN:0-553-24245-8
• Hale Dwoskin : based on the work of Lester Levenson: *The Sedona Method, Your Key to Lasting Happiness, Success, Peace and Emotional Well-being,* published 2003 ISBN: 0-9719334-1-3
• Elly Roselle: *Changing the Mind, Healing the Body* SBN 0-9738175-0-X Elly was the founder of Core Belief Engineering www.corebelief.ca
• Gary Craig: EFT (Emotional Freedom Technique) Gary Craig founded EFT and retired in 2010 www.emofree.com and www.eftuniverse.com carry on his work
• Byron Kadie: *Loving What Is, Four questions that can change your life* published 2002 ISBN: 1-40000-4537-1 www.thework.com
• Ellena Lieberman; web site called www.dynamicmanifestation.com

CHAPTER 5 PHYSICAL KEYS - BODY AND HEALTH

• Elliot D. Abravanel, M.D. and Elizabeth A. King: *Dr. Abravanel's Body Type Program for Heath, Fitness and Nutrition* published 1985 ISBN 0-553-25332-8
• Dr. Peter J. D'Adamo with Catherine Whitney *4 Blood Types, 4 Diets, Eat Right 4 Your Type, The Individualized Diet Solution to Staying Healthy, Living Longer & Achieving Your Ideal Weight* ISBN 0 399- 14255-X
• Dr F Batmanghelidj M.D. *You Are Not Sick You Are Thirsty WATER: for Health For Healing For Life* published 2003 ISBN: 0 446-69074-0
• *ABC of Asthma Allergies & Lupus, Eradicate Asthma – Now!* published 2000 ISBN: 0-9629942-6X
• *Obesity Cancer Depression, their Common Cause & Natural Cure* published 2005 ISBN: 0-9702458-2-3
• *Your body's many Cries for WATER, You are not sick, you are thirsty! Don't treat thirst with medications* published 1992-2006 ISBN: 0-9629942-5-1
• *How to Deal With Back Pain & Rheumatoid Joint Pain*

Dr. Batmanghelidj died in 2004 at the age of 74 of complications of pneumonia. web site run by his former secretary continues to make his message, books, DVD's and CD talks available. His web site, www.watercure.com

• Louise L. Hay *You Can Heal Your life* published 1984 ISBN: 0-942494-94-6

• *The Power is Within You* published 1991 ISBN:1-56170-023-1

• Theo Gimbel DCE, MIACT,MLHRC,NFSH,CERT.ED: *Form, Sound, Colour and Healing* published 1987 ISBN 0-85207-146-9

• M. Sara Rosenthal: *The Thyroid Source Book* ISBN 1-56565-087-5

• Pete Egoscue with Roger Gittines: *Pain Free, A Revolutionary Method for Stopping Chronic Pai*n published 1998 ISBN: 0-553-37988-7

• Mildred Carter: *Helping Yourself With Foot Reflexology* Library of Congress Catalogue Card Number 74-81784

• J. V. Cerney A.B., D.M., D.P.M.,D.C. *Acupuncture Without Needles* published 1974-1999 ISBN 0-7352-0035-1

• Deepak Chopra: *Perfect Health- Revised and Updated: The Complete Mind Body Guide* published 1991-2000 ISBN 0-609-80694-7

• *Quantum Healing: Exploring the Frontiers of Mind body Medicine* published 1990 ISBN o-553-34869-8

• Denie and Shelley Hiestand: *Electrical Nutrition* published 2001 ISBN 1-58333-106-9

• Ron Garner, B.Ed. Msc. ND. *After the Doctors... What Can You Do? Straight Talk about.. how you lose your health, How you can restore it.* published 2001 ISBN 0-9688362-1-6

• Bernard Jensen, DC, PH.D. *Come Alive!, Total Health Through an Understanding of Minerals, Trace Elements, & Electrolytes* published 1997 ISBN 0-932615-64-3

• Caroline Myss: *Anatomy of the Spirit: The Seven Stages of Power and Healing* published 1996 ISBN 1-800-263-1063

• *Why People Don't Heal and How they Can* published 1997 ISBN -0-609-80224-0

• Hilarion: *Body Signs* published 1982-1987 ISBN 0-919951-02-3

• Robert Masters Ph.D. and Jean Houston, Ph.D.: *Listening to the body, the Psychophysical Way to Health and Awareness* published 1978 -1979 ISBN: 0-440-54960-4

• Jean Houston The Possible Human, A course in enhancing your Physical, Mental, and Creative Abilities published 1982

ISBN 0-87477-219-2

• Dorothy Hall: *Iridology, How The Eyes Reveal Your Health and Your Personality* published 1980 ISBN: 0-87983-241-X

• George Vithoulkas: *The Science of Homeopathy* published 1980- 1985 ISBN 0-394-50866-1

• Valerie Ann Worwoood: *The Complete Book of Essential Oils & Aromatherapy* published 1991 ISBN 0-931432-82-0

• Jacob Liberman, O.D., Ph.D.: *Light, Medicine of the Future* ISBN 0-939680-80-7

• Donald M. Epstein with Nathaniel Altman: *The 12 Stages of Healing, A Network Approach to Wholeness* published 1994 ISBN1-878424-08-4

• Stephen Co & Eric B. Robbins, M.D. with John Merryman: *Your Hands Can Heal You, Pranic Healing Energy Remedies to Boost Vitality and Speed Recovery from Common Health Problems* published 2002 ISBN -13:978-0-7432-3562-4

NUETRACEUTICALS

• For further information about the Avena Originals and Mannatech Inc. nuetraceuticals and supplements that Helen used to restore health and how to purchase products please contact helen@nanawisewoman.com

CHAPTER 6 PHYSICAL KEYS - WEIGHT LOSS STRUGGLES

• Herman Aihara: *Acid & Alkaline* published 1971 -1986 ISBN -0-918860-44-X

• Dr. Paavo Airola: *How to Keep Slim, Healthy and Young with Juice Fasting* published 1971 - 1982 ISBN 0-932090-02-8

• Judith A. DeCava, MS, LNC: *The Real Truth About Vitamins And Antioxidants* No ISBN number available

• Dr. Vasant Lad: Ayurveda, *The Science of Self-Healing* ISBN 0- 914955-00-4

• Amadea Morningstar with Urmila Desai: *The Ayurvedic Cookbook* by ISBN 0-914955-06-3

• Bob Schwartz: *Diets Don't Work* ISBN 0942540026

• Dr. M.O Bircher-Benner M. M.A: *Bircher -Benner Handbook*
Bircher-Benner Nutrition Plan for Raw Fruits and Vegetables published 1977 ISBN 0879831421

• Dr. John Matsen N. D:. *Eating Alive, Prevention Thru Good Digestion* published 1988 ISBN 0-9693586-0-1

• Gene and Joyce Daoust: *The Formula, A Personalized 40-30-30 Weight Loss Program* ISBN 0-345-44305-5 (Post it notes placed at the beginning of each recipe section helped me find the recipes I wanted to use).

• Formula 101, Maintaining 40-30-30 Nutrition for a Lifetime ISBN 0-345-45059-0 (Since the recipes were scattered among the text sections I hand copied their titles into the front index in order to easily locate the recipes).

• Barry Sears, Ph.D: *Enter The Zone, A Dietary Road Map* published 1995 ISBN 0-06-039150-2

• *Zone Perfect Meals in Minutes* published 1997 ISBN 0-06-039241-X

• *Mastering the Zone, Zone Food Blocks* published 1996
ISBN 0-06-092903-0

• *Zone Food Blocks* published 1998 ISBN 0- 06-039242-8

• Dr. Howard M. Shapiro: *Dr. Shapiro's Picture Perfect Weight Loss* ISBN 1-57954-241-7

• Herman Aihara : *Acid & Alkaline* published 1986 ISBN 0-918860-44-X

• Patrick Holford: *The Holford Low GL Diet, Lose Fat using the Revolutionary Fatburner System* published 2005 I SBN-13: 978-0-7432-8722-7

• Dr. Paavo Airola: *How to Keep Slim, Healthy and Young with Juice Fasting* published 1971 ISBN 0-932090-02-8

• Dr. Richard F. Heller and Dr. Rachael F. Heller: *The Carbohydrate Addict's Life Span Program* published 1997 No ISBN

• Arthur Agastston M.D.: *The South Beach Diet* published 2003 ISBN:0-312-99119-3

• John Gray Ph.D: *The Mars and Venus Diet & Exercise Solution, Create the Brain chemistry of Health, Happiness, and Lasting Romance* published 2003 ISBN: 0-312-31864-2 www.marsvenus.com

• Dr. Eric C. Westerman, Dr. Stephen D. Phinney, and Dr. Jeff S. Volek *The New Atkins for a New You* ISBN978-1-4391-9027-2

• Harvey and Marilyn Diamond: Fit for Life published 1985 No ISBN

• Ann Louise Gittleman, M.S. with James Templeton and Candelora Versace: *Your body Knows Best* published 1996
ISBN: 0-671-87591-4

• Jordan S. Rubin N.MD, Ph.D.: *The Maker's Diet* published 2004 ISBN: 0-88419-948-7

• Floyd H. Chilton, Ph.D. with Laura Tucker: *Win the War Within, the Eating Plan that's Clinically Proven to Fight Inflammation- the Hidden Cause of Weight Gain and Chronic Disease.* ISBN 1-59486-317-2

• Optimum Health Institute, San Diego, CA. www.optimumhealth.org

• Kevin Trudeau: *The Weight Loss Cure "they" Don't Want You to Know About* published 2007 ISBN 13: 978-0-9787851-0-9

• Denise Lamothe, Psy.D. H.H.D.: *The Taming of the Chew, A Holistic Guide to Stopping Compulsive Eating* published 1998 ISBN 0 14 20.0237 2

• Jenny Craig: Weight loss program www.jennycraig.com

• Overeaters Anonymous: Local meeting locations and program at www.oa.org

• Alcoholics Anonymous World Services Inc.: *Alcoholics Anonymous, the Story of How Many Thousands of Men and Women Have Recovered from Alcoholism* ISBN0-916856-00-3

• Weight Watchers Publishing Group: *Weight Watchers New Complete Cook Book* published 1998 ISBN: 0-02-862449-1

Canadian Food Companion published 2009

Dining out Food Companion published 2009

www. weightwatchers.ca

• Nathan Pritikin: *The Pritikin Program for Diet and Exercise* published 1981 Pritikin Institute www.pritikin.org

• Geneen Roth: *Women Food and God* published 2010
ISBN: 978-1-4165-4307-7

CHAPTER 7 MENTAL KEYS

• Dr. Schuller: *Move ahead with Possibility Thinking* published 1967 ISBN: 0-515-07935-9

• Dr. Daniel G. Amen, M. D. *Change Your Brain, Change Your Life, the Breakthrough Program for Conquering Anxiety, Depression, Obsessiveness, Anger, and Impulsiveness* published 1999
ISBN 0-8129-2998-5

• *Change Your Brain Change Your Body: Use your Brain to Get and Keep the Body You Have always Wanted* published 2010 ISBN978-0-307-46357-9
www.amenclinics.com.

• Omraam Mikhael Aivanhov: *The Powers of Thought* published 1988 ISBN: 2-85566-436-5

• John Kehoe: *Mind Power into the 21St Century, Techniques to Harness the Astounding Powers of Thought* published 1997 -2004 ISBN: 0-9697551-4-7

• Dr. Brian J. Gorman: *Attitude Therapy for Stress disorders*, ISBN 0-920490-03-4

• *Fog' Em All!* supplement published 1985

• Napoleon Hill: *Think and Grow Rich* published 1960

ISBN: 1-58063-205-X
• Masaru Emoto: *The Hidden Messages of Water* published 2003 ISBN: 1-58270-114-8
• *Water Crystal Healing, Music & Images to Restore Your Well-Being* published 2006 ISBN: -13:978-1-58270-156-1
• *Love thyself, the Message From Water III*, published 2004
ISBN: 978-1-4019-0899-7
• Neil Douglas -Klotz translated and with commentary: *Prayers of the Cosmos, Meditations on the Aramaic Words of Jesus* published 1994 ISBN 0-06-061994-5
• Annie Besant: *Thought Power, Its control and culture* published 1988 ISBN: 0-8356-0312-1
• *Man and His Bodies* published 1896 -1983
ISBN 0-8356-7083-X
• Annie Besant and C.W. Leadbeater: *Thought Forms* published 1925- 1986 ISBN: 8356-0008-4
• C. W. Leadbeater. *Man visible and Invisible* published 1925 -1987 ISBN: 0-8356-0311-3
• Robert A. Johnson: *Inner Work, Using Dreams & Active Imagination for Personal Growth* published 1986
ISBN: 0-06-250437-1
• Edward de Bono: *The 5-Day Course in Thinking* published 1967 No ISBN
• Jose Silva: *Silva Mind Control, Key to Inner Kingdoms Through Psychorientology* published 1972 -1976 No ISBN
• Jose Silva and Philip Miele: *The Silva Mind Control Method* published 1977 ISBN 0-671-83045-7
• Jack Ensign Addington: *The Perfect Power Within You* published 1973 -1997 ISBN 0-87516-179-0
• Bevy C. Jaefers: *Psychometry, the Science of Touch* published 1979 No ISBN
• Bill Harris: *Thresholds of the Mind, Your Personal Roadmap to Success, Happiness, and Contentment 2002* ISBN 0-9721780-0-7
• Holosync Audio Technology available from www.centerpointe.com
• Enid Hoffman: *Huna, A Beginner's Guide* published 1976, 1981 ISBN 0-914918-03-6
• Brad Steiger: *Kahuna Magic* published 1971-1981 ISBN 0-914918-34-6
• Rhonda Byrne: *The Secret* published 2006 ISBN-13: 978-1-58270-170-7
• Lynne McTaggart: *The Field, The Quest for the Secret force of the Universe*

published 2008 ISBN 978-0-06-143518-8
• *The Intention Experiment, Using Your Thoughts to Change your Life and the World* published 2008 www.livingthefield.com
Bob Procter web site www.sixminutestosuccess.com

CHAPTER 8 RELATIONSHIP KEYS

• Allan Pease: *Signals, How to Use Body Language for Power, Success and Love* ISBN 0-553-34019-0
• Robert L. Whiteside: *Face Language* published 1974
ISBN 0-671-43905-7
• Gerard I. Nierenberg and Henry H. Calero: *How to Read a Person Like a Book* published 1973 ISBN 671-78593-1
• Boye De Mente: *Face Reading for Fun & Profit* published1968-1978 ISBN 0-914778-19-6
• Geraldine Smith co-author Miki Andres: *Human Auras* published 1978
• Sherry Sleightholm: *Slow Motion Miracles, Geraldine Smith Stringer* published 1983 ISBN: 0-919921-00-0
• W. E. Butler: *How to Read the Aura, Practice Psychometry, Telepathy and Clairvoyance* published 1963 no ISBN
• Mikol Davis and Earle Lane: *Rainbows of Life, the Promise of Kirlian* Photography published 1978 ISBN: 0-06-090624-3
• Geoffrey Hodson: *Seven Human Temperaments* published 1952-1981 no ISBN
• Ernest Wood: *The Seven Rays* published 1925-1976 ISBN: 0-8356-0481-0
• Lucis, compiled from the writings of Alice A. Bailey: *The Seven Rays of Life* published 1995 ISBN: 0-85330-142-5
• John Gray Ph.D.: *Men are From Mars, Women are from Venus* published 1992 ISBN: 0-06-092642-2
• Beth Hedva, Ph.D. *Journey From Betrayal to Trust, a Universal Rite of Passage* published 1992 ISBN: 0-89087-660-6
• David Keirsey and Marilyn Bates: *Please Understand Me, Character & Temperament Types* published 1984 ISBN 0-9606954-0-0
• Robert A. Johnson: *He, Understanding Masculine Psychology* published 1977 ISBN: 0-06-080415-7
• *She, Understanding Feminine Psychology* revised published 1989 ISBN: 0-06-096397-2
• Don Miguel Ruiz: *The Four Agreements* published 1997 ISBN 1-878424-31-9

• *The Mastery of Love, a practical Guide to the Art of Relationship* published 2002

CHAPTER 9 INSTINCTUAL KEYS

• Kathy Kolbe: Go to www.Kolbe.com for information on the various Kolbe Conative Index tests and their online testing. Another source for information is http://knol.google.com/k/conation. In addition to used copies of the book, with the test that helped me understand my Action Modes® called, *The Conative Connection, Uncovering the Link Between Who You Are and How You Perform* (ISBN: 0-201-51795-7). a new revised updated edition is about to be released. I recommend obtaining Kathy Kolbe's current book called *The Conative Connection, Acting on Instinct* which includes updated and improved understandings of the Action Mode® qualities.

• Barbara Sher with Annie Gottlieib: *Wishcraft* published 1979-1983 ISBN 0-345-31100-0

• Barbara Sher with Barbara Smith: *I Could do ANYTHING If I Only Knew What It was, How to Discover What You Really Want and How to Get it.* published 1994 ISBN 0-385-30788-8

• *Refuse to Choose!, Use ALL! of Your Interests, Passions, and Hobbies to Create the Life and Career of Your Dreams* published 2006 ISBN-13 978-1-59486-303-5

• Dr. Marsha Sinetar: *Do What You Love The Money Will Follow, Discovering Your Right Livlihood* published 1987 ISBN 0-8091-2874-8

• Mark Thurston: *Discovering Your Soul's Purpose* published 1984 ISBN 87604-157-8

• Claude M. Bristol: *The Magic of Believing* published 1948 ISBN: 0-671-55394-1

• Robert T. Kiyosaki with Sharon L. Lecter C.P.A.: *Rich Dad Poor Dad, what the Rich Teach their Kids about Money- That the Poor And Middle Class Do Not!* published 1997-1998 ISBN 0-9643856-1-9

• Og Mandino: *The Greatest Secret in the World* published 1968 ISBN 0-553-27757-X

• *The Greatest Miracle in the World* published 1973 -1981 ISBN 0-553-20551-X

Dr. Ellie Drake M.D. can be reached through braveheartwomen.com

CHAPTER 10 ACTIONAL KEYS

• Jack and Cornelia Addington: *All About Goals and How to Achieve Them* published 1983

All About Prosperity and How You Can Prosper published 1984
The Perfect Power Within You published 1973
ISBN: 0-87516-179-0

• Jack Ensign Addington; *Psychogenesis: Everything Begins in Mind* published 1987

• Mark Victor Hansen: *Future Diary* published 1980 ISBN: 0-88205-226-8

• Charles F. Haanel: *The Master Key System* re-published 2006 ISBN 956-291-382-1

• Andrew Barber Starkey; teaches Pro-Coach www.procoach systems.com

• Raymond Aaron: Monthly Mentor course www.aaron.com

• Shakti Gawain: *Creative Visualization* published 1982 ISBN 0-553-24147-8

• Sean Stephenson: *Get Off Your Butt, How to end Self-Sabotage and Stand Up for Yourself* published 2009 ISBN 978-0-470-39993-4

• T. Harv Eker: *Secrets of the Millionaire Mind, Mastering the Inner Game of Wealth* published 2005 ISBN 0-06-076328-0

T. Harv Eker offers Peak Potentials course Success Tracs as well as many others I took part in: Millionaire Mind, Warrior, Wizard, Guerilla Marketing, Life Direction, Train the Trainer and others www.peakpotentials.com.

• Bill Bartmann: *Billionaire Secrets to Success* published 2007 ISBN 1-933285-31-1 Bill also teaches business courses. www.billbartmann.com

CHAPTER 11 SPIRITUAL KEYS

• Spiritual Teachers Imre Vallyon, Foundation for Higher Learning Ashram at Waitetuna, near Hamilton, North Island, New Zealand.The Magical Mind published 1991 ISBN: 0-921590-11-3

The circle of Love, The Lightning-Struck Tower of Wisdom, You really are a Beautiful Person, Heavens and Hells of the Mind, The Divine Plan, Heart to Heart Talks, The Art of Meditation. Books available through www.planetary-transformation.org and Amazon.ca

• John de Ruiter, College of Integrated Philosophy,10930 -177 Street, Edmonton. Alberta, Canada. *Unveiling Reality*, published 1999 ISBN: 1-894538-00-5
Audio and DVD's available at www.johnderuiter .com

• Eckhart Tolle: *The Power of Now, a Guide to Spiritual Enlightenment* published 1999 ISBN: 1-57731-480-8

• *Stillness Speaks*, published 2003 ISBN: 978-1-57731-400-4

• *Findhorn Retreat, Stillness Amidst the World*, published 2006
ISBN-13 978-1-57731-509-4 with DVD

• *A New Earth, Awakening to Your Life's Purpose* published 2005
ISBN: 0-525-94802-3

• *Practicing the Power of Now* published 1999 ISBN:1-57731-195-7

• *Oneness with All Life* published 2008 ISBN: 978-0525-95088-2
Audio and DVD's available at www.eckharttolle.com

• Dr. David R. Hawkins M.D., Ph.D.: *Power VS Force, the Hidden Determinants of Human Behavior* published 1995
ISBN; 1-56170-933-6

• *The Eye of the I* published 2001 ISBN 0-964-3261-9-1 *I Reality and Subjectivity* published 2003 ISBN: 0-97150007-0-3

• *Truth VS Falsehood, How to Tell the Difference* published 2005
ISBN: 0-9715007-2-X

• *Iranscending The Levels of Consciousness, The Stairway to Enlightenment* published 2006 ISBN; 0-9715007-4-6

• *Discovery of the Presence of God, Devotional Nonduality* published 2006 ISBN: 0-9715007-7-0

• *Reality Spirituality, and Modern Man* published 2008
ISBN-13:978-193330189-2 Audio and video available at www.veritaspub.com

• Adyashanti: *Emptiness Dancing* published 2004 ISBN: 1-59179-459-5

• *True Meditation, Discover the Freedom of Pure Awareness,* published 2006 ISBN-10: 1-59179-467-6 and ISBN-13: 978-1-59179-467-7

• *The End of Your World, Uncensored Straight Talk on the Nature of Enlightenment,* published 2008 ISBN: 978-1-59179-963-4 Audio and DVD's available at www.adyashanti.org

• Bruce H. Lipton, PhD: *The Biology of Belief* is an internationally recognized leader in bridging science and spirit www.brucelipton.com ISBN: 978-1-4019-2312-9

• Michael Baigent, Richard Leigh & Henry Lincoln: *Holy Blood, and the Holy Grail* published 1982-92 Corgi book 0-552-12138-X

• Barbara Thiering: *Jesus and the Riddle of the Dead Sea Scrolls, Unlocking the Secrets of His Life Story* published 1992ISBN 0-06-068286-8

• Michael Baigent: *The Jesus Papers, Exposing the Greatest Cover-up in History* published 2006 ISBN-13:978-0-06-082713-7

• Michael Wise, Martin Abegg, JR., & Edward Cook translation: *The Dead Sea Scrolls* published 1996 ISBN 0-06-069200-6

• James M. Robinson translation: *The Nag Hammadi Library In Englis, the Definitive translation of the Gnostic Scriptures Complete in One Volume* published 1990 ISBN 0-06-066934-9

• Laurence Gardner: *The Magdalene Legacy, The Jesus and Mary Bloodline Conspiracy* published 2005 ISBN-13 978-0-00-720085-6

• Annie Besant: *The Ancient Wisdom* published in 1897 by the Theosophical Society

• Baird T. Spalding: *Life & Teaching of the Masters of the Far East*, volumes 1-6 published 1924 and copyright renewed 1964 ISBN: 0-87516-084-0

• Richard Maurice Bucke: *Cosmic Consciousness* published 1961
Library of Congress number 61-11100

• Franklin Jones (Da Free John) *The Knee of Listening* published 1972 -1973 ISBN 0-913922-00-5

• J. G. Bennett: *Enneagram Studies* 1974 (Edition 1983) Library of Congress Catalogue number 82 -60166

• Patrizia Norelli-Bachelet: *The Gnostic Circle, a Synthesis in the Harmonies of the Cosmos* published 1975 ISBN: 0-87728-411-3

• Neale Donald Walsch: *Conversations with God book 1* published 1995 ISBN: 1-57174-025-2

• G. I. Gurdjieff: *Meetings With Remarkable Men* published 1963 -1988. *Life is Real Only Then, When "I am"* published 1975 -1978 ISBN 0-525-24617-7

• Charles W. Leadbetter: *The Hidden Side of Things* published 1913-1986 ISBN: 0-8356-7007-4

• *Invisible Helpers* published 1896-1980 ISBN: 0-8356-7160-7

• *The Chakras*, published in 1927 and 1985 ISBN: 0-8356-0422-5

• *The Inner Life* published 1978- 1987 ISBN: 0-8356-0502-7

• *The Astral Plane* published 1933 ISBN 0-8356-7093-7
The Masters and the Path published 1975

• Bhagwan Shree Rajneesh: *I am the Gate* published 1975
ISBN 0-06-090573-5

• Swami Muktananda: *Play of Consciousness,* published 1978 ISBN: 0-914602-36-5 (or - 3)

• Swami Sivananda Radha: *Gods Who Walk the Rainbow* published 1981 ISBN 0-931454-07-7

• Ramana Maharshi: *The Spiritual Teaching of Ramana Maharshi* ISBN: 0-87773-024-5

• Huang Po translated by John Blofeld: *The Zen Teaching of Huang Po* published 1958 ISBN: 0-8021-5092-6

• Dan Millman: *Way of the Peaceful Warrior, A Book That Changes Lives* published 1980-2006 ISBN-10: 0-915811-89-8

Sacred Journey of the Peaceful Warrior published 2004 ISBN 1-932073-10-8
Journey of Socrates published 2005 ISBN: 978-0-06-083302-2
• Arthur E. Powell, Lieut.-Colonel: (compiled from Theosophical teachers: Charles Leadbeater, Annie Besant, Madame Blavatsky and others)
• *The Etheric Double* published 1925 to 1979 ISBN: 0-7229-5087 or 5088
• *The Astral Body* published 1997-1992 ISBN: 0-8356-0438-1
The Mental Body, published 1927 and 1984 by the Theosophical Publishing House, London Ltd. The Causal Body published 1928-1978 no ISBN by the Theosophical Publishing House, London Ltd. The Theosophical Society www.ts-adyar.org
• Hannah Hurnard: *Hinds' Feet on High Places* published 1975 ISBN: 0-7394-0564-0
• Deepak Chopra: *How to Know God, the Soul's Journey into the Mystery of Mysteries* published 2000 ISBN: 0-609-80523-1
• Caroline Myss: *Entering the Castle, an Inner Path to God and Your Soul* Published 2007 ISBN-13: 978-07432-5532-5
• Paramahansa Yogananada: *Autobiography of a Yogi* published 1946-1987 ISBN: 0-87612-079-6
• *Whispers From Eternity* published 1935 -1959 ISBN -0-87612-100-8
• *Sayings of Paramahansa Yogananda* published 1952-1986 ISBN 0-87612-115-6
• *Where There is Light, Insight and Inspiration for Meeting Life's Challenges* Published 1988 ISBN 0-87612-275-6
• Kriyananda (J. Donald Walters) *The Essence of Self Realization, the Wisdom of Paramhamsa Yogananda* published 1990 ISBN: 0-916124-29-0
• Omraam Mikhael Aivanhov: *The Symbolic Language of Geometrical Figures* published 1985 ISBN 2-85566-366-0
• James Wasserman: *Art and Symbols of the Occult* published 1993 ISBN: 1-85501-301-305-3
• Swami Prabhavananda and Frederick Manchester translated from Sanskrit: The Upanishads, Breath of the Eternal published 1957 No ISBN
• Swami Rama: *Living with the Himalayan Masters* published 1978 ISBN: 0-89389-034-0
• Swami Sri Yukteswar: *The Holy Science* published 1984
ISBN 0-87612-051-6
• Swami Venkatesananda: *The Concise Yoga Vasistha* published 1984 ISBN 0-87395-954-X

• Kyriacos C. Markides: *Fire in the Heart, Healers, Sages, and Mystics* published 1990 No ISBN

• *Homage to the Sun, the Wisdom of the Magus of Strovolos* published 1987 No ISBN

• Sri Nisargadatta Maharaj translated from the Marathi tape recordings by Maurice Frydman: *I Am That, Talks with Sri Nisargadatta Maharaj* published 1973 ISBN:0-89386-022-0

Saratoga/ Kirin Baugher (channeled Telstar) *The Final Elimination of the Source of Fear.* Published 1995 ISBN: 0-9619235-1-2

• R. M. French translated from Russian: *The Way Of the Pilgrim, and the Pilgrim Continues His Way* published1954 ISBN: 0-06-063017-5

• Alice A. Bailey: *The Light of The Soul, Its Science and effect, the Yoga Sutras of Patanjali* published 1927 -1983 by Lucis Publishing company No ISBN

• Thomas A. Kempis, translated by Stephen MacKenna: *The Imitation of Christ* published 1896 - 02006 ISBN-10: 1-84483-343-7

• Biographies and autobiographies *Madame Guyon, St Augustine, Julia of Norwood, Hildagarde Bingen, Dark Night of the Soul - St John of the Cross, Thomas Aquinas, Madame Blavatsky, Annie Besant, the Jewish Mystics, Forbidden Journey, the Life of Alexandra David-Neel, Saint Teresa of Avila*, plus many other spiritual books too numerous to list.

CHAPTER 12 LOVE AND ENJOYMENT KEYS

• Jack and Cornelia Addington: *How to Love and Be Loved, Drawing the Larger* circle ISBN: 0-87516-558-3

• *Your Miracle Book, A Magic like Way to Thinking Yourself to Abundance and - Happiness* ISBN 0-87516-649-0

• *Your Needs Met* published 1966-1999 ISBN: 0-87516 -490-0

• The Dalai Lama and Howard C. Cutler, MD.: *The Art of Happiness* published 1998-2009 ISBN: 978-159448-889-4

• Deepak Chopra: *The Ultimate Happiness Prescription: 7 Keys to Joy and Enlightenment* published 2009 ISGBN 978-0-307-58971-2

• Leo F. Buscaglia: *Living, Loving and Learning* published 1983 ISBN: 0-030615526

• *Loving Each Other, the Challenge of Human Relationships* published 1984 ISBN: 0-449-90157-2

• Hale Dwoskin and Lester Levenson *Happiness is Free, ... and it's easier than you think!* Books 1-5, published 2001 ISBN: 0-915721-02-3 Sedona Method workbook and training course available from www.sedona.com

• Harold H. Bloomfield M.D. & Robert B. Kory: *Inner Joy, New Strategies for Adding (more) Pleasure to Your Life* published 1980 ISBN: 0-87223-603-X

• Marci Shimoff with Carol Kline: *Happy for No Reason, 7 steps to Being Happy from The Inside Out* published 2008 ISBN-13:978-1-4165-4772-3

• Glenda Green: *Love Without End, Jesus speaks* ... published 1999-2002 ISBN: 0-9666623-1-8

• Writings from the Philokalia (G.E. H. Palmer, Philip Sherrard and Kallistos Ware translators): *Prayer of the Heart* published 1993 ISBN0-87773-890-4

• Ron Scolastico Ph.D.: *Healing the Heart, Healing the Body, A spiritual Perspective on Emotional, Mental and Physical Health* published 1992 ISBN 1-56170-039-8

POETRY ABOUT LOVE AND SPIRIT

• Coleman Barks with John Moyne (translators): *The Essential Rumi* published 1997 ISBN 0-7858-0871-X

• Rabindranath Tagore: *Gitanjali* published 1971 ISBN 0-02-089630-1

• Sir Edward Arnold M.A., K.C.I.E.,C.S.I. translation: *The Song Celestial or the Bhagavad-Gita* published 1961 Lao Tzu (John C. H. Wu translator): *Tao Teh Ching* published 1990 ISBN 0-87773-942-5

CPSIA information can be obtained at www.ICGtesting.com
Printed in the USA
239335LV00002B/2/P